Engineering Modeling Languages

Turning Domain Knowledge into Tools

Chapman& Hall/C RCI nnovationsin Softw areE ngineering andSoftw areD evelopment

SeriesEditor

RichardL eBlanc

Chair,D epartmentofC omputerSc ienceandSof twareEngi neering,Se attleU niversity

AIMS AND SCOPE

This series covers all aspects of software engineering and software development. Books in the series will be innovative reference books, research monographs, and textbooks at the undergraduate and graduate level. Coverage will include traditional subject matter, cutting-edge research, and current industry practice, such as agile software development methods and service-oriented architectures. We also welcome proposals for books that capture the latest results on the domains andc onditionsinw hichpra cticesa remos te ffective.

PUBLISHED TITLES

CHAPMAN & HALL/CRC INNOVATIONS IN
SOFTWARE ENGINEERING AND SOFTWARE DEVELOPMENT

Engineering Modeling Languages

Turning Domain Knowledge into Tools

Benoit Combemale
University of Rennes 1, France

Robert B. France
Colorado State University, USA

Jean-Marc Jézéquel
University of Rennes 1, France

Bernhard Rumpe
RWTH Aachen University and Fraunhofer FIT, Germany

Jim Steel
AEHRC, CSIRO, Australia

Didier Vojtisek
Inria, France

CRC Press
Taylor & Francis Group
Boca Raton   London   New York

CRC Press is an imprint of the
Taylor & Francis Group an **informa** business

A CHAPMAN & HALL BOOK

First published 2017 by Chapman & Hall

Published 2019 by CRC Press
Taylor & Francis Group
6000 Broken Sound Parkway NW, Suite 300
Boca Raton, FL 33487-2742

First issued in paperback 2020

© 2017 by Taylor & Francis Group, LLC
CRC Press is an imprint of Taylor & Francis Group, an Informa business

No claim to original U.S. Government works

ISBN 13: 978-0-367-57421-5 (pbk)
ISBN 13: 978-1-4665-8373-3 (hbk)

Library of Congress Cataloging-in-Publication Data

Names: Combemale, Benoit, author. Title: Engineering modeling languages / Benoit Combemale, Robert France, Jean-Marc Jezequel, Bernhard Rumpe, James Richard Heron Steel, Didier Vojtisek. Description: Boca Raton : Taylor & Francis, CRC Press, 2017. Identifiers: LCCN 2016026666 | ISBN 9781466583733 (hardback : alk. paper) Subjects: LCSH: Engineering--Data processing. | Modeling languages (Computer science) | Computer software--Development. | Computer simulation. Classification: LCC TA343 .C67 2017 | DDC 620.001/13513--dc23 LC record available at https://lccn.loc.gov/2016026666

Visit the Taylor & Francis Web site at
http://www.taylorandfrancis.com

and the CRC Press Web site at
http://www.crcpress.com

to our co-author, our colleague and our friend,
rest in peace Robert.

Contents

List of Figures

List of Exercises

List of Sidebars

List of Listings

Preface

The digital age is around us. More and more sectors of our societies are becoming digital. It started for example in the late seventies in the telecom industry, where first the signals were digitized and then more and more network functions were implemented with software, right up to today's Software Defined Networks (SDN). It completely changed the banking and finance industries. It carried on with aerospace and automotive industries, and it is now turning the building industry upside down (see chapter 15 on the Building Information Model in this book).

The process is always the same: first software is written to monitor and record what's going on in the real world, and reflect on it (introspection). Then people realize that they can run computations on the collected data, and that the results of these computations can be used to act on the real world (intercession). Once this loop is closed, more and more human know-how and knowledge is transferred to software. The final step is when software *becomes* the real world. You already know that your bank account only exists in software, but it is more and more true that an available hotel room is not really available unless it is available on Booking.com or Expedia. AirBnB or Uber are other well-known examples of turning full industry sectors upside down with software playing the leading role, and many more are to follow.

Of course one of the biggest challenges in the software industry has always been to turn human knowledge, know-how and procedures into software. When the domain of expertise is close enough to computer science, the software engineers typically can manage it because they can understand the full spectrum of the problems, ranging from the problem domain to the solution space in the computer.

However, when the domain stands far away from the software engineer's expertise, it's much more difficult to do the right thing. A lot of approaches have been developed over the years to handle this gap. In this book we provide an overview on one of these approaches, based on the idea of using *models* to capture domain knowledge at the right level of abstraction, and software tools to transform it into technical solutions. The software engineers then need to provide the domain experts with the right tool-supported *modeling languages*; that is, *turn domain knowledge into tools*.

This book proceeds from the collective expertise of the authors, who are working in the field of engineering modeling languages for more than 15 years. It draws from both state-of-the-art research, typically published at leading conferences and journals such as MODELS or *SoSyM*, but also on more than a decade of collaboration with many industrial partners from many different sectors and countries who tried these new approaches on many different projects and brought us inestimable feedback.

TRIBUTE TO ROBERT B. FRANCE

By the time we were finalizing this book, we were devastated to learn about the passing of Prof. Robert B. France, on the evening of Sunday, February 15th, 2015. His passing was painless, after a battle against cancer. He was 54 years old.

Robert B. France was one of the initial key authors of this book, and was fully devoted to its writing while enduring his illness.

Robert was a co-founder of *SoSyM* and served as its editor-in-chief since its inception in 1999. He passionately believed that the modeling community needed their own journal to be able to read and publish innovations in the areas of modeling, model languages, use of models, tooling, and related topics. Throughout the past 16 years, Robert has been a major driving force behind the journal as well as the whole modeling community. We dedicate this book to his memory.

Robert's Scientific Life

Robert started his scientific life at the University of the West Indies, St. Augustine, Trinidad and Tobago, in the Caribbean. He graduated in 1984 and began working as a computer specialist in a project called USAID Census in the St. Vincent office of a US company. In 1986, he moved on to the Massey University in Palmerston, New Zealand, where he received his PhD in computer science in 1990. From 1990–92, he worked as a postdoctoral fellow at the University of Maryland, Institute for Advanced Computer Studies.

Robert was appointed as an assistant professor at the Computer

Science and Engineering Department, Florida Atlantic University in Boca Raton, Florida, and stayed there for six years (1992–1998).

In 1999, he moved to the Colorado State University (CSU) in Fort Collins as a tenured associate professor and was promoted to a full professor in 2004.

In 2006–2007, Robert spent his sabbatical year at Lancaster University in the United Kingdom and at IRISA/INRIA in Rennes, France. He also made a number of extended scientific visits to the University of Nice in 2009 and 2012, to SINTEF in Norway in 2009 and 2011, and the University of Pau in 2003. From 2011, he held a position as a visiting adjunct professor at the University of the West Indies. In his visits and travels, he was often accompanied by his wife Sheriffa.

Robert was active at CSU in both organizational and scientific positions for as long as his health allowed him and even helped to organize the Modularity conference, which took place in Fort Collins in March 2015.

During his scientific life, Robert made a remarkable number of research contributions. His CV (last updated in August 2014) lists 33 journal articles, 10 book chapters, 1 invited paper, 107 refereed conference papers, 40 refereed workshop papers, and 13 proceedings and journal editorials. As of May 22, 2015, DBLP lists 251 published entries co-authored by Robert, and an astonishing list of 230 collaborating authors. Google Scholar lists 387 entries! Since he was an editor-in-chief of *SoSyM* from its inception, Robert was never allowed to publish his work there. So his modeling papers were mostly published at conferences.

In addition to his amazing research productivity and a 16-year labor-intensive commitment to *SoSyM*, Robert was also an active member of IEEE-CS, ACM, and the OMG. In addition, he served on one of the UML task forces as part of his OMG participation. Robert served as a keynote speaker, invited panelist, panel moderator, invited speaker, summer school lecturer, and in addition, gave numerous talks at companies and conferences all around the world. He also served as an associate editor of *IEEE Computer* (2006–2012) and the *Journal of Software Testing, Verification and Reliability* (2006–2015). Furthermore, he cared deeply about the computer science educational curriculum, serving on the IEEE Computer Society Educational Activities Board (2011–13). However, his most sustainable scientific service achievement was the role he played in establishing the

UML/MODELS conference series. He was the general chair and the local arrangements chair of the first UML/MODELS conference held in Fort Collins in 1999, right after an initial UML workshop in France in 1998. This conference series brought together a research community that eventually made *SoSyM* the success it is today.

Robert was an Outstanding Researcher

He was a pioneer in the cross-fertilization of formal methods and informal or semi-formal specification languages used in software engineering. His work provided the scientific foundations of the "integrated methods", which have evolved into a rigorous Model Driven Engineering (MDE). His contributions in the fields of languages, verification, and modeling have provided the mathematical tools used in the design of critical systems. The exceptional quality of his work on modeling and his contribution to the object-oriented programming and modeling community, was honored in 2014 with the AITO Dahl-Nygaard Senior Prize, awarded at the ECOOP conference. The steering committee of the MODELS conference also awarded him in January 2015 the first MODELS Career award.

Robert was a Recognized Teacher

He was recognized both for his teaching skills, the proximity with the students, and his ability to share his vision. Sharing knowledge with students always concerned him. He actively participated in the democratization of computer science education, being a member of the steering committee of the "IEEE/ACM Computer Science Curriculum Recommendation, CS2013" and head of the "IEEE Curricula" committee. He was responsible for the international program REUSSI and a mentor for many researchers around the world and helped them to develop a culture and scientific rigor, as well as appreciating the richness of this job. Since 2014, he was "Professor Laureate" at Colorado State University (CSU), the highest honor that can be awarded to a teacher, recognizing his qualities.

Robert was Passionate about the Animation of the Scientific Community

He was a founding member of the pUML initiative to define a formal semantics for the UML standard. As already mentioned, he organized the first UML conference in 1999 in Denver, the first edition of the newly renamed MODELS conference in 2005 at Montego Bay, Jamaica, and was also a founding editor-in-chief of the *SoSyM* journal. More recently, he promoted various initiatives to take a new step in MDE through a maturation phase: the ReMoDD initiative, which aims at the creation of a repository of models to build experimental results that are sound and reproducible, and the GEMOC initiative, which aims to develop the foundations, methods, and tools to facilitate the creation, integration, and automated processing of heterogeneous modeling languages.

Robert was a Child of the Caribbean

Always concerned with providing excellent training, he worked a lot to enable young researchers to access studies, build their academic networks, and benefit from exceptional collaborations. He devoted his energy to allowing Caribbean students to access their expected studies. These efforts join the heritage of the Caribbean, awarded in 2014 by the Institute of Caribbean Studies.

Acknowledgments

We thank all our colleagues for the years of fruitful and interesting discussions and collaborations that finally led to this book.

We in particular thank the member of our groups for helping in developing concepts and their empirical implementations as well as for constructive reviews on parts of this book. For this we are very grateful to Kai Adam, Arvid Butting, Robert Eikermann, Sylvia Gunder, Timo Greifenberg, Robert Heim, Gabriele Heuschen, Katrin Hölldobler, Oliver Kautz, Evgeny Kusmenko, Markus Look, Klaus Müller, Pedram Mir Seyed Nazari, Dimitri Plotnikov, Deni Raco, Alexander Roth, Christoph Schulze, Michael von Wenckstern, and Andreas Wortmann.

Chapter 10 is largely based on common work with Clémentine Nébut, Tewfik Ziadi, Paul Istoan and Mathieu Acher, and could not have been written without all their contributions to the variability modeling field.

Chapter 15 is largely based on common work done with Robin Drogemuller, Keith Duddy, and Jörg Kiegeland.

Cédric Brun (CTO Obeo) for the three side bars about tools.

A special word of thanks also goes to our respective families for having the patience with us for having taken yet another challenge which decreases the amount of time we can spend with them.

Introduction

The more we try to understand the world in which we live, the more complex it appears. From far away galaxies and black holes, to human social behaviors, biological processes, and down to sub-atomic particle physics, complexity prevails. Scientists and engineers engage in modeling activities to better understand the complex processes, artifacts, and other phenomena they are studying or constructing. These models make explicit, among other things, the assumptions made, logical consequences of the assumptions, and the data on which current understanding is based. Using models, scientists and engineers can of course make predictions as to how processes will respond to certain events, but also use them for many different purposes, such as playing out "what-if" scenarios (e.g., what happens when assumptions are changed) [36].

Software systems are increasingly playing critical roles in complex real-world contexts and thus it should not be surprising that the development of these software systems is also a very complex endeavor. In his seminal book *The Mythical Man-Month* [16], Fred Brooks identifies two types of software complexity: *essential* and *accidental* complexity. Essential complexity is software complexity that is inherent in the problem targeted by the software or in the solution provided by the software. This inherent complexity can arise, for example, from the variety of input events and data that must be correctly handled by the software, and the critical functional and quality concerns that the software must address. For example, software in autonomous road vehicles is inherently complex from both a problem and solution perspective. Accidental complexity arises as a result of the use of inappropriate technologies, or the non-use of technologies, which leads to significant human effort being spent on developing the software. For example, manually inspecting a million lines of code for errors is a source of accidental complexity.

In the software domain, *Model Driven Engineering* (MDE) is the discipline that focuses on how modeling can be used to better manage essential complexities and reduce accidental complexities associated with developing complex software-intensive systems [46]. MDE technologies support development of models that capture software functionality and properties at different levels of abstraction and from different perspectives, as well as rigorous analysis of models, and transformation of models into software artifacts that serve specific development purposes (e.g., test cases, implementations, software configuration scripts, user manuals). Various experience reports provide evidence that MDE technologies are being integrated into industrial software development processes, and that such integration has led to improved quality and productivity [147].

Modeling languages are at the core of MDE, and an interesting trend that is emerging in the MDE research community is a broadening of the focus from technologies that manipulate models to technologies that enable software developers to create and evolve their own modeling languages, aka *Software Language Engineering* (SLE). Such languages provide developers with abstractions that are directly related to the application-specific concerns that they are addressing in their software projects. For example, there are modeling languages for expressing security, distributed real-time systems, and user interface concerns, in addition to languages that are specific to the automotive and aeronautic software domains. These languages tend to be smaller, focus on a particular domain, serve a smaller user community, and evolve at a faster rate than traditional modeling or programming languages, since the concern domains are continually evolving. The engineering of these languages thus presents special challenges when compared with the development of traditional languages. For example, unlike traditional programming languages defined in terms of grammars that describe concrete syntax, modeling languages base their definitions on abstract syntax described in a metamodel. The MDE community has developed a rich integrated collection of generative technologies that are based on standardized metamodeling facilities such as OMG's MetaObject Facility (MOF) [112]. These technologies use metamodels to facilitate and drive the generation of parsers, compilers, code generators, checkers, simulators, and other integrated development environment services.

This book includes end-to-end coverage of the engineering of modeling languages to turn domain knowledge into tools. This includes the definition of different kinds of modeling languages, their instrumentation with tools such as editors, interpreters and generators, the integration of multiple modeling languages to achieve a system view, and the validation of both models and tools. These elements of modeling are illustrated through industrial case studies across a range of application domains, attesting to the benefits offered by the different techniques, as well as through a variety of simple worked examples that introduce the techniques to the novice user.

This book is thus meant for both master's and PhD students working in the field of modeling languages, as well as for practicing engineers who want to get both a conceptual and a very practical understanding of the subject matter.

This book is structured in two main parts. The first part is organized around a flow that introduces readers to MDE concepts and technologies in a pragmatic manner. It starts with definitions of modeling and MDE, and then moves into a deeper discussion of how to express the knowledge of particular domains using modeling languages to ease the development of systems in this domain, and their dedicated tooling to automate or increase the quality of some part of the development, configuration or deployment of such systems. Each chapter concludes with a small set of exercises to help the reader reflect on what she just learned, or dig further into some of our examples.

Throughout the main flow introduced in this first part, an extra flow will be woven to provide informational, technical, or foundational background content. Foundational sidebars are meant to provide scientific and advanced details for master's and PhD students, as well as researchers. A more practically oriented reader should be able to safely skip them all.

The second part of the book presents examples of applications of the model-driven approach to different types of software systems. In addition to illustrating the unification power of models in different software domains, this part demonstrates applicability from different starting points (language, business knowledge, standard, etc.) and focuses on different software engineering activities such as requirement engineering, analysis, design, implementation, and verification and validation (V&V).

Finally, many examples of models and code snippets are presented throughout the book. The reader is of course most welcome to try them for real. To help that, we set up a website at `http://mdebook.irisa.fr` where all the models and programs (and their associated tooling) discussed in this book are available for download.[1] Have fun!

NOTATIONAL CONVENTIONS

This book uses notational conventions. There are several kinds of highlighted bars.

> **Tip**
>
> This is the tip area, which usually contains useful extra tips, how to use the tooling or for example, how to read the book.

> **Foundation**
>
> While the book concentrates on practical issues, it is sometimes helpful to understand the foundations and formal definitions behind the practical concepts. Foundation bars concentrate on theoretical background. They are not necessary for the understanding of the rest of the book, but helpful for foundational discussions.

> **Note**
>
> Notes contain extra information that might be useful to read but are not essential.

> **Tool**
>
> Some notes are used to present information about a tool that is of particular interest.

> **Exercise**
>
> A book dedicated to practical use comes with tooling. Examples describe how the tooling is used. But to gain really practical insight, it is necessary to exercise yourself. The provided exercises are suggestions to gain more experience and can be used in teaching courses as well.

---

[1] A specific part of the website storing the solutions to our exercises is also open to teachers upon request.

> [www] ✎ Exercise
>
> Some exercises require that you get and install some tools and resources. This icon indicates that the book companion website (`http://mdebook.irisa.fr`) provides additional instructions for the exercise.

Models come in textual and graphical forms. To easily understand the kind of model, the model is normally marked by the modeling language to which it belongs. For example, the ⌐CAIR⌐ tag stands for a DSL called `CAIR`. The same kind of marker is used to identify listings content. The following table lists the tags used in this book.

Tag	Description
Acceleo ⌐	Acceleo template
CAIR ⌐	Cellular Automata Initialization Rule DSL
CAER ⌐	Cellular Automata Evolution Rule DSL
Class Diagram ⌐	Class Diagram
EBNF Grammar ⌐	EBNF grammar
Java ⌐	Java program
Kermeta ⌐	Xtend program with Kermeta active annotations support
Object Diagram ⌐	Object Diagram
OCL ⌐	OCL constraints
StateMachine Diagram ⌐	StateMachine Diagram
Xtend ⌐	Xtend program
Xtext ⌐	Xtext grammar

In listings, the lines containing only an ellipsis (. . .) indicate that less relevant lines have been removed from the full running listing.

What's a Model?

CONTENTS

THIS chapter introduces the notion of the *model* as an abstraction of an aspect of reality built for a given purpose. It also introduces the cellular automata that are used as running examples throughout the first part of this book. It concludes with a discussion on the semantic foundations of MDE.

After reading this chapter you will:

- have an understanding of the different roles models play in science and engineering;

- understand how modeling of software-intensive systems handles problem and solution complexity through separation and abstraction of concerns;

- be familiar with cellular automata and how they can be modeled; and

– have a basic understanding of the semantic foundations of MDE.

1.1 INTRODUCTION

Building a model of some real-world phenomenon seems to be an intrinsic human technique to understand and predict occurrences in the world. Many disciplines use models to help navigate through complex concepts in order to gain a better understanding of their target of study. For example, physicists build models to postulate and examine consequences of the big bang; chemists use models to study atoms and molecules; mathematicians use models to study the abstract nature of numbers, functions, and other concepts; mechanical and electrical engineers build models of engines to predict how they will behave when built; architects build models to analyze structural integrity of buildings, sociologists and psychologists use models to understand human behavior; biologists use models to understand the impact that a phenomena have on a particular species; medical researchers build models to better understand human bodies and the brain; economists use models to describe and predict market behaviors, geologists and climatologists use models to understand the behavior of the Earth and climate; and finally, astronomers use models to better understand the universe.

While it may seem to some in the MDE community that modeling was invented by computer scientists or software engineers, clearly modeling has long been an essential mechanism for coping with the complexity of reality. In fact, one can venture to say that models have been used since the dawn of humanity, where early humans used cave drawings to communicate, for example, hunting instructions to novices or to establish communication with the spirit world (e.g., see `http://www.bradshawfoundation.com/clottes/index.php`). However, the use of models in software engineering has unique characteristics. First, models are used to provide explicit form to the immaterial nature of software (as will be discussed later, source code can be considered to be a model). Second, the medium for expressing models and the medium for defining software implementations are one and the same, and thus software developers do not have the additional complexity of changing medium when moving from models to implementations. This has led to considerable work on automated model transformations (in particular, code generators) in the MDE domain. However, the common medium does not necessarily imply that the task of generating reliable implementations from models is straightforward. In fact, such generation may sometimes be more complex than transforming paper-based artifacts into physical artifacts such as bridges. Software is considered by many to be very malleable (easy to change) and there are no physical laws that restrict what computable behaviors can be implemented, and thus software often takes on many responsibilities that are anticipated to change over the software's lifetime, even when those responsibilities can be handled by hardware. In addition, large software systems that play critical roles in society and that serve a diverse user base are required to have many qualities, some of which may be at odds with each other. These and other factors related to the growing complexity of software makes generating complete implementations from models challenging. On the other hand, producing implementations without the help of models is a considerably more complex task; that is, it leads to significant accidental complexity.

The above indicates that modeling plays a much more important role in software development than in other disciplines, and is (or at least can be) more intricately connected to the final software implementation. Therefore, it is worth answering the following questions in the context of software development:

– What is a model?

– When and why should models be used?

– What is the benefit of modeling?

– What are the relationships between models and the real products?

– Which tools allow us to successfully use models?

– How do we build such tools?

To help answer these questions, we compare modeling in software development with modeling in other disciplines because, on the one hand, some phenomena are similar to those found in software development, and on the other hand, we will build more and more software-intensive systems that are engineered in an interdisciplinary manner, that is, systems that involve developers from science, engineering, and other disciplines. Examples of software systems that span disciplines are the currently upcoming cyber-physical systems [87].

While in science, models are used to describe and predict existing phenomena of the real world, in engineering, models are used to describe a system that is to be developed in the future. Thus engineering models are typically *constructive* while science models are *descriptive*. In the following, we more closely examine the way models are used in science and engineering.

1.2 MODELING IN SCIENCE

Scientists handle the complexity of the phenomena they are studying through *modeling*. According to Joshua M. Epstein [36]:

> *The modeling enterprise extends as far back as Archimedes; and so does its misunderstanding. Anyone who ventures a projection, or imagines how a social dynamic— an epidemic, war, or migration—would unfold is running some model. But typically, it is an implicit model in which the assumptions are hidden, their internal consistency is untested, their logical consequences are unknown, and their relation to data is unknown. But, when you close your eyes and imagine an epidemic spreading, or any other social dynamic, you are running some model or other. It is just an implicit model that you haven't written down.*

Of course, to be useful as a means of communication, models have to be made *explicit*, that is, assumptions about the world must be made explicit, and communicated in a language that can be understood by other stakeholders. According to Jeff Rothenberg [127]:

> *Modeling, in the broadest sense, is the cost-effective use of something in place of something else for some cognitive purpose. It allows us to use something that is simpler, safer or cheaper than reality instead of reality for some purpose. A model represents reality for the given purpose; the model is an abstraction of reality in the sense that it cannot represent all aspects of reality. This allows us to deal with the world in a simplified manner, avoiding the complexity, danger and irreversibility of reality.*

Stachowiak provides a more detailed definition of modeling [135], in which the three main characteristics of a *model* are described as follows:

- There is an original.

- The model is an abstraction of the original.

- The model fulfills a purpose with respect to the original.

Scientific models are typically used to understand the real world and predict some aspects of the real world: using Newton's laws of gravitation we can predict the time it will take for an apple to fall from a tree. That led the philosopher K. Popper to the characterization of scientific theories as *falsifiable models* [121], i.e., models that can be compared to some observable reality to assess whether and where they fit. Thus the *original* is part of this world. Scientists abstract away from complex details and typically the models they construct only hold within certain boundaries that need to be explicitly understood too. For example, Newton's laws of gravitation only hold near the surface and for objects of certain sizes. Some models are known to be wrong in the general case, but still explain certain phenomena quite well, e.g., Kepler's geocentric model of the solar system.

Abstraction always means that certain properties are lost while (hopefully) the relevant ones are captured in enough detail to fulfill the model's purpose. Whether a model is helpful can therefore only be answered with knowledge about its purpose.

1.3 MODELING IN ENGINEERING

Like other scientists, engineers (including software engineers) use models to address complexity. However a key difference is that the phenomenon (engine, process, software, building) they model generally does not exist *at the time the model is built*, because the engineers' goal is to build the phenomenon according to the model. That is, the model acts as a blueprint.

In this book we distill the various notions of models to obtain the following short definition of *model* that is applicable to software development:

Definition 1.1 (Model) *A model is an abstraction of an aspect of reality (as-is or to-be) that is built for a given purpose.*

As an aside, the word *model* was knowingly used for the first time for 1:10 versions of cathedrals in medieval Italy. Such a 1:10 miniature could still be analyzed, e.g., to walk in and see the light flow and thus customers could understand what they would buy. The building's stability could only be roughly estimated, but that was still better than nothing.

In engineering, one wants to break down a complex system into as many models as needed in order to address all the relevant concerns in such a way that they become understandable, analyzable and finally can be constructed. This *separation of concerns* engineering principle has stood the test of time.

In the remainder of this section we will focus on how modeling supports abstraction and separation of concerns principles for complex software systems, that is, complex systems in which software plays a primary role. Complex software systems are often required to interact with elements in their environments, and thus two major types of models can be produced in an engineering project:

- Models that each describe a part/abstraction of the software to be built.

- Models that each describe a part/abstraction of the environment to be controlled, monitored, responded to, or augmented.

This distinction is important. Models that describe the internal structure of a system—for example, software architectures and data structures—are often used to fulfill some constructive purpose. By contrast, there are, for example, models that describe the business process that should be supported by the software, or the plant to be controlled. From a software development perspective, these models describe existing entities. These kinds of models are used to understand how software interacts with its environment. These models can also be used for defining tests to check that the software actually accomplishes its goals with respect to interactions with the environment.

As already indicated, models can be used for a variety of purposes that are related to the various activities defined in software development processes. Each activity or phase in a project may be associated with its own kinds of models. For example, requirements models are used to express, organize, and analyze gathered requirements in the requirements phase, while logical architecture models are associated with high-level/logical design activities. In early phases it is particularly interesting to model the interplay between a software product and its environment to precisely understand what the final product shall do, as the interfaces between system and environment are typically complex and need to be precisely and correctly defined for the system to be of use.

A model in software engineering can have one or more of the following purposes:

– The model serves as an exploration of the solution possibilities.

– The model is used for construction of the system.

– The model serves as a source for tests.

– The model helps the customer to understand the final product.

– The model is used to generate code.

– The model is used to customize the system to be designed.

– The model serves as documentation of the system.

– The model is used for simulation of the not-yet-existing system.

– The model is used to simulate a phenomenon in the real world.

Defining models to fulfill the above purposes will be discussed in detail later in this book. However, it is worth describing some aspects of the code generation purpose as it provides further insight into the nature of software models. Due to the immaterial nature of a software system, a model describing a piece of software and the software itself can be more tightly coupled than in any other engineering discipline. If a model is represented digitally, with a predictable form, then it can be used to generate other digital forms, including executable, meaning that the model as a draft of the system can be tightly connected to the system's implementation. One can even argue that the model is the system, which is a convenient simplification that programmers usually take when they do not distinguish between the source code, the compiled files, and the running system. In fact, executable code in a high-level programming language can quite reasonably be considered a model. So if the model is sufficiently detailed or (even better) the generator is intelligent enough, we can conveniently regard a model to be the system.

> **Note 1.1 Defining a Modeling Language: Metamodeling**
>
> The core idea of Model Driven Engineering is to also use models for explicitly defining a modeling language: this is called *metamodeling* and will be discussed in details in the following chapters.

Code generation, generation of testing infrastructure, as well as checking of context conditions and high-level analysis, all make it necessary that the modeling language developers are using be precisely defined. Only with an explicit definition of a model's syntactic form is it possible for machines to interpret and manipulate the models. The benefits that come from an explicitly defined modeling language are particularly significant in the software engineering discipline, more than any other, due to the advantages that come from tightly coupling the models and the artifacts being built. This is one of the reasons that computer science was one of the first disciplines to come up with explicit, operational language definitions.[1]

As computers become engineering tools in other domains, there is a growing trend in which domain experts define and use their own languages, referred to as domain-specific (modeling) languages (DSLs), for modeling phenomena unrelated to software development. This trend makes it even more important to have support for explicitly defining modeling languages. Having well-defined languages makes it possible to develop reusable tools that manipulate the models expressed in these languages.

The UML [113] is an explicitly defined language, although it can still be argued that it is not yet precisely defined [39]. However the UML consists of a substantial set of sublanguages whose union is general purpose enough to describe large parts and aspects of a system in a relatively accurate manner, and thus can act as a lingua franca in the software development domain. The UML can thus be regarded as a general-purpose modeling language.

By contrast, domain-specific modeling languages (DSML) are typically more problem-oriented and allow smaller and more concise

---

[1]Of course, Chomsky's works on grammars in the field of linguistics or Russell's attempts at explicitly defining the language of mathematics had strong influence on computer science.

> **Foundation 1.2 Models Created Using the Same Medium as the Thing They Model**
>
> Usually in science and engineering, a model is created using a different medium than the thing it models (think of a bridge drawing vs. a concrete bridge). Only in software and perhaps linguistics and nowadays also 3D printing is a model created using the same medium as the phenomenon it models. In software, at least, this opens up the possibility of automatically deriving software from its model and thus leads to a more tightly coupled relationship between model and original.

models. However, extra effort is needed to develop a DSML and its accompanying tooling. The overhead of such an undertaking must be considered against the advantages of using a DSML.

Models defined in the UML, and those defined in a DSML, can all be seen as the abstraction of an aspect of reality for describing a certain concern. The provision of effective means for handling such concerns makes it possible to establish critical trade-offs early on in the system life cycle.

Identifying the abstractions that fit the model's purpose is not always straightforward. Currently, developers rely on their experience in the application domain to identify suitable abstractions, that is, abstractions that can be effectively manipulated to satisfy a model's purpose. If this experience is not available, the use of unsuitable abstractions can be a significant source of accidental complexity in a model-based project. The quality of the abstractions captured in models is critical to successful application of modeling in software development.

1.4 ILLUSTRATIVE EXAMPLE: CELLULAR AUTOMATA

For illustrating the various ideas presented in this book, we are going to use the running example of cellular automata. It is simple enough to be explained in a few lines, and still rich enough to allow us to illustrate all the concepts presented in this book; it has been shown [47] that some of the rule sets were Turing-complete, which means in essence that they can simulate any computer program. Cellular automata is a simple example used for pedagogical purposes in this book. However, in the second part of this book, we will see that the various principles that we demonstrate through this simple example can be extended to handle the full complexity of real-world case studies.

Cellular automata were originally proposed in the 1940s by Stanislaw Ulam and John von Neumann, and popularized in the 1970s by Conway's Game of Life, based on a simple two-dimensional cellular automaton.

1.4.1 Cellular Automaton Topology

A cellular automaton consists of a universe of cells organized in some topology (typically a regular grid, in any finite number of dimensions). Each cell is in one of a finite number of states, such as *empty* or *occupied*. Defined by the universe topology, each cell has a set of cells called its neighborhood.

For regular two-dimensional Cartesian grids, the two most common types of neighborhoods are the von Neumann neighborhood (consisting of the four orthogonally adjacent cells) and the Moore neighborhood (adding the four diagonal adjacent cells to the von Neumann neighborhood). Another point of variation is also the *depth* of the neighborhood, i.e., whether the neighbors of the direct neighbors (and so on) are considered.

The universe can be either finite or infinite. For finite universes (e.g., in two dimensions, the universe would be a rectangle instead of an infinite plane), a problem arises with the cells on the edges, because their neighborhood is different (fewer neighbors). One possible method is to allow the values in those cells to remain constant. Another one is to use a toroidal topology, i.e., in 2-D to use a torus instead of a rectangle (the cells at the top are considered to be adjacent to the cells at the corresponding position on the bottom, and those on the left adjacent to the corresponding cells on the right).

1.4.2 Cellular Automaton Evolution Rules

An initial state for the automaton is selected by assigning a state for each cell. Each new generation is created according to some rule that determines the new state of each cell as a function of the current state of the cell and the states of the cells in its neighborhood. Typically, the rule for updating the state of cells is the same for each cell, does not change over time, and is applied to the whole grid simultaneously, though exceptions are known, such as probabilistic cellular automata and asynchronous cellular automata.

As an example, the rules for Conway's two-state, two-dimensional cellular automaton called the Game of Life are as follows: If a cell has 2 black neighbors, it stays the same. If it has 3 black neighbors, it becomes black. In all other situations it becomes white. According to Wikipedia[2]:

> *Despite its simplicity, the system achieves an impressive diversity of behavior, fluctuating between apparent randomness and order. One of the most apparent features of the Game of Life is the frequent occurrence of gliders, arrangements of cells that essentially move themselves across the grid. It is possible to arrange the automaton so that the gliders interact to perform computations, and after much effort it has been shown that the Game of Life can emulate a universal Turing machine.*

Of course one may design many variants of rules for evolving cellular automata.

1.4.3 Modeling Cellular Automata

Cellular automata are used as the running example in the following chapters of this book. It is used to illustrate how one can build a modeling environment that allows a modeler to define cellular automata topologies, to design rules, to simulate cellular automata evolution, and more generally to perform a wide spectrum of computations on cellular automata. To provide concrete illustrations of the MDE principles, we will use the Eclipse environment[3] as a particular technological environment, and more specifically the Eclipse Modeling Framework (EMF) [140].

The first thing we can remark on is that modeling cellular automata involves taking into account the many variations that exist among such automata, including:

– variation in topology (typically a regular grid, in any finite number of dimensions);

– different types of neighborhoods (von Neumann, Moore);

---

[2]Cf. `http://en.wikipedia.org/wiki/Cellular\_automaton`
[3]Cf. `http://eclipse.org`

- different depths of the neighborhood;

- whether the universe is finite or infinite, with special rules for border cells in finite universes; and

- variation in rules for updating the state of cells.

Different choices made on each of these variation points will produce a large family of cellular automata. This is typical of modern systems, which increasingly can no longer be shipped with the assumption that one-size-fits-all, and thus frequently take the form of product lines. While the basic vision underlying *Software Product Lines* (SPL) can probably be traced back to David Parnas's seminal article [116] on the Design and Development of Program Families, it is only quite recently that SPLs are emerging as a distinct approach for modeling and developing software system families rather than individual systems [106]. SPL engineering embraces the ideas of mass customization and software reuse. This approach focuses on the means of efficiently producing and maintaining multiple related software products, exploiting what they have in common and managing what varies between them. This notion of product lines will be further explored in Chapter 10.

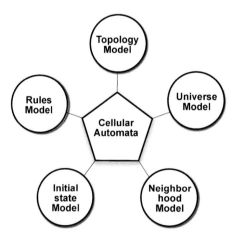

Figure 1.1 Modeling cellular automata: separating concerns.

Since modeling is the activity of separating and abstracting concerns of the problem domain, an activity often called *analysis*, it is not surprising that it typically produces at least one model per concern. In the cellular automata example, we would thus find a model for describing the topology, another one for the universe, and yet others describing the notion of neighborhood, the initial state of the cellular automata and the rules (see Figure 1.1). For instance, in a topology model we would find its number of dimensions (1, 2, 3 or more) and whether it is a grid or a torus. These models may be expressed with a general-purpose modeling language such as the UML, or with a DSML when available.

If modeling is separating concerns, the design process can be characterized as a weaving[4] of these model aspects into a detailed design model (also called the solution space). This is not a new idea: it is what designers have been doing forever. Most often, however, the various aspects are not explicit, or when there are, they are expressed as informal descriptions. So the task of the designer is to do the weaving in her head more or less at once, and then produce the resulting detailed design as a big tangled program (even if one decomposition paradigm, such as functional or object-oriented, is used). While it works pretty well for small problems, it can become a major headache for larger ones.

The real challenge here is not how to design the system to take a particular aspect into account: there is a wealth of design know-how for that, often captured in the form of design patterns. Taking into account more than one aspect at the same time is a little bit trickier, but many successful large-scale projects are there in industry to show us that engineers do ultimately manage to sort it out (most of the time).

The real challenge in a product-line context is that the engineer wants to be able to change her mind as to which version or which variant of any particular aspect she wants in the system. And she wants to do it cheaply, quickly, and safely. For that, repeating by hand the tedious weaving of every aspect is not an option.

We do not propose to make this problem go away, but to mechanize and make repeatable the process that experienced designers already follow by hand. The idea is that when a new product has to be derived from the product-line, we can automatically replay most of this design process, just changing a few things here and there.

This is really what model-driven design (MDD) is all about.

---

[4]Some also say: combining

1.5 SEMANTIC FOUNDATIONS OF MDE: THE MEANING OF MODELS

In this section, we introduce the primary concepts that are needed to formally and therefore precisely define not only the syntactic shape, but also the semantics (in terms of meaning) of a modeling language.

> **Note 1.3 Semantic Foundations of MDE**
>
> If you are a practically oriented reader, you may safely skip this section. On the other hand, if you are interested in an even deeper discussion of semantics, you might also look at [128, 60]. The following is a compact summary of these discussions and is needed to understand the forthcoming foundation bars.

1.5.1 Basics of Denotational Semantics

As explained above, computer science benefits significantly from, and even relies upon, explicit models. That means it needs explicitly defined languages, such as the UML. To define a modeling language we need to define the *set of models* that belong to it, their *syntactic shape*, their *meaning* (semantics) and how to use these models (purpose).

Please note that the *semantics* of a model definitely describes its meaning, which may be behavior or also structural constraints, depending on the language that we describe. For example, class diagrams are a structural modeling language and therefore their semantics is given solely in terms of structural constraints (in terms of which object structures are considered to be valid expressions in the language).

We will, in Section 2.4, use a denotational semantics that explicitly defines the *set of well-formed models* $\mathbb{L}$, a *semantic domain* $\mathbb{S}$, and a *semantic mapping* $\mathbb{M}$ between them. Often mathematics is used to describe the concepts of such a language definition, because mathematics allows a very concise description of the concepts of denotational semantics.

In particular, the *semantic domain* $\mathbb{S}$ is often a precisely defined set of mathematical entities representing what we want to describe. In the case of class diagrams, this should be object structures, while in case of Mealy machines (which are state-machines with output), this could be allowed input/output relations, maybe together with their state changes.

The *semantics mapping* $\mathbb{M}$ can be described mathematically, but becomes more practical with an algorithmic, executable implementation using, e.g., a generator.

The above is the essence of denotational semantics, which can be used both for programming and modeling languages. Based on this essence, we can look at variants and specific problems.

1.5.2 Underspecification and Interpretation in the Real World

Underspecification is used when specifying requirements in an abstract way or when the behavior of a model may not be fully determined at design time, but might be dependent on particular implementations chosen afterward. Underspecification can be captured using a set-based semantics, i.e., mapping one model to a set of semantic entities it describes.

This technique is used, for example, when defining the semantics of recognizing state machines with a semantic domain that consists of all words over an alphabet. The semantics of a concrete nondeterministic state machine, then, is exactly the set of recognized words. Consistency of a model is in this case easily defined by demanding that its semantics is not empty (i.e., there is an implementation).

For example, if we examine class diagrams, we identify a set of object structures as the semantic domain. Each class diagram describes the set of all possible object realizations. However, there are variations in this semantic interpretation.

We might think of a class diagram to be a view, i.e., an abstraction of the full object structure, because certain classes, associations and attributes are not shown. That means object structures may be much more detailed than the class diagram predicts. In this interpretation the class diagram is just a constraint. In a stricter form, we might only be interested in the object structures that belong to "minimal" implementations, in terms of having exactly the attributes and associations as defined and no additional surprises. While the latter is more oriented toward an implementation, the former allows us to use several class diagrams as views (and merge them accordingly). Please note that an implementation-oriented semantics is always much stricter than a specification-oriented semantics, i.e., it is a subset.

Please also note that the *semantic domain* $\mathbb{S}$ is a formal mathematical construct that does not necessarily, but hopefully, reflects the concepts of the real world that we want to describe. Thus the semantics of a language is always the same, regardless of how the semantic domain should be interpreted in the real world. For example, the recognized set of words of the state machine can be used for lexical analysis in compilers as well as for describing the allowed set of incoming messages for a communication component. This interpretation in the real world is left open to the modeler and is not (and cannot be) part of the formalization of the modeling language itself.

Class diagrams in turn might be interpreted as a requirements specification, where a class typically is an abstraction of a phenomenon of the real world, e.g., the class **Person** stands for the set of real people. But it might also be used to describe the architecture of a software implementation, where **Person** stands for a Java class. Unfortunately, the UML tries to cover both: language semantics as well as all the possible interpretations in the real world.

1.5.3 Operations on Models

In this book we will identify a number of semantically interesting operations on models, such as refinement, refactoring and model composition. Given our semantic definition, we can define semantics for the composition of models.

Foundation 1.4 Model Composition

Formally a composition of (two) models has this signature:

$$\otimes : \mathbb{L} \times \mathbb{L} \to \mathbb{L}$$

Composition of the syntactic models must be compatible with the composition of the semantics:

$$\forall m_1, m_2 \in \mathbb{L} : \mathbb{M}(m_1 \otimes m_2) = \mathbb{M}(m_1) \,\bar{\otimes}\, \mathbb{M}(m_2)$$

where $\bar{\otimes}$ denotes the semantic composition operation.

To understand the meaning of a syntactic composition operator, it is very helpful to have a clear understanding of what the composition should mean on the semantics.

Please note that the semantic domain often has a much simpler structure than the language and therefore it is much easier to define and understand a composition operation on the semantic domain than defining on the syntax. Furthermore, there are often many syntactic operations that map to the same semantic composition.

Refinement and refactoring are other helpful transformations that allow us to adapt models during the development process. Refinements will be discussed in more detail in Chapter 8, but we already have enough information to state the main idea underlying the semantic foundations of MDE: modeling is separating and abstracting concerns, enabled by composition and refinement techniques, that allow us to combine them into a single, hopefully coherent, system late in the development process, instead of from the beginning.

1.6   EXERCISES

Exercise 1.1 Models in Civil Engineering

List all the models that might be needed for the construction of a house.

Exercise 1.2 Models in Politics

List all the models describing a modern democracy from the political point of view.

Exercise 1.3 Advantages of Separating Concerns

List the advantages of separating concerns in the development and runtime management of software-intensive systems.

Exercise 1.4 Conway's Game of Life

Taking the example of Conway's Game of Life (see above), describe in English what information should be present in each of the 5 models of Figure 1.1.

What's a Modeling Language?

CONTENTS

IN this chapter we show how the use of domain-specific modeling languages allows us to create explicit models enabling discussion, analysis, and further processing of the models. We learn what a modeling language consists of: it comes with concrete syntax for the user, and abstract syntax for all the tools supporting the modeling language and the core mechanisms for defining meaning (semantics) of the language. We also learn to distinguish the different variants of concrete syntax and their advantages and disadvantages.

2.1 WHY WE NEED MODELING LANGUAGES

In the first chapter we discussed what models are. We also found out that while many disciplines use models to develop their products, most of them have a rather informal understanding of what a model actually is. In software engineering, this is different. We not only use models for communication among developers and with the client, we also want to automatically process and analyze these models, and in particular to generate code and tests from them. For this reason, we need a clear notion of what a valid model is and what a given model means.

Computer science and in particular software engineering therefore needs an explicit definition of the notion of a *model*. Mathematics and some ISO specifications share some of these characteristics, but do not specify their notion of model as explicitly or completely as software engineering must. Only when this is done, can we talk about the validity, consistency, quality, and semantics of the models in a sufficiently precise and automatic way.

A precise characterization of the notion of a model can be given by explicitly defining the set of all possible models in the form of a *modeling language*. A modeling language is defined like any other language but has a specific purpose, i.e., modeling.

Definition 2.1 (Modeling Language) *A modeling language defines a set of models that can be used for modeling purposes. Its definition consists of*

- *the syntax, describing how its models appear,*

- *the semantics, describing what each of its models means, and*

- *its pragmatics, describing how to use its models according to their purpose.*

Modeling languages are typically complex in their internal structure and are therefore usually defined in several layers. We usually distinguish between the *concrete syntax*, which is visible to the modeler, and the *abstract syntax*, which is used for the internal representation within the tools. This distinction between concrete and abstract syntax is typical for software engineering, because we do want tools to be able to read and manipulate our models.

To further understand how a modeling language is defined, we will look at illustrative example models for our cellular automaton. We will look at the concrete and the abstract syntax as well as the semantics of two languages being used in the cellular automata example.

2.2   CONCRETE SYNTAX

It is important to distinguish between the essential information a model conveys to its reader, and the concrete *representation* necessary for the human reader in order to grasp and/or manipulate this essential information. Although humans do have many input sensors, most of the time when we are choosing a concrete representation for a model we focus on visual representations. In most contexts we can safely neglect other sensor channels, such as haptic and audio, for effective model understanding.

Definition 2.2 (Concrete Syntax) *The concrete syntax of a modeling language is used to describe the concrete representation of the models and is used by humans to read, understand, and create models. The concrete syntax must be sufficiently formal to be processible by tools.*

Models can be visualized in a variety of forms. It is common to categorize them into graphical (or diagrammatic) and textual forms. Among these there are many variations, such as box-and-line diagrams, function graphs, trees, and tabular forms on the graphical side as well as ASCII- or XML-based textual forms.

Graphical visualization generally has the advantage that the reader gets an easy overview of the model, and particularly of the relationships between different parts of the model. At the same time, it also has the disadvantage that it often needs more presentation space than a textual syntax to convey the same content. Big models, therefore, are often easier to "read" by browsing through them using an advanced graphical visualization tool. Text, on the other hand, is sequential by nature and therefore easier to navigate in detail, but also needs assistance when specific information needs to be found. Tabular form is generally useful, but can only be applied if the information to be shown is structured in a regular form. We distinguish between tabular and graphical form, because the tabular form shares some characteristics with textual representation too.

While for some kinds of information it is preferable to use visual models, for example in state machines or the cellular automaton grid values; for other kinds of models a textual representation is preferred. For example, mathematical models as well as programs, which can also be regarded as a form of model, are usually represented textually. The most important point is that the model and therefore its language must be fit for purpose in terms of both its characteristics—easy to understand, readable, easy to construct—and its target audience, whether novice or advanced users. For this reason, the choice of the concrete syntax of a modeling language is crucial for the adoption of the language by a broader range of human users.

Note that we can also provide several concrete syntaxes for otherwise identical languages, for different purposes. For example, it is common to have a graphical representation for communication and understandability, and a textual representation to ease the edition of the models.

2.2.1 Textual Concrete Syntax

Processing textual concrete syntax is nearly as old as computing. Nowadays it has well established theories and tools, including grammars and parser generators (e.g., ANTLR[1])).

In the textual case, we indeed rely on an underlying alphabet like ASCII or Unicode as a basis, and group the characters available in two phases: First, we define lexical terms, like keywords (e.g., `init`), operators (e.g., `x`), numbers (e.g., `5`), or names (e.g., **Person**). Second, we group these lexical elements into full sentences of our language using a grammar. Listing 2.1 shows a complete sentence of the *Cellular Automaton Initialization Rules* language (CAIR). CAIR is used to describe the geometry and initial values of the universe for cellular automata. This listing tells us about a regular 5×5 geometry and how the values in that two-dimensional matrix shall be initialized. The initialization uses ranges for each dimension. More on the meaning of this CAIR-Lite version can be found in Section 2.4.

CAIR

```
regularGeometry {5 x 5}       // 2 dimensions 5x5 bounded world
init {[1..5] x 1}     = { 1 } // assign 1s on first line
init { 1     x [1..5]} = { 1 } // assign 1s on first column
init {[2..5] x [2..5]} = { 0 } // assign 0s to the rest
```

Listing 2.1 Example of universe initialization rules.

---

[1]Cf. http://www.antlr.org/

It is typically the case that the editing tool used to view/edit the text, as well as printed representations (like the ones in this book), use additional highlighting and fonts to ease the reading of the model. In Listing 2.1, for example, we see keywords being typeset in bold font and comments using a slanted font. This highlighting, however, has no influence on the essential information, the meaning of this listing, but is purely part of the representation and thus of the concrete syntax only.

The CAIR language has two further characteristics that many recent textual languages share. First, it allows comments of two forms. The line comment starts with // and the multi-line comment is enclosed in /* and */. Comments do not add essential information to the model, but help the reader understand what is being described within the model. No model will ever be more useful without comments, but modeling languages, quite similar to programming languages, try to keep the number and size of comments needed compact by defining a number of layout and naming guidelines.

Secondly, languages are typically agnostic to white spaces, which include real spaces, tabulators, and line breaks. This allows the modeler to freely add indentation or line breaks wherever she feels it useful to make the model more readable. In our example, we have arranged the main text in four lines, where each line conveys a compact piece of information. Please note that there are languages where indentation does play a role, as in Haskell, Python, or in makefiles.

As there is quite a variety of possible representations of the same information, any useful language typically provides a set of guidelines on how to describe a concrete model. This is very well elaborated in programming languages, where even comments, indentation, size and semantics of names, etc. are often guided by agreed-upon conventions. When deriving a new language, just as one draws upon other languages' syntaxes when designing the concrete syntax, it is also useful to derive the guidelines of usage from such a previously existing language. Violations of these guidelines do not result in an invalid model, but a less readable one. Because these guidelines can be detected by tools it is also possible to use *pretty printing* to rearrange the layout as well as add empty comments to highlight their absence. This improves the *representation quality* of a model. Please note, though, that the *quality of the essential information* remains the same.

The textual concrete syntax of a language is generally best described using a grammar. We show the EBNF grammar of a subset of the CAIR language in Listing 2.2, which we call CAIR-Lite. We are going to discuss the different elements of a language using this CAIR-Lite example. The version shown abstracts away from white spaces and comments that are, of course, necessary, but does, e.g., incorporate lexicals and keywords. We refer to [88] for the interested reader to learn more about grammars.

EBNF-grammar

```
/*
 * EBNF grammar describing the simplified version of the CAIR language:
 *   CAIR-Lite
 */
CAIR-Lite     = Geometry Rule*
Geometry      = 'regularGeometry' '{' (Dimension, 'x')+ '}'
Dimension     = Int 'circular'?
Rule          = 'init' Position '=' '{' Value '}'
Position      = (PositionRange , 'x')+
PositionRange = '[' Int '..' Int ']' | Int
Value         = 0 | 1
```

Listing 2.2 EBNF-grammar for the CA Initialization Rule Language.

The grammar-based definition of textual languages only allows for the definition of so-called *context-free* languages. Therefore, the definition of *context conditions* is needed as a third layer to prevent all possible inconsistencies that would disqualify the model from being meaningful. In our example we have defined the geometry as a 5×5 bounded world. This immediately imposes the context condition on the developer to describe all positions to be within the borders between 1 and the maximum (5) as well as that the number of position ranges is the number of initial dimensions (in our case 2). Other typical context conditions occur when names are being used to refer to elements that have been defined elsewhere. This is not the case in CAIR, but programming languages and many modeling languages do have references to types, classes, methods, attributes, variables, states, actions, associations, roles, and the like.

As a second example for a textual language, Listing 2.3 shows the listing of two evolution rules that implement the Game of Life. The *Cellular Automaton Evolution Rules* (CAER) language is similar in its style to CAIR, in that it similarly allows comments, is agnostic to white spaces, and consists of lexical elements that are grouped together hierarchically using a context-free grammar. However, it differs in the keywords it provides, the structure of how these rules are defined, and

Note 2.1 XML-Based Languages

With XML we, in principle, have another mechanism that allows us to describe modeling information. XML is a carrier language like ASCII that becomes meaningful when using a concrete grammar on top. In the case of XML, a grammar is defined using an XML Schema Definition (or XSD). It allows us to define a specific XML-based language that can be used to encode essential information. For simple structured information, like large lists of similar data, it might be reasonable to consider XML data to be human readable and even understandable. However, XML-based languages cannot really be considered human readable when they try to capture highly complex data structures such as those needed for complex modeling languages. From a technical point of view, defining parsing/printing tools for XML is only slightly more complex than defining a grammar-based language. However, from a user's perspective, there is a lot more effort involved to find and interpret essential information between the tags. It is also worth noting that although XML is, on the one hand, a textual language, on the other hand, it embodies a tree-like structure, which enables us to view and manipulate XML data using a tree browser.

of course its semantics, which will also be discussed in detail later.

CAER

```
/*
 * Game of life Cellular Automata rules
 * Universe: 2D grid, cells have 8 neighbors, 0 represent a dead cell,
 * 1 a living one
 */
// Rule for living cells (if a cell has 2 or 3 living neighbors
// it will live, otherwise it will die)
when [1,1] nextValue = {
  if neighborsSum == 2 | neighborsSum == 3 {1} else {0} }

// Rule for dead cells (if a cell has 3 living neighbors it will
// be reborn, otherwise it will remain dead)
when [0,0] nextValue = {
  if neighborsSum == 3 {1} else {0} }
```

Listing 2.3 Example of evolution rules implementing the Game of Life.

When we define a grammar for CAER we can reuse a number of the lexical and grammar definitions from the CAIR language, but the CAER grammar would be considerably more complex and would have a different overall structure.

2.2.2 Graphical Concrete Syntax: Box-and-Line Diagrams

Graphical modeling languages use both dimensions available on paper and screen. These languages may have three dimensions in the future. These diagrams are typically augmented with pieces of text to represent the essential information in the model. Many of the modeling diagrams used today are combinations of boxes and lines in various shapes or styles, and often allow hierarchical nesting. StateCharts [58] are basically state machines that allow additional nesting of states. Class diagrams [113] are another example of diagrams that use boxes, with three compartments to describe class structures and a variety of lines to relate boxes for composition, association and subtyping. Sequence diagrams use a special form of lines, namely *lifelines*, that only have a beginning and continue downward forever.

In Figure 2.1 we see a UML object diagram. Object diagrams are typical box-and-line diagrams that are used to describe concrete object structures. In this case we have 25 objects of class `Cell`, each of them equipped with the attribute `val` carrying a concrete value, which is either 0 or 1. This graphical representation describes the situation directly after the initialization defined in Listing 2.1 has been completed. Not only are the contents of the cells important, but also their linking structure, which describes the relationship of being a neighbor between them.

Just as a textual language defines its primitives as lexical terms, a diagrammatic representation of models also has a set of diagram primitives that are combined to describe the model elements. In the case of a box-and-line diagram, these primitives are various shapes of boxes (e.g., rectangles, ovals, circles, clouds and the like often equipped with additional symbols) and lines in dashed, continuous, and other broken forms as well as with various line ends (e.g., arrows, triangles, diamonds) to distinguish different kinds of elements that a model can have. While these shapes allow us to distinguish between different kinds of model elements and therefore contribute to the essential information of the model, we typically abstract away from the layout and size of these elements, just as a textual representation abstracts away from

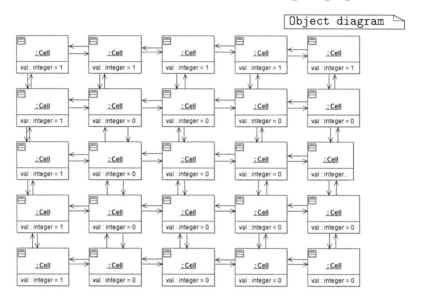

Figure 2.1 Graphical representation of a two-dimensional universe (object diagram).

white space. For example, in class or object diagrams, diagrammatic proximity of two boxes (i.e., classes, objects) and their size has no significance to a tool that processes the model. However, layout and placement has a lot to do with readability for humans, as we can easily see in Figure 2.1. Here the position of the objects suggests a two-dimensional tabular structure that is actually defined in the diagram by using the neighbor links.

We also typically do not use color, highlighting and, for example, line thickness to transport essential information. This is partially because misinterpretations could then easily happen especially on copies in black and white. Please note that there are exceptions to this rule[2]: for example, Statemate [59] uses the clockwise order to resolve underspecified transitions going from one state, and Live Sequence Charts (LSCs) [30] incorporate red and blue messages to describe different intentions, as well as lifelines that convey a temporal ordering of their messages.

As in the case of textual syntaxes, it is important to agree on a set of guidelines that describe how a good model should look.

---

[2]In general, most approaches of *live modeling* would break with this rule.

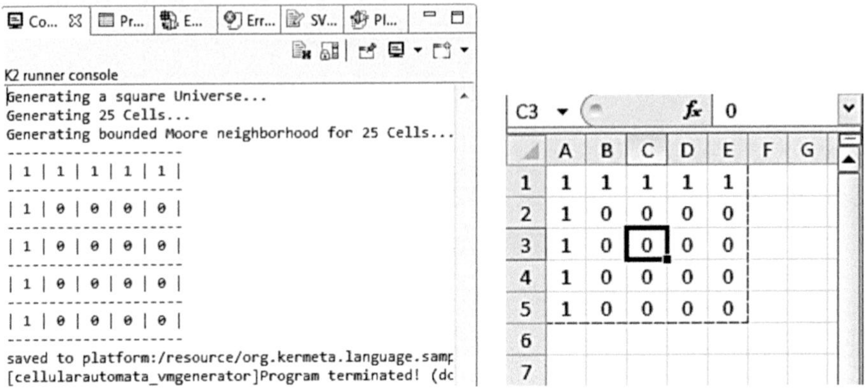

Figure 2.2 Tabular representations of a two-dimensional universe (ASCII and spreadsheet).

These guidelines are typically specific to the diagrammatic language in question. In class diagrams it is common to place the most important classes in the middle, because we are then able to arrange all associations around these classes. In state machines we place the initial state(s) on the top left and try to arrange transitions to go clockwise. Unfortunately, the style guidelines for graphical syntaxes are often much more involved and/or subjective than those for textual syntaxes, and less well supported by editing tools, such that pretty printing often only exists in very limited forms (such as autolayout).

2.2.3 Graphical Concrete Syntax: Tabular Notations

A special form of graphical notation that actually shares quite a number of characteristics with textual notations is the tabular syntax. Tables can be used in various forms, including being hierarchically nested as discussed in [115]. In our example, we can use a two-dimensional grid to describe a concrete tabular layout of a Cartesian universe. Figure 2.2 shows possible tabular layouts of the situation in our universe again right after initialization.

The tabular visualization on the left uses rather simple mechanisms, namely ASCII characters (| and -) to mimic the grid. The visualization on the right illustrates that mechanisms similar to Microsoft's well-known Excel are possible as well. The content of each cell is depicted with its current value in text form (0 or 1). Again, the concrete form of the grid, such as width or height of the cells, does not constitute essential information, and elements other than ASCII characters could be used. The position of a value within the grid, however, is very significant. One has to know the index of the value to understand the cell to which the value belongs. This is why a grid in our case can be much more compact than an object diagram, since the neighbor relation is actually shown through the adjacency of the cells.

In larger grids, of course, it is often useful to number the rows and columns and possibly to provide a visualizer with scrolling and zooming functionality. Fortunately, the layout of models such as this tends to be rather fixed and therefore not many guidelines are necessary to improve the readability of tabular data. On the other hand, these kinds of models are also very limited in their expressivity and can only be used in regularly structured situations, such as the cell contents of our Cartesian grids.

2.2.4   Graphical Concrete Syntax: Trees

A second special form of diagrammatic representation is that of *trees*. Such a representation is only possible, of course, when the essential information to be represented is internally organized in a hierarchical tree. This is quite often the case, because it is often relatively easy to define a spanning tree over a graph structure.

Trees share some characteristics with text and some with ordinary box-and-line diagrams. First of all, trees can of course be depicted with a box-and-line diagram, where each node becomes a box and the relations to children become links.

But it is also quite easy to define an automatic layout and to navigate trees in a graphical way, as for example in the usual file and directory navigators that can be found in operating systems such as Windows or Linux.

The graphical representation of a tree is much easier because we know that the root node is placed on top of the diagram. Therefore an accepted way of inspecting a tree is by starting to read at the top and navigating through the children hierarchically. Most tree editors exhibit one of two representation conventions. In one, the children at the same depth in the tree are aligned horizontally, and placed symmetrically below their parent. The second commonly used form of hierarchy (e.g., seen in the Windows file explorer and many other tools), is very commonly used to show file and folder hierarchies, where children are depicted sequentially below each other, i.e., are aligned vertically, and the depth of a child within the tree determines its (horizontal) indentation. These conventions are often combined with common tools for manipulating the tree representation, such as hiding/folding and revealing subtrees, in what is generally accepted as an easy way to view and manipulate trees. XML structures, which as we have learned can also be seen as trees, are also often shown and manipulated this way.

Later, when we discuss internal representation of various modeling languages using metamodeling as well as grammars, we will talk about the conceptual difference between trees and ordinary graphs, the possibility to extend a tree with additional links such that it becomes an ordinary graph with a spanning tree embedded, as well as the necessity to map a graph structure into a tree (e.g., for storage) using identifiers to break up the links. We will see that trees as opposed to box-and-line diagrams not only have differences in concrete syntactical representation, but also in their internal representation in the form of abstract syntax.

Note 2.2 Other Kinds of Diagrams

There are other kinds of diagrams, for example typical function graphs for mathematical functions $f : \mathbb{R} \rightarrow \mathbb{R}$, pie charts, candlestick charts, bar plots, and many others. While they of course convey essential information and also fulfill our definition of being a model from 1.1, they are less commonly used for software development, serving more often for communication among humans. We leave the consideration of these kinds of diagrams as an exercise to the reader.

2.3 ABSTRACT SYNTAX

In Section 2.2 we have already identified that humans need a readable representation of a model. The very same holds for tools that need an internal representation of a model, which includes all of the essential information of a model, but abstracts away as much as possible from unnecessary details (aka syntactic sugar). As mentioned above, information such as layout or comments are typical representation information that are present and useful in the concrete syntax, but should be abstracted away in the abstract syntax.

Definition 2.3 (Abstract Syntax) *The abstract syntax of a modeling language contains the essential information of a model, disregarding all details of the concrete syntax that do not contribute to the model's purpose. It is of particular interest for use by software tools.*

2.3.1 Abstract Syntax of Textual Languages

Textual languages are defined using grammars and use trees as their internal representation. In Figure 2.3 we see the tree resulting from the abstract syntax from the CAIR model in Listing 2.1. Typically, the abstract syntax tree is structurally equivalent to the grammar's productions. However, sometimes optimizations, rearrangements, and extensions are made in order to allow efficient storage and retrieval of information from the abstract syntax tree. In particular, the resolution of names by explicit links is an extension that leads to an ordinary graph with a spanning tree covering it.

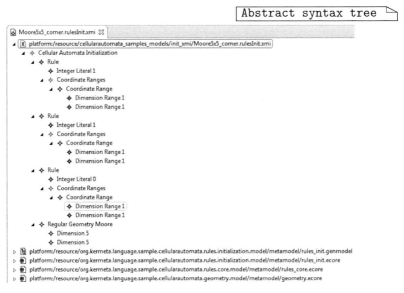

Figure 2.3 Abstract syntax tree of a cellular automata initialization rule.

While the grammar in Listing 2.2 describes the concrete syntax of the CAIR language quite well, we have two (not fundamentally different) approaches for the abstract syntax. We can either derive the abstract syntax tree directly from the grammar, something that e.g.,

> ## Note 2.3 Abstract Syntax Tree Representations
>
> Figure 2.3 actually only depicts a representation of the abstract syntax tree. Humans are generally in trouble with abstract syntax, as this is a tool-internal form of storage and any presentation in a book or a website needs a concrete representation of the abstract syntax. A quite different form of actually the same essential information would be to use an object diagram that would then reflect the tree structure through its form of linkage.
>
> As a convention in this book, we will nonetheless use this form of trees, as well as object diagrams, to depict the abstract syntax of our models.

compilers and language tool benches such as MontiCore [80] do, or we can use class diagrams on the so called "meta-level" to describe the set of possible CAIR models on the abstract syntax level, i.e., the CAIR metamodel (see Chapter 3).

2.3.2 Abstract Syntax of Graphical Languages

Diagrammatic languages are typically defined using the metamodeling approach that was mentioned earlier, and which will be discussed in detail in Chapter 3. Here class diagrams are used to describe the graph structures behind the boxes and lines that are visible in the concrete syntax. Thus any given model is an instance of such a class diagram, describing the abstract syntax of the model. A class diagram describing the abstract syntax (which is actually a metamodel) for the cell structure in Figure 2.1 is given in Figure 2.4.

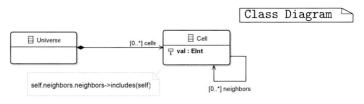

Figure 2.4 Abstract syntax for the cell structure.

A modeling language, by definition, describes a set of models.

However, the set of abstract syntax structures permitted as instances of this class diagram is not the same as the set of abstract syntax structures we wish to allow to be considered as valid models in our modeling language. Many of the structures permitted by the class diagram will include illegal structures, wrong combinations of attributes, and other such problems. In order to eliminate the possibility of these problems, the class diagram must be accompanied by information defining the well-formedness of the models. The well-formedness of a model is described using context conditions, which are in this case called *constraints* and can be formulated using languages such as the OMG standard called OCL (Object Constraint Language), which is explained in Chapter 3.

In our example, we can identify a number of potential constraints relating to the structures of the universe that we are going to allow. Two obvious constraints in our CAIR-Lite language are that the `neighbor` links are symmetric or that the cell values are 0 or 1. Further constraints might deal with the structure of the grid, e.g., limiting the number of neighbors, enforcing some regularity, etc. Please note that these constraints are to some extent artificial and for a general cellular automaton we may give up any of them including constraints on values or the symmetry of the neighboring relationship. We might even start to distinguish between "kinds" of neighbors, e.g., using *upper*, *left*, etc. neighbors.

2.3.3 Concrete and Abstract Syntax Relationship

The abstract syntax is used for efficient tool internal representation and domain analysis, allowing computers to check, assess, and manipulate models, or to derive or synthesize executable programs from them, while the concrete syntax helps the user to assess models. In the last sections we have seen several examples for concrete syntax (CS) and abstract syntax (AS) of modeling languages. Both have a strong relationship. Furthermore, it is often not a simple task to identify AS and CS and therefore we need methodological guidance. We therefore distinguish between these three dimensions: (a) how to denote CS and AS, (b) how AS and CS are related, and (c) the method to derive AS and CS.

As already discussed, there are different forms of concrete syntax, most importantly the textual, the diagrammatic, and the tabular forms. For textual languages, a grammar is used to describe the CS.

The very same grammar also describes the AS, by just ignoring the syntactical sugar present in the grammar. For diagrammatic languages, a metamodel, which is a certain form of class diagram, is used to describe the essential concepts of the language and their relationships. This class diagram is then augmented with information on how to represent these essential concepts on screens.

In both cases, textual and diagrammatic, the relationship between CS and AS is primarily defined as abstraction. The abstract syntax is derived from the concrete syntax by removing all the semantically irrelevant parts of the syntactic representation. In the textual case, this is done by removing the tightly integrated syntactical sugar from the grammar. In the diagrammatic case, we just ignore the layout and representation of augmentation, which is usually not directly part of the metamodel. This augmentation-based approach also has the advantage, that it is possible to attach different CS to the same metamodel, depending on different forms of interests and preferences by users.

Formally, the relation between CS and AS can be captured by a mapping between the concrete and the abstract syntax. This mapping is normally a relatively straightforward, structure-preserving abstraction. Depending on the actual use, the AS is sometimes enriched and potentially modified, for example for efficient navigation, quick lookup of symbols, and other data structures, e.g., for efficient consistency analysis, or assistance of evolution. This means that a modeling language may actually have several CSs and several ASs. In such a case, we still think of one modeling language in different syntactic shapes, regardless according to our Definition 2.1 these are different modeling languages that, however, share their semantics and should be at least very similar in the AS.

Both the pure abstract syntax as well as the enriched data structure are usually called metamodels.

The third dimension addresses the question of how to derive both forms of syntaxes. In practice, defining a new language is often a complex task. One potential approach would be to use the following (high-level) method:

1. Let users create an abstract description of the domain in which models should be described, and let the users define an appropriate set of examples (which are obviously defined in concrete syntax).

2. Derive the essential concepts of the language, which make up the core classes of the metamodel (= abstract syntax).

3. Define the relationships between essential concepts to bring structure into the language. This extends the metamodel by associations.

4. Constrain the metamodel by appropriate (context) conditions to ensure that each instance of a metamodel reflects a valid model.

5. Decorate the AS according to examples to define the CS.

When the domain is complex, and possibly with no common understanding and various stakeholders involved, or when different CSs have to be supported (e.g., one textual for edition and one graphical for communication and understanding), it's easier to first reason on the domain at the AS level as a graph of concepts and extend this later on in both directions (a) adding the CS and (b) adding tool-internal data structures.

In general, it is possible to define AS and CS in independent artifacts and in fact in independent order. It is also possible, as discussed above, to come up with several CSs for the same AS. For example, state machine tools often provide a diagrammatic and a tabular representation. However, abstract syntax is always a structure-preserving abstraction of the concrete syntax (as the name says) and therefore serves quite well as a starting point for a semantic definition of a modeling language.

2.4 SEMANTICS OF A MODELING LANGUAGE

Given a model, we need to ensure that the model has a consistent meaning for all involved persons and tools. The same syntactic representation, be it concrete or abstract, can have quite a variety of interpretations. If people are not aware of this problem, then the model is very likely to be misinterpreted at some point during the project. This misinterpretation could lead to implementing the wrong system, which in turn might lead to a project failure.

This is why the language definition always comes not only with the definition of the syntax that the user is going to manipulate, but also with the *semantics*, which gives each model of the language a *meaning*.

Definition 2.4 (Semantics) *The semantics of a modeling language captures the essential information of its models in the form of an explicitly defined*

- *syntactic domain that describes all well-formed models,*

- *a semantic domain that captures all essential information that the models can describe, and*

- *a semantic mapping that relates the syntactic constructs of the models to the semantic domain.*

Semantics can be defined in various forms. Computer science generally distinguishes between *denotational*, *operational* and *axiomatic* semantics. Furthermore semantics can be defined mathematically or in algorithmic form (both approaches converge continuously, but with expressiveness and computational complexity). All these variants of semantics have their advantages and disadvantages.

2.4.1 Denotational Semantics

Denotational semantics describe what a model means, without talking about how this meaning is actually achieved. Denotational semantics is typically defined using mathematical constructs. As a result, it is quite abstract and typically requires some training in mathematics to understand. Its advantage is that because we have the full power of mathematics at hand, we do not have to suffer from computational limitations.

For the CAIR-Lite language defined in Listing 2.2, let us examine how such a denotational semantics can be defined in a compact mathematical form.

The first part of CAIR-Lite deals with the geometry and size of the underlying structure. CAIR allows us to define a grid of a fixed dimension $n \in \mathbb{N}$ and a size of $s_i \in \mathbb{N}$ for each $0 \leq i \leq n$. We regard s to be this vector of dimensional sizes.

The second part of CAIR deals with the question of how to fill the grid with values. Mathematically, the grid can be defined as a vector space G over its values (see Foundation 2.5). To be able to talk about individual values, we also define the set of positions P as an extension to the core semantic domain. As an additional piece of essential information, we have to reflect which of the dimensions

Foundation 2.4 Denotational Semantics

Denotational semantics explicitly defines the *set of models*, a *semantic domain*, and a *semantic mapping* between them. We use mathematics to describe the concepts of such a language definition, because doing so allows us a very concise description of the concepts of denotational semantics.

Let $\mathbb{L}$ be the *set of models* in their syntactic shape. For example, these could be all class diagrams, state machines, etc.

Let $\mathbb{S}$ be the *semantic domain*, which is a precisely defined set of mathematical entities representing what we want to describe. In the case of class diagrams, this should be object structures, and in the case of Mealy machines, this could be the allowed input/output relations together with their state changes.

A *semantics mapping* $\mathbb{M}$ is then a mathematical function that relates one model of our modeling language with its meaning:

$$\mathbb{M} : \mathbb{L} \to \mathbb{S}$$

This is the essence of denotational semantics, which can be used both for programming languages as well as general-purpose and domain-specific modeling languages.

are circular. This is information that does not directly correspond to changes in the grid itself, but will become important later when we describe evolution in the state of the grid. Here we again use an n dimensional vector c with Boolean values.

The complete essential information is then stored in a tuple (n, s, c, G, val) reflecting exactly one universe. Each concrete model of CAIR-Lite corresponds to exactly one such tuple. The *semantic domain* $\mathbb{S}$ is therefore the set of all these universes U defined in Foundation 2.5.

We are now able to define the *semantic mapping* $\mathbb{M}$ that relates the syntax with the semantic domain. This mapping becomes a mixture between metamodels or grammars on the one hand and the above defined mathematical construct U on the other side. We can describe the mapping informally as done here or even more formally as, e.g., discussed in [60, 128]. In Foundation 2.6 we use a more informal argument, but it is sufficiently detailed and precise that we could derive an explicit definition of the mapping from it.

Foundation 2.5 Semantic Domain for CAIR-Lite

The semantic domain $U = \{(n, s, c, G, val)\}$ of CAIR-Lite is defined by:

- the dimension of grid $n \in \mathbb{N}$;

- s as a vector of dimensional sizes, i.e. $s_i \in \mathbb{N}$ of each dimension $(0 \leq i \leq n)$;

- vector space $G = \{0, 1\}^{s_1 \times \cdots \times s_n}$;

- grid positions $P = \{ (p_i)_n \mid 1 \leq p_i \leq s_i \}$,

- retrieval function $val(g, p)$ for the value of $g \in G$ at position $p \in P$; and

- vector on circularity $c = \{\texttt{true}, \texttt{false}\}^n$ for each dimension.

One of the advantages of an explicit definition of semantics is that it also provides a fresh view of the language itself. When defining this mathematical structure, one very quickly notices that it is unclear what happens if two init clauses conflict, or if no init clause is given at all. Foundation 2.7 describes this formally and applies it to an enhanced semantics of CAIR.

We can also select a specific semantics now by saying that the first matching init clause has higher priority. Furthermore, we define the semantic mapping such that if a position is not initialized at all, we use 0 as the default initialization. Please note that our choice of priority does not allow us to read to the init clauses as a sequential program. It is an advantage of denotational semantics that we don't have to care about operational or implementation issues.

The underspecification technique is used, for example, when defining the semantics of (recognizing) state machines where the semantic domain is set of accepted words.

While the equality definition for $=$ looks pretty simple, it is a core value of a good theory to know, which representations are semantically equivalent and can thus be used for optimization, simplification, refactoring, or restructuring to embrace later extensions. In Section 8.1.2 we will discuss the relationship between underspecification and

---

Foundation 2.6 Semantic Mapping for CAIR-Lite

The mapping relates syntactic elements to the universe (n, s, c, G, val) as an element of the semantic domain.

The first part of a CAIR-Lite model will be a syntactic clause like

CAIR with placeholders

$$\texttt{regularGrammar } \{ \ a_1 \ o_1 \ \texttt{x} \ a_2 \ o_2 \ \texttt{x} \ \ldots \texttt{x} \ a_k \ o_k \ \}$$

This line incorporates "placeholders" like a_i for integers that denote dimensions, and o_i, which is either keyword 'circular' or empty. This line determines $n = k$, $s_i = a_i$ and $c_i = (o_i = \text{'circular'})$.

All further syntactic clauses look like

CAIR with placeholders

$$\texttt{init } r_1 \ \texttt{x} \ r_2 \ \texttt{x} \ldots r_k \ \texttt{= } \{ \ v \ \}$$

with r_i as single position x_i or a position range $[l_i, u_i]$. For any grid position $p = (p_i)_n \in P$ with $(l_i \leq p_i \leq u_i)$ or $x_i = p_i$, we get $val(g, p) = v$.

Note that this definition is valid when there is exactly one clause for each position (this is a context condition here).

---

the possibilities to use it for refinement of models, which is a little weaker than equality, but also very powerful in understanding how to evolve models over time.

Let us apply the general principle of underspecified semantics for CAIR-Lite.

Unfortunately, the above definition of universe U is pretty specific to the simplified version of CAIR-Lite that has been defined in Listing 2.2. We need a more general semantic domain in order to define the semantics of the full CAIR language,[3] or even use a direct implementation for any kind of irregular cellular automaton. It needs a semantics using graphs as the underlying mathematical constructs. One characteristic of this approach is that all information about circularity is directly embedded in the structure of the edges. This is an advantage, as circularity does not need to be handled or stored as a special case

---

[3]CAIR will be introduced in detail in Section 3.6.

🎓 Foundation 2.7 Underspecification Reflected in Semantics

Underspecification is a technique for leaving details open when variability is explicitly desired in the specification. Underspecification can be captured using a set-based semantics i.e., mapping one model to a set of semantic entities ($\wp$ denoting the powerset):

$$\mathbb{M} : \mathbb{L} \to \wp(\mathbb{S})$$

Two models $m_1, m_2 \in \mathbb{L}$ are semantically equal when the following equation holds:

$$\mathbb{M}(m_1) = \mathbb{M}(m_2)$$

Model m_1 is a refinement of model m_2 when the following inequation holds:

$$\mathbb{M}(m_1) \subseteq \mathbb{M}(m_2)$$

A model is exactly *consistent* if its semantics is not empty (i.e., there is an implementation):

$$consistent(m) \Leftrightarrow \mathbb{M}(m) \neq \emptyset$$

🎓 Foundation 2.8 Underspecification in Semantics of CAIR-Lite

Universe U stays the semantic domain, but each model is now mapped to a set of universes U reflecting underspecification:
From the above, the meaning of syntactic lines l_k is adapted

> CAIR with placeholders 🔖
> init r_1 x r_2 x...r_k = { v }

such that each line l_k describes a set of grids S_k, where only the specified ranges are constrained. The semantics of the overall CAIR model is then an intersection $\bigwedge S_k$ of all initialization lines. The result is exactly nonempty if the initializations are non-overlapping or consistent at the overlaps. The result contains more than one possible initialization, when the init rules do not cover the full grid, i.e., have been underspecified.

anymore, but also a disadvantage, as it is not as easy to see whether a given graph has a regular structure.

2.4.2   Operational Semantics

In the above case, we have used a denotational semantics for a textual language. The same approach would work for a graphical language in a very similar way. Denotational semantics only cares about the result, and is not always very helpful when the language is to be used for execution. In this case an operational semantics is of better help.

An *operational semantics* is typically defined by mapping an input model to some executable code, which then executes on an appropriate data structure. Quite often it is a case that this execution is assisted by a *virtual machine* that manages the data storage, assignment of any kind of variables, method calls and returns, etc. It typically also provides a number of predefined generic procedures that can be reused.

For the initialization language CAIR, such an operational semantics is not that interesting. By contrast, for the evolution language CAER it will be very interesting, and we will discuss a simulator for this evolution language in Chapter 7. It will embody a virtual machine specifically designed for cellular automata and will be written in such an operational way that we can actually run the derived engine. With such a simulator, CAER exhibits characteristics not only of a modeling language, but also of a high-level programming language.

Having an executable operational semantics allows us, for example, to run the code as a simulation. This has the big advantage that we can experience the behavior of the system very early in the development process and identify possible misbehaviors and errors before they become expensive. We can also use the simulated system for behavioral analysis and for automated testing. In both cases the shifting of the verification process from a late phase to the early development phases considerably enhances quality, development predictability, and reduces costs.

It may be the case that the resulting code is not only suitable for simulation, but can directly be embedded in the final product. This has additional advantages: first of all, assuming that the generator works correctly, the whole process of implementation becomes correct by default. This considerably reduces the development costs both for implementation and testing. Secondly, it allows engineers to evolve the system much more easily, as we can always go back to the models to

Foundation 2.9 Graph as Semantics for CAIR

The *semantic domain* is a graph structure $(V, E \subseteq V \times V)$ that describes cells as nodes V and the neighboring relation as edges E. Function $val : V \to \mathbb{R}$ assigns a value to each node.

The *semantic mapping* maps the clause

CAIR with placeholders

```
regularGrammar { a₁ o₁ x a₂ o₂ x ...x aₖ oₖ }
```

as follows: The set of positions P is again constrained by $s_i = a_i$. We use these positions as nodes: $V = P$. Edges are then defined in several steps using these core relations:

Math

$$F_j^{reg} = \{ (p, q) \in P \times P \mid p_j = q_j - 1 \wedge (\forall i \neq j \Rightarrow p_i = q_i) \}$$

for the regular edges, and this relation for the edges that occur when the dimension is circular:

Math

$$F_j^{circ} = \{ (p, q) \mid p_j = s_j \wedge q_j = 1 \wedge (\forall i \neq j \Rightarrow p_i = q_i) \}$$

We add these relations together in form of F as a union of all regular F_j^{reg} and all circular F_j^{circ} where $o_j =$ 'circular'.

Math

$$F = \bigcup_j F_j^{reg} \cup \bigcup_{j, o_j = \text{`circular'}} F_j^{circ}$$

As neighboring structures are symmetric, when defined using CAIR-Lite, we use the symmetric closure for our edges $E = F \cup F^{-1}$.

The semantics for the init clauses is almost the same as previously given and is thus omitted in this example.

understand evolution and directly map those to the evolving system again.

2.5 EERCISES

Exercise 2.1 Experiencing Cellular Automata Structures

Install the Eclipse environment for this exercise as explained in the book companion web page.

- Go to project `ca.game_of_life.samples` which contains several CAIR models. Run these models by using the *Cellular Automata interpreter* and the `game_of_life.caer` model.

- CAIR model `spaceship_01.cair` has a replicating pattern that slowly moves. Extend the grid such that you can watch it moving for a longer period of time. What happens if you make the grid become circular?

Exercise 2.2 The CAIR Language

Install the cellular automata sources for this exercise as explained in the book companion web page.

- File `cair.xtext` contains the full CAIR grammar. Understand the full CAIR grammar in an implementable way. What are the main differences?

- Replace keyword "regularGeometry" with "cube." Make relevant changes in the implementation. Adapt one of the CAIR models. Rerun.

- Adapt the CAIR grammar in such a way that curly brackets ("{" and "}") becomes optional.

Exercise 2.3 Semantics of CAIR-Lite 1/2

- For each CAIR-Lite model in `cair_lite.exercise`, indicate how many cells they declare and how many links between the cells. How many cells have value 1?

 Exercise 2.4 Semantics of CAIR-Lite 2/2

- Define a CAIR-Lite model that will have 41 cells, all with value 1. How many links can such a model have?

- How many different CAIR-Lite models can you define that have 27 cells?

- CAIR provides a keyword "Neumann" that indicates that all diagonal neighbors are also connected (as opposed to the default "Moore" wiring). What would be an appropriate form of semantics? Define it precisely.

- Adapt the semantics definition for CAIR-Lite such that it has a default value when underspecified.

- Adapt the semantics definition for CAIR-Lite such that it reflects priorities of init rules from top to bottom.

Metamodeling with MOF and Ecore

CONTENTS

THIS chapter presents how to characterize a particular (technical or business) domain as a metamodel in terms of its essential concepts and their relations. If the users want to explicitly model specific information within this domain, then the metamodel can at the same time be used as a description of the essential part of domain-specific modeling language (DSML) dedicated to this particular domain.

The chapter introduces the MOF (*Meta-Object Facility*), which is dedicated to modeling the structural concern of domains. Then the chapter presents how to use a modeling environment such as EMF (*Eclipse Modeling Framework*) to automatically translate the domain model into the metamodel describing the DSML for this domain. We also discuss tools for serializing models for tool processing, based on an XML-representation. The concepts introduced in this chapter are illustrated by the definition of the abstract syntax of the different DSMLs of the cellular automata example.

After reading this chapter you will know how to obtain the abstract syntax of a DSML from the model of a particular domain. In practice, you will learn the OMG standard MOF and the EMF, including Ecore.

3.1 METAMODEL AND META-LANGUAGE

Let us consider the model shown in Figure 3.1, which represents a traffic light control system. This model aims to describe the behavior of the system, i.e., the possible states of a traffic lights (*red*, *green* and *orange*), including the initial one (*orange*), and the possible transitions from one state to another.

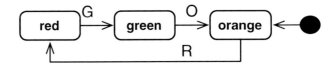

Figure 3.1 State machine (i.e., a model) of a traffic light.

The picture shown in Figure 3.1 is just a graphical representation of a model, just a normalized *drawing*. That can be suitable for human communication, but it is hard (although possible) to be processed by a computer program. Since we want to write programs to process models (i.e., the DSML tooling), our models must be *formalized* and should be easily and efficiently processible. Practically speaking, this means that our models must be put in a form that is readable, understandable, and modifiable, by a computer program. For such a purpose, we need a formal description of the structure of the model (i.e., the possible elements that can be in the model and their possible organization). This structural definition of the models, is interestingly at the same time a structural characterization of the domain, and a description of the abstract syntax of the language used to define the model.

There are several possible ways to achieve this. In this chapter we concentrate on the aforementioned approach called *metamodeling*. The core idea is that we are going to use the very same notion of a model to help us formalize models. We call such a special kind of model a *metamodel*.

Definition 3.1 (Metamodel) *A metamodel is a model describing the abstract syntax of a language.*

Consequently, metamodeling is a form of modeling the structure of the language in a precise way in order to characterize the valid models of the language (in the same way that a class diagram characterizes the valid object structures). As said, the resulting metamodel describes the abstract syntax of the language. MDE uses an object-oriented approach to model such a structure (e.g. MOF and Ecore) describing the possible elements and links between them. All model elements are thus classified in terms of the concepts that can be instantiated in the model, and the relations that organize them.

A model is valid with regard to a given language if the model *conforms* to the metamodel of this language.

Definition 3.2 (Model conformance) *A model conforms to a given metamodel if each model element is an instance of a metamodel element. Then a model is **valid** with respect to the language represented by the metamodel.*

Figure 3.2 shows a metamodel where the traffic light state machine shown in Figure 3.1 conforms to. The metamodel in Figure 3.2 contains the metaclass `StateMachine`, which is composed of metaclasses `State` and `Transition`. A state has references to a set of `outgoing` transitions. Transitions themselves refer to a `next` state. Finally, one of the states in the state machine must be an `initial` state.

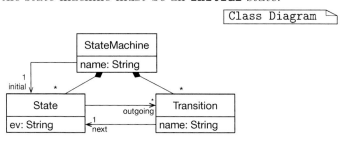

Figure 3.2 **A possible metamodel for a state machine.**

Note that Figure 3.2 represents only one of the possible metamodels to describe the structure of state machines. For example, Figure 3.3 shows another metamodel that also describes state machines correctly.

This metamodel includes the same concepts (`StateMachine`, `State` and `Transition`), but uses a different form of relation to connect transitions to their `source` and `target` states.

Dependent on the purposes that a metamodel has, different metamodel variants have individual advantages. Thus choices have to be made, which have a major impact, e.g., on how to navigate and manipulate models that belong to the DSML. This is a way to capture and capitalize on the knowledge of a particular domain. For example, in the metamodel given in Figure 3.2 it is easy to retrieve the outgoing transitions of a given state, but it is difficult to get the source state of a given transition, and vice versa in Figure 3.3. Another metamodel could use bidirectional associations respectively associations in both directions, but that would introduce memory overhead and redundancy that is difficult to maintain, when modifying the model. Consequently, a metamodel must be defined according to the particular needs in a given domain.

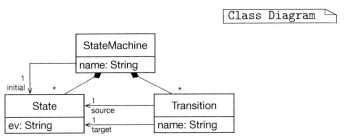

Figure 3.3 Another possible metamodel for a state machine.

Note also that by definition, a metamodel is often only an abstraction of a modeling formalism for a given purpose. Hence, a metamodel is *not* supposed to handle every possible aspect of a modeling language: it can be formal, yet incomplete. Depending on the purposes of the computer programs we want to write to process models, their metamodel might need to be complemented with other aspects, such as advanced consistency rules, execution data and rules if we are interested in building an interpreter or a compiler for our modeling language, or concrete representations (textual or graphical) if we expect to build an editor allowing a human to manipulate the conforming models. These aspects will be addressed in the following chapters.

In the following sections, we discuss, how and in which language to write a metamodel.

3.2 METAMODEL, META-LANGUAGE, LANGUAGE WORK-BENCH, AND META-METAMODEL

Of course the reader would have noticed that since a metamodel is a model, it must be formalized by another language. In the last decade, several dedicated languages have been proposed for describing metamodels. These languages can be seen as DSMLs whose domain is a particular concern of a language. Such languages are called *meta-languages*. In metamodeling, a meta-language is also called a metamodeling language.

Definition 3.3 (Meta-language) *A meta-language is a language dedicated to language modeling, i.e., for defining metamodels.*

In practice, most of the current MDE approaches leverages the object-oriented paradigm and most of the meta-languages are derivatives of UML's class diagram often extended by related languages, e.g., the Object Constraint Language (OCL).

Figure 3.4 (middle) shows the two metamodels of two languages, a (simplified) class diagram and a state machine. These metamodels describe the abstract syntax of both languages, using itself a simplified form of class diagram. We will later discuss the fact in greater detail, that the metalanguage class diagrams is used to describe the modeling language class diagrams.

The Figure 3.4 also illustrates the relation between a model and a metamodel, called *conformance* (cf. Def. 3.2. Conformance is applicable on the model in total, but also ensures that each model element is an instance of an appropriate metamodel element. State green is instance of metaclass State, G is instance of metaclass Transition, etc.

Meta-languages are usually supported by dedicated tools for language development called *language workbenches*. The term was initially popularized in 2005 by Martin Fowler.[1] Some prominent language workbenches are JetBrains's Meta-Programming System (MPS), MetaCase's MetaEdit+, the Eclipse Modeling Framework (EMF), MontiCore [94, 53], and the Microsoft's Visualization and Modeling SDK (formerly DSL Tools).

---

[1]Cf. http://martinfowler.com/articles/languageWorkbench.html

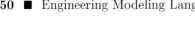

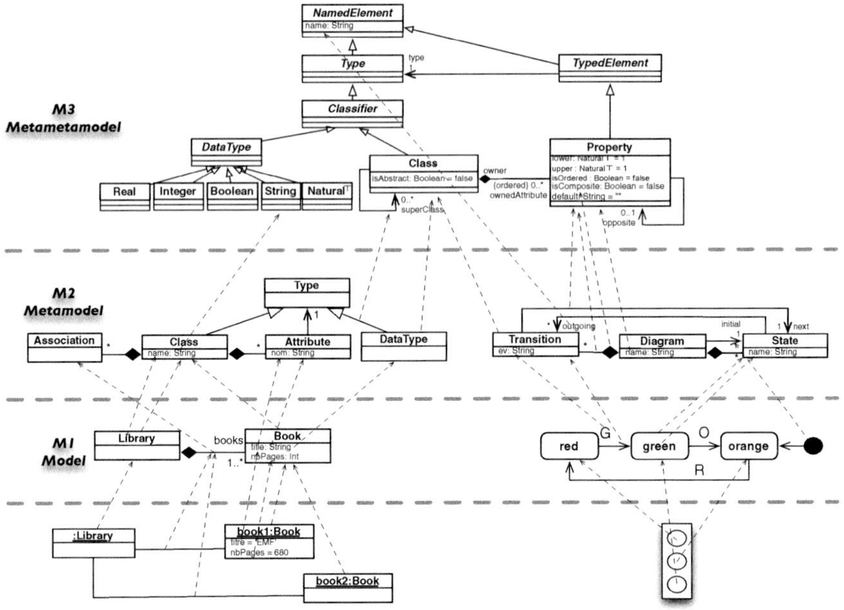

Figure 3.4 A hierarchy of metamodels describing models.

Definition 3.4 (Language Workbench) *A language workbench provides a set of tools and meta-languages supporting the development and evolution of a language and its associated tooling, including design, implementation, deployment, evolution, reuse, and maintenance.*

Supporting a meta-language in a language workbench requires an explicit description of the meta-language. Similar to a language, the meta-language itself is defined by a metamodel, namely a *meta-metamodel*.

Definition 3.5 (Meta-metamodel) *A meta-metamodel is a model describing a meta-language.*

Figure 3.4 (top) shows a simplified version of a meta-language for modeling the abstract syntax of languages. This meta-metamodel defines the concepts Class and Property, used to define the concepts of the language, and the relationships between them. In the same way that a model conforms to a metamodel, a metamodel conforms to a meta-metamodel.

As a meta-metamodel is itself a model, it can be formalized using a *meta-meta-metamodel*, and thus we could see ourselves in an infinite recursion. The solution to escape this kind of infinite recursion is to resort to metacircularity. That means, we use a metamodel to model its own shape. An example of such a metacircular metamodeling language is the Meta-Object Facility (MOF), discussed further below. Metacircularity just means that all the concepts available in a language can be modeled using the language itself. This is not an issue. In practice, this circularity helps tool infrastructures to construct themselves. Theoretical complaints can be handled by understanding that using a reflexively defined metamodel must not necessarily be the only way to describe itself. If another precise form of description exists, the circularly defined metamodel can comfortably model itself too. For example, EBNF can model any kind of textual language, including itself, and this is not a threat to EBNF's usability or precision.

3.3 META-OBJECT FACILITY (MOF)

The Meta-Object Facility (MOF) is a modeling formalism standardized by the OMG to specify the concepts and the relationships between these concepts for a particular domain. As MOF talks about the domains of modeling, these MOF descriptions, which are normally called metamodels also describe the abstract syntax of the corresponding DSML. For these descriptions MOF uses object-oriented techniques and, therefore, MOF descriptions are a form of UML class diagrams.

MOF has evolved considerably since its original standardization, and has for some time been associated with the UML specification, as the metamodeling language used by all OMG specifications. However, MOF is largely independent of UML, even if it shares some important structural concepts. Figure 3.5 displays an excerpt of the structure of MOF [112] (i.e., the meta-metamodel).

MOF allows specifying the concepts of a particular domain in a `Package`. Such a `Package` contains `Class`es and `Property`s to model the DSML concepts and relationships. A `Property` of a `Class` can be: an `Attribute` or a `References` to other another `Class`.

An `Attribute` is typed by an `Enumeration` or a primitive type, such as `Boolean`, `String`, `Integer`, `Real` or `UnlimitedNatural`.

MOF also allows for the specification of the services supported by

Foundation 3.1 The Pyramidal View of MDE

The modeling foundations can be, and often are, represented in a pyramidal way (see figure below). The real world (i.e., the system being modeled) is shown in the base of the pyramid (aka the M0 level). Models representing this system correspond to the M1 level. Metamodels for the definition of these models (e.g., the UML metamodel) correspond to the M2 level. Finally, meta-metamodels are shown at the top of the pyramid (M3 level). Each level corresponds to a particular use/purpose of models (M1 for modeling systems, M2 for modeling languages, and M3 for modeling meta-languages) and represents the capitalization of the body of knowledge for a particular domain used at the level below.

It should be noted that such a hierarchical arrangement of models according to their particular purposes is not specific to MDE, since it has been used in areas of computer science. For example we see such hierarchies in other *technological spaces* [81] such as grammarware (technical space of grammars defined by languages such as BNF or EBNF) or databaseware (technical space of databases).

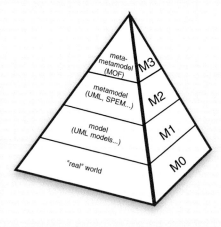

Note 3.2 Model-Driven Architecture

The OMG has defined the *Model Driven Architecture* (MDA) in 2003 [108] to promote good practices of modeling and to fully exploit the advantages of models. The latest version of the specification [110] gives a detailed definition of the architecture. This approach aims to highlight the benefits of models, such as sustainability, productivity, and the consideration of execution platforms. For such a purpose, MDA includes the use of several other OMG specifications, including UML, MOF, and XMI.

The initial and key principle of MDA consists of leveraging UML for defining separately the models of the different steps of the software development process. In particular, MDA promotes the definition of the following models:

- the *Computation Independent Model* (CIM) corresponding to a requirement model without consideration of the machine, computability or resource restrictions,

- the *Platform Independent Model* (PIM) corresponding to the design model, and

- the *Platform Specific Model* (PSM) corresponding to the code model, especially including machine specific issues and deployment on target hardware.

The MDA aims to support sustainable models (PIM), independent of all technical details of a particular execution platform (J2EE, .Net, PHP, etc.), to enable automatic generation of all code models (PSM) and a significant gain in productivity.

Moving from PIM to PSM involves transformation and composition mechanisms based on an explicit or implicit *Platform Description Model* (PDM).

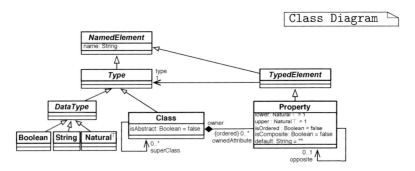

Figure 3.5 The MOF core with class diagram notation (excerpt from MOF 2.0 [112]).

a particular domain in terms of **Operation** (not depicted in Figure 3.5) signatures defined in the concepts of the domain model. Note that MOF does not support the definition of the operations' behaviors, but only their declaration (i.e., signatures).

MOF enables to define the abstract syntax of a language by instantiating its concepts, i.e., the concepts described in the MOF meta-metamodel. By convention, a class diagram is used as the graphical representation for this purpose. It should be noted that it would be possible to provide a different graphical representation, e.g. one similar to an object diagram (as instance of the metamodel) and to explicitly represent instantiation links between the metamodel elements and their instances. Figure 3.4 presents examples of instantiation links crossing the levels represented by dotted arrows.

3.4 ECORE AND EMF

As the field matures, there have various modeling frameworks been developed. Among others, the *Eclipse Modeling Framework* (EMF) is becoming more prominent to implement metamodels in the Eclipse workbench. It benefits from a set of tools such as reflective editors or XML serialization of models, as well as a uniform way of accessing models from Java.

EMF provides its own meta-language, namely Ecore, which can be seen as an implementation of MOF. Figure 3.6 shows an excerpt of the most important concepts of Ecore, which are very close to the ones of MOF presented in Section 3.3. For example, the **EClass** metaclass is equivalent to the `Class` metaclass in MOF. `Property` from MOF is, however, split in two metaclasses in Ecore: `EReference` for links between `EClass`es and `EAttribute` for properties which are typed by primitive datatypes such as `Integer` or `String`. The `containment` attribute in `EReference` specifies composition links in Ecore. MOF uses the `isComposite` attribute for this. Other attributes have been factorized and placed into abstract metaclasses. For example, `upper` and `lower`, which defines multiplicities of links, are extracted into the abstract class `ETypedElement`.

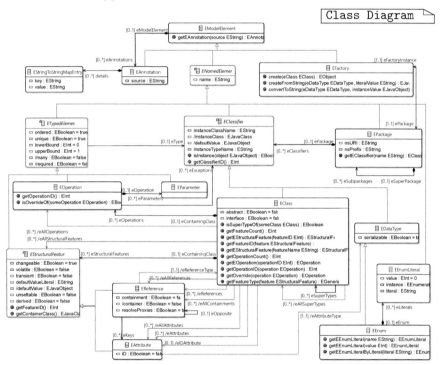

Figure 3.6 Ecore metamodel main concepts.

For avoiding confusion, not only with MOF, but also with the underlying Java implementation, the designers of Ecore have prefixed all the name of the concepts with an `E`. This is convenient when writing transformations and also helps to identify on which level (M1, etc.) a class resides.

EMF provides a number of tools that allow to specify metamodels and then to instantiate models conforming to them. The instantiation

> **Tip 3.3 Derived Properties in the Ecore Metamodel**
>
> Ecore has a set of operations and properties to help in manipulating Ecore models. This includes several derived properties (see attributes and references with a name starting with a / in Figure 3.6). They are comfortable, but can be used only for model navigation purposes.

of these models can be done either in a reflexive way or through the generation of a set of Java interfaces and implementation classes. Finally, the framework offers several services on these models such as basic manipulation, load and save in formats such as XMI, and event notification. Among others, EcoreTools provide an advanced graphical editor for Ecore models (Cf. Tool 3.4). As a feature specific to Ecore, EMF uses a registry of Ecore metamodels in order to uniquely identify a metamodel. More precisely, each **EPackage** defines a Uniform Resource Identifier (called nsURI). When loading models, the framework is able to create the Java objects implementing the correct Ecore definition.

> **Tool 3.4 EcoreTools**
>
> EcoreTools provides a comprehensive environment to create, edit and maintain Ecore models. It offers specific editors and tools to assist the design of a metamodel while applying the best practices of the EMF world. All classical Ecore constructs, such as **EClasses**, **EDatatypes**, **EReferences** are defined using a diagram editor. It also helps the language designer to document, review and specify constraints through specific layers that can be activated in each diagram.
>
> EcoreTools also provides editors for navigation and exploration of existing Ecore models and analysis of cross-model dependencies. It is an open-source software part of Eclipse and ready to use in the Eclipse Modeling Package: **https://www.eclipse.org/downloads/**.

EMF provides extensive generation facilities. The top right part of Figure 3.7 shows the popup that triggers the EMF code generator. It generates the Java structure presented on the left part of the figure. This popup is launched from a **genmodel** file that contains generator

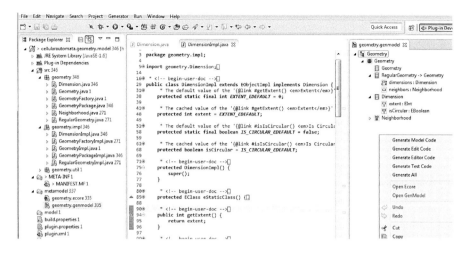

Figure 3.7 Screenshot: Generation of a metamodel implementation with EMF.

configuration information, which is itself seen as a model. It allows specifying some customization of the generated code. The generator creates four projects:

- A *model* project with the implementation of the metamodel. The generated Java code offers a type-safe way to navigate and manipulate models conforming to this metamodel. For example, it ensures the notion of opposite reference or the notion of containment. In Figure 3.7, for each class of the model, it creates an interface and an implementation Java class.

- an *edit* project that contains a reusable part for creating editors. More precise it offers a support for the presentation (text or icons) of each model element.

- An *editor* project that implements a basic tree editor for the Eclipse IDE.

- A *test* project that offers a host structure for testing the *model* project implementation using JUnit.

EMF also offers a notification service. This service enables a program to register on events such as model element creation, modification, or deletion. This is particularly useful for visualization

> **Tip 3.5 Protecting Hand-Coded Operations in EMF**
>
> The classes generated by EMF support an *@generated* annotation. When set to *@generated NOT*, the default generated code can be overridden and the generator will maintain the handwritten changes if the code is generated again. In the *model* project, this powerful feature should be limited to the implementation of operations or derived references/attributes.
>
> Chapter 6 discusses another more flexible approach for achieving similar goals.

and generation. Some editors based on this notification mechanism will be detailed in Chapter 5. For further details on EMF see the EMF Book [140] and the help in the Eclipse IDE.

Currently, EMF is extended by other frameworks and used by many model-based tools that need to collaborate using EMF as a cornerstone. This includes server solutions, persistence frameworks, UI frameworks, and support for transformations. Those extansions add services such as transaction, serialization in database, common model manipulation, comparison, or validation. Many of these frameworks can be found at the Eclipse Modeling project website[2] or in the Eclipse Market Place.[3]

> **Tip 3.6 EMF Is Not Tied to Eclipse**
>
> While the use of EMF is well integrated into the Eclipse IDE, the model manipulation part generated by the Eclipse Modeling Framework is independent of the Eclipse IDE. Any Java application with the EMF runtime jars in its classpath can use the *model* project to manipulate models.

3.5 REPRESENTATIONS FOR MACHINE CONSUMPTION

To avoid a complete lock-in of the development projects in a single tool infrastructure, it is also important that either the tooling provides

---

[2]Cf. http://eclipse.org/modeling/

[3]Cf. http://marketplace.eclipse.org/ mostly in Modeling, Modeling tools and UML categories.

an open API for model examination or manipulation and/or a model has a documented, and accessible stored representation that can be processed by other programs. This greatly improves the possibilities for example for exchanging, analyzing, executing and modifying the model. The abstract syntax of the model (see Section 2.3), thanks to the metamodel, can be serialized in various ways.

> ### Note 3.7 CRUD Access to Models
>
> A basic interface to access and manipulate a model is the CRUD interface, consisting of the four operations create, read, update, and delete, which are applicable to any model element.
>
> However, higher-level interfaces may –and ideally should– hide these low level operations in order to help maintaining the consistency of the model.
>
> In addition to providing a means to manipulate the abstract syntax of the model, these CRUD operations can also be used to create basic generic editors (see Section 5.2).

As primary interface EMF offers access to models via an API including methods for all of the CRUD operations necessary to that model. This includes:

- methods for adding and removing objects to and from a model;

- factory methods for creating objects of all non-abstract classes representing concepts in the modeling language;

- getter and setter methods for single-valued attributes and references;

- methods for accessing objects collections for multi-valued attributes and references, into which new objects can be added and from which existing objects can be removed; and

- abstract method signatures for storing models to and loading models from whichever persistent format is preferred.

The actual implementation for model storage is abstracted behind what EMF terms a *Resource Implementation*. This abstraction allows developers to select their variants of models storage concepts.

In addition to these methods, the framework also offers a reflective API, which can be used to inspect and modify models without prior knowledge of their metamodels. This allows reuse generic algorithms, such as counting objects or calculating transitive closures.

3.5.1 Textual Representations for Machine Consumption

As an alternative to the primary API used by EMF for accessing models it is possible to directly access the stored, linearized model. This allows for example to exchange models between different programs or develop own, pretty specific tools serving a specific problem. The most commonly used standard for this is the XML-Based Model Interchange (XMI) standard, which defines a mapping from any EMOF (or Ecore) model to an XML syntax (defined using an XML Schema). XMI is defined as an OMG specification [107] and is supported as a model interchange format by many tools, including EMF. Since XML is a tree structure, XMI uses a tree interpretation of a model-based on containment, in much the same way as the generic tree-based editor discussed earlier.

However, XMI is a pretty inefficient representation. In syntactically complex languages such as UML only 2–5% of the data is actually content and the rest is XML infrastructure. Furthermore, XML-based representations suffer from looking textual, but being neither really readable, nor well suited for version control. Versioning often fails because the usual line-based resolution of conflicts sometimes leads to syntactically invalid XML code and furthermore, the textual write-out of graphs can easily rearrange lists in different orders, which makes a tracing of the real changes in version control impossible.

Figure 3.8 shows an XMI representation of a Cellular Automaton universe. It shows the model elements in its XML syntax and how they reference each other. Except for the root elements, XML tags are used to follow containment links. In the example, which is conforming to the Ecore presented in Figure 2.4, an `Universe` contains `Cells` via an `EReference` named `cells`. The `EAttribute`s are directly stored as XML attributes (See the `val` of the `Cells`). The cross-references are stored in XML attributes and use a path expression to identify the target elements. By default in XMI, the path expression uses URI fragments of the form: `@feature-name[.index]`.

A more visual representation of the model in Figure 3.8 is presented on the right part of Figure 5.6 in Chapter 5.

```
x  Neumann5x5_corner.vm.xmi

    <?xml version="1.0" encoding="ASCII"?>
  <vm:Universe xmi:version="2.0" xmlns:xmi="http://www.omg.org/XMI" xmlns:vm="http://vm/1.0">
    <cells neighbors="//@cells.1 //@cells.5" val="1"/>
    <cells neighbors="//@cells.2 //@cells.6 //@cells.0" val="2"/>
    <cells neighbors="//@cells.3 //@cells.7 //@cells.1"/>
    <cells neighbors="//@cells.4 //@cells.8 //@cells.2"/>
    <cells neighbors="//@cells.9 //@cells.3"/>
    <cells neighbors="//@cells.0 //@cells.6 //@cells.10" val="2"/>
    <cells neighbors="//@cells.1 //@cells.7 //@cells.11 //@cells.5" val="3"/>
    <cells neighbors="//@cells.2 //@cells.8 //@cells.12 //@cells.6" val="2"/>
    <cells neighbors="//@cells.3 //@cells.9 //@cells.13 //@cells.7" val="1"/>
    <cells neighbors="//@cells.4 //@cells.14 //@cells.8" val="1"/>
    <cells neighbors="//@cells.5 //@cells.11 //@cells.15"/>
    <cells neighbors="//@cells.6 //@cells.12 //@cells.16 //@cells.10" val="2"/>
    <cells neighbors="//@cells.7 //@cells.13 //@cells.17 //@cells.11" val="1"/>
    <cells neighbors="//@cells.8 //@cells.14 //@cells.18 //@cells.12"/>
    <cells neighbors="//@cells.9 //@cells.19 //@cells.13"/>
    <cells neighbors="//@cells.10 //@cells.16 //@cells.20"/>
    <cells neighbors="//@cells.11 //@cells.17 //@cells.21 //@cells.15" val="1"/>
    <cells neighbors="//@cells.12 //@cells.18 //@cells.22 //@cells.16"/>
    <cells neighbors="//@cells.13 //@cells.19 //@cells.23 //@cells.17"/>
    <cells neighbors="//@cells.14 //@cells.24 //@cells.18"/>
    <cells neighbors="//@cells.15 //@cells.21"/>
    <cells neighbors="//@cells.16 //@cells.22 //@cells.20" val="1"/>
    <cells neighbors="//@cells.17 //@cells.23 //@cells.21"/>
    <cells neighbors="//@cells.18 //@cells.24 //@cells.22"/>
    <cells neighbors="//@cells.19 //@cells.23"/>
  </vm:Universe>
```

Figure 3.8 XMI example of a Cellular Automaton universe (von Neumann 5x5).

3.5.2 Database Representation

While XMI can be used in various situations for the persistent storage of models, there are occasions where XML is no longer a viable form for storing models. This is particularly true when the models are large and monolithic (and not decomposed into individual parts). In specific domains such as modeling the genome or medical data, modeling buildings or cities, or large data sets gathered from traffic, or permanently running sensors in general, models can easily contain billions of elements. Those forms of models and model data cannot be usefully stored in XML structures anymore, because they result in unacceptably large delays in loading, navigating, or storing a model. If a more scalable solution is called for, one possibility is to move to storing the information in database.

Frameworks such as CDO, Teneo, or MORSA allow the user to store models in a database — including traditional relational and NoSQL databases. The used framework takes responsibility for managing the loading and storing of model objects between the database and in-memory versions when demanded by programs accessing the models. In the simple case, this can be done without providing any information about the way the model is stored. Unfortunately, it is often necessary, to improve performance by using domain-specific knowledge about the models to adapt the mapping to the database.

3.6 ILLUSTRATIVE EXAMPLE: METAMODELS FOR THE CELLULAR AUTOMATON

As seen in Section 1.4, a system based on cellular automata combines several points of view depending on the purpose. For the Cellular Automaton example, we consider two variants of a rule language: one variant is used to define the actual evolution rules that drive how an automaton state will change over time (CAER); a second variant is used to specify the initial state of the automaton in a declarative way (CAIR). This second language is an alternative way to set the initial state. The other alternative would be to use an editor representing the automaton state and manually set each cell value.

As these two languages are very similar in structure (they both share some concepts), the proposed design factorizes common concepts in a kind of reusable language library. Other tools discussed in the following chapters will benefit from such a structure. This illustrates one way to combine and reuse languages. Other language composition approaches will be discussed in Chapter 11.

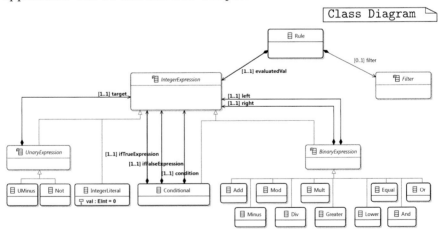

Figure 3.9 Reusable metamodel for rule expression (CACore).

Figure 3.9 shows the core structure of the expressions of the evolution language for cellular automaton (CAER). It is composed of rules with an expression and an optional filter. For the sake of conciseness in this book, all expressions are `IntegerExpressions`, because we encode the Booleans as Integers) (we will later see how to adapt the interpreter for this language accordingly).

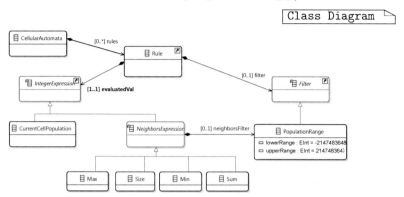

Figure 3.10 Evolution rules metamodel (CAER).

Figure 3.10 shows the extension of the core expression language used to allow to compute values based on the neighborhood of a `Cell`.

It is a typical problem for structural metamodels, that they don't directly describe the full meaning. While the meaning of the core expression language shown in Figure 3.9 is relatively straightforward, because its language concepts are well known, the extension of the expression language, which adds additional syntactic constructs in form of subclasses of `IntegerExpression` and `Filter`, needs extra explanations. This can for example be done in systematic explanations based on examples and looks similar to the following explantion: `Sum` will return the sum of the value of its neighbors. If a `PopulationRange` is applied, it will sum only the neighbor's values that match the range.

As suggested in Section 1.4.2, CAIR is a second DSML for our example that can be used to initialize a universe. In Figure 3.11, the `Filter` and `IntegerExpression` are subclassed into `Area` and `PositionLiteral` in order to offer some coordinate system so we can write rules based on the position in the universe.

Figure 3.12 describes the possible regular topologies of the universe that will be used to run the rules. It will be used in Chapter 7 to define the geometry of the universe and to initialize a part of the runtime model by generating the cells and their neighboring links. The values

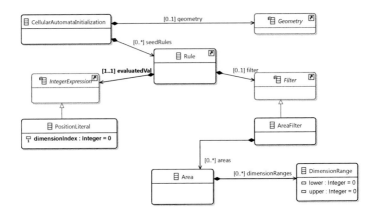

Figure 3.11 Initialization rules metamodel (CAIR).

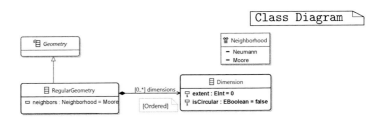

Figure 3.12 Topology metamodel.

in the cells will then be initialized thanks to the CAIR language.

All these metamodels have been implemented using EMF in Eclipse, see Figure 3.13, in order to provide the necessary tooling for these languages.

3.7 EXERCISES

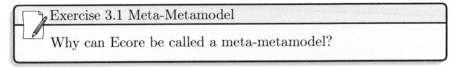

Exercise 3.1 Meta-Metamodel

Why can Ecore be called a meta-metamodel?

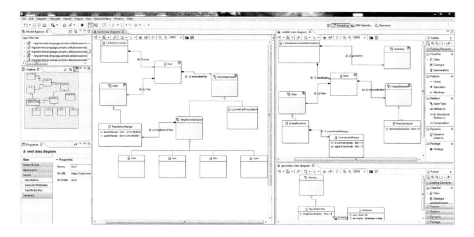

Figure 3.13 Example of Evolution rules, Initialization rules, and Topology metamodels in Eclipse.

Exercise 3.2 Topology Metamodel as Object Diagram

Draw the Topology metamodel above as an instance of Ecore, i.e., using the object diagram notation.

Exercise 3.3 Minimal Meta-Metamodel

Define the absolute minimal meta-metamodel that is able to both describe itself and the Topology metamodel above.

Metamodeling with OCL

CONTENTS

I N this chapter we learn how to describe additional properties that cannot be modeled with the structure-oriented MOF directly. We examine the Object Constraint Language (OCL), what invariants written in OCL mean and how these invariants are integrated into other kinds of diagrams, in particular MOF metamodels. We are then able to model fine-grained constraints on any kind of model including the shape and meaning of modeling languages.

With graphical notations such as MOF's class diagrams we cannot conveniently model every possible fact or requirement. This is why the OCL is a usable textual notation to describe complex properties in a rather concise and yet understandable, abstract form.

OCL is a derivate from logic languages and, thus, developers are not necessarily well familiar with some of the language concepts. In fact OCL shares a number of characteristics with expressions in ordinary programming languages, but also provides a number of extra concepts. It also looks a little unfamiliar due to its own syntactic form. But the modeling user will find OCL convenient to describe certain forms of system properties.

For this purpose we will introduce the language in the forthcoming section and demonstrate the use of OCL with MOF and cellular automata later on.

4.1 THE OBJECT CONSTRAINT LANGUAGE

The core idea of OCL is to allow the definition of properties of a data structure made of a set of objects in an abstract form, without caring too much about executability, while at the same time allowing use of the defined constraints during system executions. OCL constraints can be used for different purposes, including

- invariants on classes in a class diagram;

- pre- and post-conditions on methods;

- body in a query (i.e., operation without side effect); and

- guards on transitions in state machines, and on alternatives in sequence diagram.

In the rest of this section we will introduce generalities about OCL independent of any context of use, and will focus on the next section on the use of OCL in the metamodeling activities. For a more comprehensive introduction to OCL, we refer the reader to [19].

4.1.1 Invariant and Its Context

Each OCL constraint is defined in a context. The context provides type information, variables that are accessible, and usually also methods (queries) that can be used. When used in a class diagram, an OCL constraint is defined in the context of one class, allowing the constraint to formulate properties about the attributes of the objects of that class.

Let's have a look at the following simple example that is based on the class diagram given in Figure 2.4. This class diagram describes the abstract syntax of the cell structures and contains two classes, Universe and Cell.

OCL ⌐

```
context Cell inv PositiveUniverse:
       self.val >= 0
```

This OCL constraint is an invariant (keyword **inv**) and has a context (Cell), a name (PositiveUniverse), and a (simple) Boolean expression as the body. All attributes as well as associations from Cell are available within the constraint body. The body now forces each cell to contain an integer value larger or equal to zero. As an invariant, this OCL constraint quantifies over one instance of Cell (manipulated through the optional keyword **self** if no explicit name is given), and must hold for all instances of Cell.

We can also quantify over several instances, but have to name them explicitly. The following invariant ensures that the neighbor relation is symmetric[1]:

OCL ⌐

```
context Cell a,b inv SymmetricNeighborhood:
       a.neighbors->includes(b) = b.neighbors->includes(a)
```

As an invariant, it quantifies over two cells, a and b, i.e., it must hold over all pairs of cells a,b.

4.1.2 Basic Operations

The expression part of OCL provides types and operators quite similar to other ordinary languages. We can use, e.g., Integers or Strings and

---

[1]Note that this constraint would be directly expressed in the metamodel using the **opposite** property of a reference.

Operator	Signature	Effect
`+, -, *, /`	Integer, Real	Infix operations on Numbers
`and, or, xor, implies`	Boolean	Infix operations on Booleans
`not`	Boolean	Prefix, unary negation
`=`	all types	Equality and also Boolean equivalence
`<, >, <=, >=, <>`	Integer, Real	Further comparisons

Figure 4.1 Operations on basic OCL datatypes in descending precedence.

appropriate operations. We refer to [111] for the OCL standard forms and to [129] for OCL in Java. If OCL is used in other contexts as well, then the basic operations and datatypes are usually adapted to the available types. That happens when we later use OCL on the meta-level to define languages. So the OCL type Integer may map to Java `int` or `Integer`, C `int`, EMOF `EInt` or other possible integer representations.

Figure 4.1 contains a more detailed list of operators for basic operations. In addition OCL provides a number of typical functions, such as `abs(.)`, `max(.,.)`, but it depends on the respective concrete OCL implementation library, which functions are actually available.

Booleans are especially important, since all OCL invariants deliver results of type Boolean. As expected, standard operations on Booleans are available: and, or, xor, not, implies, = (equivalence), if-then-else. When executing an expression it might also happen that it doesn't evaluate correctly, e.g., due to a raised exception, non-termination or as a result of a database query with a 'null' result. While the UML standard [111] has a specific 4-valued interpretation for these cases, from a pragmatic point of view we just don't care about the special results here, where no database is used and we can assume that all OCL statements we use behave well and either evaluate to true or false ([129, 26] discuss this in more detail).

OCL forbids side effects for its expressions, such that execution (for example for testing purposes) does not have any effect on the underlying model. This means OCL can use method calls only if the underlying method is a *query*, which means it is side effect-free and operators like `i++` are also forbidden.

Type	Description
Collection(T)	Any collection of elements of type T
Set(T)	sets: no order, no duplicates
Sequence(T)	lists: order of elements is retained, duplicates possible
Bag(T)	"sets" with duplicates, no order
OrderedSet(T)	"sets" with order, but no duplicates

Figure 4.2 Collection datatypes in OCL.

4.1.3 Collections

OCL has good support for collections, namely sets, ordered sets, bags, and sequences as well as their operations. For example, `includes` checks whether an element is contained in a collection and `size` gives back the number of elements.

Figure 4.2 describes the available data types for collections and their specific variants, which differ in their abilities to store duplicates and the knowledge to retain an order of the elements.

> **Foundation 4.1 Collection, Ordered vs. Sorted**
>
> Please note that an order of the stored elements should not be confused with the possibility to compare the elements; such a sequence of elements retains an order, but is not necessarily sorted.

While each of the concrete types is a subtype of collection, they cannot be substituted for each other, but need to be explicitly converted.

When we want to enumerate a set, sequence, etc., we use `Set { .,... }` or `Sequence { .,... }` etc. Of course there are many more operations available manipulating collections as we can see in Figure 4.3. Here we omit specific operations for bags and ordered sets, but concentrate on general collection operations as well as operations on sets and sequences.

While many of the names are somehow unfamiliar, because they are often called differently in programming languages, they should be relatively self-explanatory. Maybe it is worth noting that positions in operations such as `subSequence(a,b)` and `at(n)` for sequences

Operator	Effect applied on any collection
size	Size of the collection (Integer)
count(elem)	Counts an element in the collection (Integer)
includes(elem)	Is the element in the collection (Boolean)
excludes(elem)	True if the element is not in the collection
includesAll(coll.)	Is this a sub-collection?
excludesAll(coll.)	Are the collections disjoint?
isEmpty	Is the collection empty?
notEmpty	Does the collection contain elements?
Operator	**Effect applied on a set**
union(set)	Union of two sets
intersection(set)	Intersection of two sets
- (infix)	Removes the elements of the second set from the first
including(elem)	Adds an element
excluding(elem)	Removes the element
asSequence()	Transforms a set into a sequence (order is unclear)
Set { .,... }	Builds a set of its given elements
Operator	**Effect applied on a sequence**
union(seq.)	Concatenates two sequences
append(elem)	Appends an element at the end
prepend(elem)	Inserts an element at the beginning
subSequence(int,int)	Selects a subsequence
at(int)	Selects an element at a position
first	Selects the element at position 0
last	Selects an element at the last position
insertAt(int,elem)	Inserts an element at a position
including(elem)	Adds an element at the end (= append)
excluding(elem)	Removes all occurrences of the element
reverse()	Reverses a sequence
asSet()	Transforms a sequence into a set (forgetting duplicates)

Figure 4.3 Operations on OCL collections.

start counting with index 1 as opposed to many languages like Java that start with index 0. Furthermore, the b-th element is included in `subSequence(a,b)`.

> OCL

```
context Cell inv:
    Sequence{21,22,23,24,25}->subSequence(2,3) = Sequence{22,23}
```

4.1.4 Quantification, Collection, Selection

Continuing the cell example, we can specify that the universe is complete in the sense that if it contains a cell, it also contains the neighbors of the cell:

> OCL

```
context Universe inv:
    self.cells->forall( c | self.cells->includes(c.neighbors) )
```

The `forall` iterator shares some characteristics with quantifiers known from logic languages, but it is actually just an ordinary function that evaluates its body (right of |) for every value c of the set `cells`. `forall` checks whether the expression evaluates to true for every element, while for `exists` it would be sufficient to have at least one. Please note that OCL remains executable even using these iterators, because they all iterate over finite collections only. However, execution might become rather slow when large collections are involved.

In the following constraint, we define the very same condition again, this time using a closed and therefore empty context, while the universe objects are explicitly quantified:

> OCL

```
inv:
  Universe.allInstances()->forall( u | u.cells->forall( c |
      u.cells->includes(c.neighbors) )
```

This constraint shows the use of the special construct `allInstances`, which derives all currently existing instances of a class and allows for an example to quantify over these instances.

There is also a possibility to apply functions, respectively expressions, pointwise using the `collect` operation:

> OCL-Expression

```
    cells->collect( c | c.val )
```

This OCL expression ranges over all cells and collects their value in a new set of integers. Again, there is a new variable c introduced and iterated over the expressions on the right. The collect operation is a very helpful statement that, for example, allows navigating along chains of associations and collecting interesting data. OCL therefore provides a shortcut (aka *auto-collect*) that can be applied in almost all practically useful cases. This expression is equivalent to the above expression:

OCL-Expression

```
cells.val
```

If the starting collection is a sequence instead, the result will also be a sequence. For sets, the number of resulting values may shrink, as different cells might have the same value, while for sequences the result is, of course, a new sequence of equal length.

Another possibility to deal with collections is to filter on a subset, respectively subsequence, using the `select` statement. The OCL expression below returns all cells with a value larger or equal to 1:

OCL-Expression

```
cells->select( c | c.val >= 1 )
```

4.1.5 Navigation along Associations

Collections are often used together with the possibility to navigate along associations of the underlying models. OCL allows collection-based navigation. For example:

OCL

```
context Cell inv:
      self.neighbors.neighbors->includes(self)
```

The OCL expression uses navigation from the initial cell, which is named `self` if it doesn't have an explicit name, to the set of its neighbors. From this initial cell, we navigate to the set of neighbors by `self.neighbors`. We continue navigating through an additional step `self.neighbors.neighbors`. This is again a set of cells that is derived as a union of cells that we get by navigating from each of the cells from `self.neighbors`.

Finally we check whether the starting cell is included. This invariant is equivalent to `SymmetricNeighborhood`, but shows that chains of navigations through associations are allowed in OCL even if the starting or elements in between are already collections.

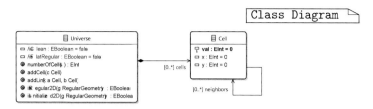

Figure 4.4 Cell Universe extended with several attributes.

4.1.6 Derived Attributes

Sometimes properties do not hold all the time, but are still of interest. Although these are no invariants, we can specify them using OCL by attaching their outcome to a virtual attribute, also known as the *derived attribute*. In the following example we define a derived attribute (keyword **derive**) named `isClean` in the class `Universe`, which is actually derived by the value of the OCL expression:

OCL

```
context Universe derive:
    isClean = cells->forall( c | val = 0 )
```

The attribute `isClean` is derived, since it is not necessarily implemented in the underlying model in that way, but only used for specification purposes. Figure 4.4 shows an adapted version of the class diagram depicting the cell structure.

A more complicated constraint would be, for example, to describe that the universe has a regular flat structure. For this purpose we can use the semantics defined for CAIR in Section 2.4. In this example, we constrain ourselves to a 2-dimensional $5 * 5$ grid by first using two attributes `x, y` for each cell that describe their position (see Figure 4.4):

OCL

```
context Cell inv:
    0 < x and x <= 5 and 0 < y and y <= 5
```

We furthermore force cells in the universe to have unique positions:

OCL

```
context Universe inv:
    cells->forall( c1, c2 | c1 <> c2 implies
        c1.x <> c2.x or c1.y <> c2.y )
```

We see that the **forall** iterator also works over several variables. Now we describe when the neighborhood relation is a flat regular one:

OCL

```
context Universe inv:
  isFlatRegular =
    let dist(a,b) = max(abs(a.x-b.x), abs(a.y-b.y))
    in (cells.size = 5*5) and
      cells->forall( c1, c2 |
        c1.neighbours->includes(c2) = (dist(c1,c2) = 1) )
```

This constraint introduces an auxiliary function **dist** by using the **let** construct. In general we can use **let** for introducing auxiliary variables and functions that can be used in the rest of the expression. While the auxiliary function describes the distinction between two cells using their position, the constraint determines that cells are neighbors if and only if their distance is 1, and that the **Universe** consists of exactly 25 cells.

4.2 ADVANCED FEATURES OF OCL

4.2.1 Nature of OCL: First Order and Expression Language?

We have seen that OCL provides the usual expression operations, although it uses its own concrete syntax for them. In addition OCL allows us to use iterators, such as **forall** and **exists** to handle elements and collections, which look similar to logical quantifiers. However OCL does not allow their application over infinite ranges such as natural numbers, so that it remains, as said earlier, an executable expression language with Boolean values as results. This means OCL expressions can be evaluated at any point in time, which greatly assists in testing of software and checking certain properties during runtime. While OCL helps in defining constraints, it does not tell us what to do if a constraint is violated, nor does it tell us how to prevent a violation directly. These things have to be clarified when using OCL in a certain context. For example, using OCL in a requirements document means that some developer has to decide how to ensure constraints during runtime. As an alternative, OCL constraints could be checked at runtime directly, so that for example the last operation (which led to the constraint violation) could be undone, or a transaction abandoned.

OCL is good at describing invariants and handling objects, attributes, and especially associations. With the exception of the **let** construct, the OCL does not provide any mechanisms to introduce new variables, methods, and in particular not any types. That is why OCL has to be applied in the context of other models that provide types, such as class diagrams.

4.2.2 Specifying Operations in OCL

Figure 4.4 also shows that the `Universe` class has a number of operations. OCL invariants, as we have used them so far, are not able to describe the effect of operations. But there is an extension to OCL called *pre-/postcondition* style that allows us to do that. It originally was implemented into Eiffel [92] and called *contract*. In this listing we see how a method is specified using such a contract:

OCL

```
context Universe::numberOfCells(): Integer
  pre: true
  post: result = cells->size
```

This very simple specification contains two conditions: the precondition, which defines when an operation can be called and the postcondition, which defines the effect on the underlying objects as well as the result. For this purpose the postcondition can use the virtual variable `result` that holds the result after the operation was executed. In our case the method can be called at any time (precondition is true). And the result is easily determined by the size of the `cells` association.

We also might omit the precondition if it is true, i.e., the operation can be called at any time. Here we count the number of cells with a certain value using a select expression to filter the desired cells only:

OCL

```
context Universe::countCells(Integer status): Integer
  post: result = cells->select( c | c.val = status)->size
```

OCL not only describes the result of an operation, but also the effect on the underlying data model. The following operation allows us to add a new cell to the universe:

OCL

```
context Universe::addCell(Cell c)
  pre: not cells->includes(c)
  post: cells = cells@pre->includes(c)
```

The precondition says that the universe should not already contain the cell. The postcondition describes the effect on the association `cells`: it says that the old association value, which is accessible through `cells@pre`, is being extended with the new cell. In general, the postcondition relates the time before execution of the operation with the time after its execution. This is why the old value of each variable is accessible by adding the `@pre` operator.

This can also be nicely seen with the following specification:

OCL

```
context Universe::injectNewCell(Cell a, b)
   pre: cells->includesAll(Set{a,b}) and a.neighbors->includes(b)
   post: let Cell n = Cell(0)
       in new(n) and
           cells = cells@pre->includes(n) and
           n.neighbors = Set{a,b} and
           a.neighbors = a.neighbors@pre->including(n)->excluding(b) and
           b.neighbors = b.neighbors@pre->including(n)->excluding(a)
```

Here we adapt the cell structure by injecting a new cell **n** between **a** and **b**. We use the `new(.)` function to describe that this value has not been existing at the start of the operation. In this example:

OCL

```
context Universe::addLink(Cell a, b)
   pre: cells->includesAll(Set{a,b}) and not a.neighbors->includes(b)
   post: a.neighbors->includes(b)
```

Subexpression `a.neighbors->includes(b)` does not hold in the precondition, but does hold in the postcondition. A common problem of this kind of specification is that in practice, people only specify the important properties or changes that they think of. There are a lot of other variables that might change too, e.g., one might change the cells association or restructure other neighbors as well. In practice we usually assume that an implementation does nothing more than necessary to establish the effect that is being described in the postcondition.

Another important question is, what to do if the precondition is not fulfilled. On the one hand, the contract doesn't specify anything, because if the caller doesn't fulfill the precondition the contract is voided. Thus the implementation doesn't have to fulfill any postcondition. It might alternatively react defensively, by immediately throwing an exception, going for the *fail quick on errors* paradigm or might be `robust` as we would like to have it in flying airplanes. For example, the `addLink` implementation might also establish its goal if the link was already there (by not changing anything).

We can use this form of defining behavior for operations both for operations of the underlying class model and for operations that we need only for defining constraints. So-called `helper` operations or in short, helpers, are superimposed on the underlying class model, and thus are not to be used by the normal implementation and in particular not present at runtime, if the OCL constraints are not in use anymore.

4.2.3 Further Concepts of OCL

In this book, we are mainly applying OCL to metamodels of languages, e.g., to define context conditions that constrain the set of well-formed models. Since metamodeling technologies like MOF and Ecore do not provide all the concepts that class diagrams have, we have omitted a number of OCL concepts as well, but would like to mention them at least for the interested user. This includes mechanisms to deal with qualified associations, ternary associations, etc. OCL also provides the concept of message, which is of no use in our context.

4.2.4 OCL Used at Different Modeling Levels

We introduced in Chapter 3 a modeling stack where models can be used to describe systems, languages, or meta-languages. Since OCL mostly applies to class diagrams, we actually can use OCL on each level of the modeling stack. Figure 4.5 shows an example with three OCL constraints on three levels of a metamodeling hierarchy.

OCL doesn't make sense on the lowest, the instance level (level 0), where the concrete objects reside. On level 1, OCL invariants describe restrictions on the domain, such as that the number of pages of a book is not negative.

```
context Book inv:
  nbPages > 0
```

On level 2, where the modeling language is being defined, OCL is used to define context conditions. In the example below it says that each two attributes of a class need to have different names.

```
context Class inv:
  attribute->forall( a1, a2 | a1 <> a2 implies
                              a1.name <> a2.name )
```

On level 3, OCL constrains the possibilities of how to define a metamodel. In our example, it says that metamodels cannot define classes having the same name.

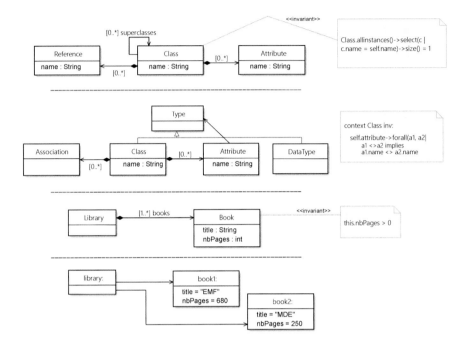

Figure 4.5 Use of OCL on the different modeling levels (class diagram, its metamodel and its meta-metamodel).

 OCL

```
context Class c1, c2 inv:
    c1 <> c2 implies c1.name <> c2.name
```

Please note that each OCL constraint is dedicated to the model on one specific level. This means the OCL constraints can only use classes and attributes on that level and mixing the levels is not allowed. Please also note that according to the MOF metamodeling hierarchy it may happen that a class name, such as **Class** in our example, can occur several times in different levels. To avoid confusion we need to recall that a class can of course be called **Class** and that the boxes one level below are their instances.

4.3   USAGE OF OCL FOR MOF

OCL is particularly interesting when the data model is complex. As discussed in Chapter 3, the abstract syntax of a modeling language is typically a pretty complex structure. Furthermore, MOF in its variants is a language-defining structure, and is not capable of describing every possible constraint.

This is the main reason why OCL is particularly of interest in defining conditions on metamodels. From an OCL point of view a metamodel is just a class diagram that describes an aspect of a modeling language. This means you can apply OCL very easily on the metamodel of a language for two purposes:

- Languages often have complex internal structures, such as typing of variables, that cannot be described using MOF. OCL can describe these context conditions. That means that if the OCL context conditions are fulfilled, a model is well formed and as such has a meaning.

- We can specify new operations for the metamodel using OCL pre-/postconditions.

In this section we will highlight what this looks like when applied to our example, i.e., languages that define cellular automata.

4.3.1 OCL for Context Conditions

In general, context conditions define whether a given model makes sense or should not be considered for further processing. We can only give semantics (meaning) to models that make sense. We call these models *wellformed.* Only wellformed models should be used for further processing, while illegal models should be rejected right away and the developer should take notice as soon as possible. Formally, well-formedness can be modeled as

OCL ⬒

```
context CellularAutomataInitialization::wellformed(): Boolean
  pre: true
  post: // conjunction of all the rules
```

Below we define a number of these rules that usually apply on specific parts of the models directly.

In Figure 4.6 we see an extension of the `Rule` metamodel from Figure 3.9 that adds a simple version of typing information to expressions. The expression language is defined so that it only uses integers, but some of them can also be used as Booleans. Thus the Boolean flag `isBoolean` is added to all expression objects and we need

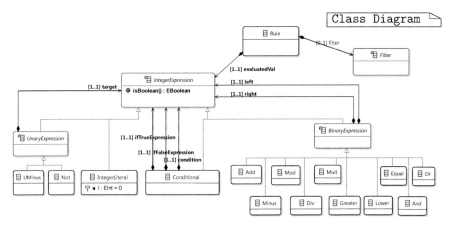

Figure 4.6 Core expression language extended with Boolean type information.

to define whether it is true or false using OCL. With this we can define the following context conditions that reveal a relatively simple typing system.

Literals 0 and 1 are used for the Boolean values in our rule language:

OCL

```
context IntegerLiteral inv:
    isBoolean = (val = 0 or val = 1)
```

Negation Not is used on Booleans only:

OCL

```
context Not inv:
    isBoolean = true       and
    target.isBoolean = true
```

UMinus and many other classes don't have a context condition, because any Boolean (0 and 1) is also an integer and thus any value is an integer.

The Conditional is interesting because it can be used on each type as long as both are equal and deliver, as a result, the same type as its arguments 2 and 3 (we omit the =true from now on). However since Booleans are also integers, we can only derive that the result is Boolean if both arguments are Booleans.

OCL

```
context Conditional inv:
    isBoolean =
        (ifTrueExpression == ifFalseExpression) and condition.isBoolean
```

For logic expressions, the infix operators enforce that their parameters are both Booleans and ensure that the infix expression delivers a Boolean as well. We illustrate this on the `Or` infix operator:

OCL

```
context Or inv:
    isBoolean and left.isBoolean and right.isBoolean
```

Comparisons operate on integers (thus no constraint) but deliver Booleans. For example:

OCL

```
context Greater inv:
    isBoolean
```

We know that some operators don't deliver a Boolean, although they could by chance evaluate to 0 or 1. We exemplify this on `Mult`:

OCL

```
context Mult inv:
    not isBoolean
```

4.3.1.1 Illustrative Example: Geometry Constraints

Let us now examine the combination of the geometry (Figure 3.12), the initialization (Figure 3.11), and the core expression metamodels. As discussed in Chapter 3, these three class diagrams are combined using a weaving technique that binds the classes with the same name to the same classes. For example class `Filter` is introduced in the expression core, but remains abstract there. It is detailed through subclassing in the initialization metamodel. We get a number of new context conditions, this time dealing with coordinates, such as:

OCL

```
context DimensionRange inv:
    1 <= lower and lower <= upper
```

and

OCL

```
context Dimension inv:
    size > 0
```

The relationship between geometry and filters is defined like the following constraint, to ensure that the boundaries of any field lay within the defined geometry. First, geometry and filter should have the same number of dimensions. The number of dimensions is encoded in the size of the **dimensions** and the **areas** associations:

OCL ⬒

```
context CellularAutomataInitialization cai, RegularGeometry rg,
      AreaFilter af inv:
  rg = cai.geometry and cai.seedRules.filter->includes(af) implies
  af.areas->forall( a |
    a.dimensionRanges.size = rg.dimensions->size )
```

This constraint shows an interesting technique: If we have to deal with links directed toward a superclass like **Geometry** or **Filter**, but we want to constrain a situation where a subclass object is there, we explicitly include the object of the subclass (here **AreaFilter af** and **rg**) in the context and link it to the main object **cai** through an appropriate navigation expression. In the case of **af** we also select one of the possibly many filters that the cellular automaton can have. With these techniques, we avoid casts and **instanceOf** expressions to distinguish between if-then-else cases. The first line of the condition works like pattern matching, while the rest defines the real constraint. While the rule is defined for one **AreaFilter af**, it actually has to hold for all possible matches.

In the following constraint, we ensure that the ranges given in a filter comply with their dimensions. This means in each dimension **i** the dimension extent is an upper bound of the upper coordinate. This comparison is possible, because of the use of **[ordered]** associations here:

OCL ⬒

```
context CellularAutomataInitialization cai, RegularGeometry rg,
      AreaFilter af, Area a, Dimension d inv:

  rg = cai.geometry and cai.seedRules.filter->includes(af) implies
    let Integer i = rg->indexOf(d)
    in a = gp.areas->at(i) implies
       a.upper <= d.extent
```

This constraint shows how to deal with a set of variables of dimensions that still has to be consistently the same at all places used. It is a little tricky to define and read, because the standard OCL unfortunately doesn't allow us to quantify over integers and it would be necessary to do that to relate position and dimension extent for each dimension. We thus use a trick: we quantify over the dimension object d.

4.3.1.2 Illustrative Example: Enhanced Versions of OCL

If we use an enhanced version of OCL as defined in [130], it would instead look like this:

```
                                        Enhanced OCL / Java-style
context RegularGeometry rg, AreaFilter af inv:
    af in rg.geometry.seedRules.filter implies
    forall i in [0 .. af.areas.size] :
        af.areas[i].upper <= rg.dimensions[i].extent
```

In this version of OCL you can navigate against the association directions (that only constrain an implementation, but not a specification), quantification over integers is allowed, especially when constrained to a finite range, and several operations have Java-like style.

The enhanced version of the OCL also integrates object diagrams as a form of constraints. Object diagrams can be used to describe a specific situation and can therefore easily be used for pattern matching. Figure 4.7 shows such an object diagram. We assume it is called DimAndRange.

```
                                                  Object Diagram
```

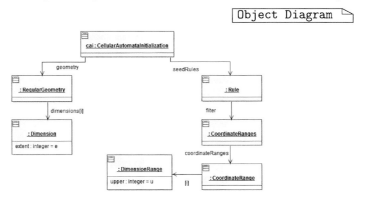

Figure 4.7 Object diagram showing a situation to be constrained by OCL.

```
                              ┌─────────────────────────────┐
                              │ Enhanced OCL / Java-style  ⌐│
context CellularAutomataInitialization cai inv:
    forall Integer i, e, u:
        OD.DimAndRange implies u <= e
```

Navigation and selection of the appropriate objects is already described through the object diagram such that the actual constraint boils down to a comparison of two integer values. The integration of the object diagram in the OCL is carried out in such a way that each variable in the object diagram is bound within the OCL (such as `cai`, `i`, `1`, and `u`). We use universal quantification over all variables, such that any matching object structure must actually comply with the given constraint.

4.3.1.3   Illustrative Example: Filter Constraints

We already mentioned in Section 2.4 that the filters in CAIR have a context condition, namely that they need to be disjoint on the positions that they are describing. Note that a robust alternative would be to give priority to the later rules, such that the more specific, later ones override the general, early ones. The constraint we define here imposes that each two filters in a CAIR model describe two disjoint areas. That means there must be at least one dimension `i` where the coordinates are disjoint. We again use enhanced OCL, because it is more convenient (we leave it open to the reader to translate that to an OCL standard constraint):

```
                              ┌─────────────────────────────┐
                              │ Enhanced OCL / Java-style  ⌐│
context CellularAutomataInitialization cai,
        AreaFilters af1, af2 in cai.seedRules.filter inv:
    af1 != af2 implies
    forall a1 in af1.areas, a2 in af2.areas :
        exists i in [1 .. a1.dimensionRanges.size] :
            a1.dimensionRanges[i].lower > a2.dimensionRanges[i].upper ||
            a2.dimensionRanges[i].lower > a1.dimensionRanges[i].upper
```

4.3.1.4   Illustrative Example: Language Constraints from Metamodel Composition

To complete the context conditions on the language we use in our cellular automaton example, we need to look at the evolution language with its metamodel defined in Figure 3.10. The only rule that we have to give is that:

OCL ◣

```
context PopulationRange inv:
   0 <= lowerRange and  lowerRange <= upperRange
```

However, the metamodel defined for the evolution language is connected to all the other CA metamodels through several classes: `Filter`, `IntegerExpression` and `Rule`. This form of composition allows undesired combinations of the languages, that we have to prevent. For example, one could now use a `PopulationRange` filter in a CA initialization rule. We forbid those undesired *language interactions* using OCL constraints:

OCL ◣

```
context CellularAutomataInitialization cai, PopulationRange pr inv:
   not cai.seedRules.filter->includes(pr)
```

Furthermore, using `NeighborsExpression` is possible, but not desired in the integer expressions in the initialization rules. Describing this is trickier, because expressions are composed hierarchically and we need to ensure that none of the expression objects actually comes from the newly added language. There are several variants: we describe the variant of checking recursive descent first, by adding a proof function `isForInitLanguage`.

OCL ◣

```
context IntegerExpression::isForInitLanguage(): Boolean
  pre: false
  post: true
```

Please note that we set the precondition to false, because the operation cannot be called on this abstract superclass at all, and as a consequence, the postcondition is of no interest. However it is now possible to specialize its behavior on each subclass individually, which includes the possibility to extend the precondition (in our case from false to true):

OCL ◣

```
context BinaryExpression::isForInitLanguage(): Boolean
  pre: true
  post: result = left.isForInitLanguage() and
               right.isForInitLanguage()
```

OCL ◣

```
context ConditionalExpression::isForInitLanguage(): Boolean
  pre: true
  post: result = condition.isForInitLanguage() and
```

```
        ifTrueExpression.isForInitLanguage() and
        ifFalseExpression.isForInitLanguage()
```

OCL ⌐

```
context UnaryExpression::isForInitLanguage(): Boolean
  pre: true
  post: result = target.isForInitLanguage()
```

OCL ⌐

```
context LiteralExpression::isForInitLanguage(): Boolean
  pre: true
  post: result = true
```

We also ensure the new expression element does not belong to our initialization language:

OCL ⌐

```
context NeighborsExpression::isForInitLanguage(): Boolean
  post: result = false
```

This trick to specialize behavior of operations in subclasses works well. Each OCL constraint only has to deal with one specific situation and is as such relatively simple. And again we avoid cascades of if-then-else expressions with `instanceOf` checks.

We now only have a constraint over the CA initialization language, but we also need to constrain the evolution language. We leave this to Exercise 4.1.

Constraints like this, where we have to ensure that a hierarchy of objects contains only certain classes, could be enforced through defining a more general operation where we collect all objects of a hierarchy and then check whether an undesired object is found in that collection. We leave this to Exercise 4.2.

As we have seen in this section, merging of metamodels of different languages leads to undesired effects, since these languages can suddenly be mixed in new ways. We therefore have defined a number of OCL constraints that forbid undesired mixtures or interactions between languages. In practice, this is not such a critical issue when we consider the construction of objects of these metamodels to come from parsers and other importing mechanisms, because they only populate the desired subset of classes.

This issue becomes more critical with a metammodel-based editor that allows the manipulation of loaded models by starting to mix language concepts. This way they might end up with an integer expression in the initialization language that does have neighbor expressions in it. Our OCL constraints prevent this, but it would be more convenient if the editor itself already knew that it should only allow a subset of the integrated metamodel language concepts.

4.3.2 OCL for the Execution Domains (Semantics)

Paper [60] discusses quite a variety of semantic forms applicable for modeling languages. While some forms of semantics can be given with mathematical constructs only, a mapping of a language model to an appropriate simulation or execution engine can also be regarded as a specific form of semantics. In Section 2.4 we have already defined a semantic mapping for CAIR-Lite in side bars and will now reuse this mathematical definition for a specification of an executable simulator. Thus we should be able to implement the actual mapping in higher quality, having a description of the effect of it.

The universe model gives us an appropriate semantic domain for the CA initialization and the evolution language. Again we use the OCL to describe the requirements for the mapping by relating the two metamodels. However this time, one of the metamodels describes the syntax language while the other one describes the execution domain. We relate the metamodel in Figure 4.4 to the already discussed metamodels of CAIR.

4.3.2.1 Illustrative Example: Evaluating Expressions

For this purpose it is necessary to describe how the CAIR is evaluated. We start with the evaluation function for expressions:

OCL ▱

```
context IntegerExpression::evaluate(): Integer
  pre: false
  post: true
```

It can be detailed for the different forms of expressions known from the expression core metamodel. Again we use a typical recursive descent approach, which we have already applied for the `isForInitLanguage` complex condition. We define some rules as examples and leave the rest as an exercise:

OCL ▱

```
context UMinus::evaluate(): Integer
  post: result = - target.evaluate()
```

OCL ⌐

```
context UNot::evaluate(): Integer
  post: result = if target.evaluate() <> 0 then 0 else 1
```

OCL ⌐

```
context Conditional::evaluate(): Integer
  post: result = if condition.evaluate() <> 0
        then ifTrueExpression.evaluate()
        else ifFalseExpression.evaluate()
```

OCL ⌐

```
context GreaterExpression::evaluate(): Integer
  post: result = if left.evaluate() > right.evaluate()
        then 1 else 0
```

It is not surprising that the evaluation of an expression actually applies the operators encoded in the expressions. However we have to carefully deal with the encoding of the Booleans as integers 0 and 1. We choose a specification that enforces a robust implementation, which means that any integer can be used as Boolean and as in the C programming language, 0 stands for false, while all other values stand for 1. We could have made a different choice by restricting the possible inputs in the precondition, for example as in this alternative:

OCL ⌐

```
context UNot::evaluate(): Integer
  pre: target.evaluate() = 0 or target.evaluate() = 1
  post: result = if target.evaluate() <> 0 then 0 else 1
```

Boolean expressions however can only have 0 or 1 as a result.

The information function is relatively simple on the core because it does not have variables or any other kind of reference to foreign values. In the general case, expressions are evaluated in the context of a set of assignments that assign values to variables. In the merged core expression and CAIR metamodel, we define a new subclass of expressions, the PositionLiteral. This expression contains the dimension number and is evaluated to the size of the dimension. We therefore don't need a general assignment infrastructure, but can use the regular geometry as context:

OCL ⌐

```
context PositionLiteral::evaluate(RegularGeometry rg): Integer
  post: result = rg.dimensions->at(dimensionIndex).extent
```

For specifying evaluations, it is common to use the context as parameter as shown above, but then unfortunately all the above defined functions have to adapt their signature as well. In this case we could also solve the transportation of the necessary information to evaluate `PositionLiteral` by a helper function. The way how it is implemented shall be left open to the developer and should not be predefined in an OCL specification.

4.3.2.2 Illustrative Example: Describing the Effect of a Regular Geometry

Although regular geometries can be of any dimension, we concentrate on the simpler case of a 2-dimensional geometry and leave the general case as an exercise. This allows us to reuse the universe of Figure 4.4 with some of the already defined invariants, such as unique positions.

We now relate the cell positions to the geometry definition:

OCL

```
context Universe::isRegular2DInRange(RegularGeometry rg): Boolean
 post:
   let Integer xdim = rg.dimensions->at(1);
       Integer ydim = rg.dimensions->at(2)
   in result = cells->forall( c | 1 <= c.x and x <= xdim.extent and
                                  1 <= c.y and y <= ydim.extent )
```

Next, we specify the cell neighbor relation, which unfortunately has to obey quite a number of special cases, which correspond to the borders. We specify the cases individually. We look at each direction individually:

OCL

```
context Universe::isRegular2DUp(RegularGeometry rg, Cell c1,c2):
    Boolean
 post:
   let  Integer ydim = rg.dimensions->at(2)
   in
     result = c2.x = c2.x and ((c2.y = c1.y+1) or
       (ydim.isCircular and c2.y = 1 and c1.y = ydim.extent))
```

OCL

```
context Universe::isRegular2DRight(RegularGeometry rg, Cell c1,c2):
    Boolean
 post:
   let  Integer xdim = rg.dimensions->at(1)
   in
     result = c2.y = c2.y and ((c2.x = c1.x+1) or
       (xdim.isCircular and c2.x = 1 and c1.x = ydim.extent))
```

After having enough helper functions, we define the regular structure as follows:

OCL

```
context Universe::isRegular2D(RegularGeometry rg): Boolean
post:
    result = cells->forall( c1, c2 |
                    isRegular2DRight(rg,c1,c2) or
                    isRegular2DRight(rg,c2,c1) or
                    isRegular2DUp(rg,c1,c2) or
                    isRegular2DUp(rg,c2,c1) )
```

Now we have ensured that the geometry of our universe is actually regular. However we still have to ensure that the cells actually do have the correct value. We introduce another helper function isInitialized2D that uses the following function to check if a cell is contained in an area:

OCL

```
context Area::isContained(Cell c): Boolean
post:
  let crx = dimensionRanges->at(1) ;
      cry = dimensionRanges->at(2)
  in result = crx.lower <= c.x and c.x <= crx.higher and
              cry.lower <= c.y and c.y <= cry.higher
```

OCL

```
context AreaFilter::isContained(Cell c): Boolean
post:
    result = areas->exists( a | a.isContained(c) )
```

OCL

```
context Universe::selectCells2D(Rule r): Set(Cell)
post:
    result = cells->select( c | r.filter.isContained(c) )
```

Based thereon we define the effect of a rule:

OCL

```
context Universe::isInitialized2D(Rule r): Boolean
post:
    result = selectCells2D(r)->forall( c |
      c.val = r.evaluatedVal.evaluate() )
```

The effect of a complete CAIR model is now described by the effect of its rules and the default 0 if no rule applies:

```
                                                              OCL
context Universe::isInitialized2D(CellularAutomataInitialization cai):
    Boolean
post:
    cai.seedRules->forall( r | isInitialized2D(r) ) and
    let definedCells = cai.seedRules.selectCells2D(r)
    in
        result = (cells - definedCells)->forall( c | c.val = 0 )
```

Here we collect the set of cells that have been initialized by a rule and specify that all other cells are initialized with 0.

Finally, we are able to specify the complete contract for the initialization function for our language CAIR:

```
                                                              OCL
context Universe CellularAutomataInitialization::doInit2D() inv:
    pre: cai.wellformed()
    post: result.isRegular2D(cai.geometry) and
          result.isInitialized2D(cai)
```

Please note that we are not using OCL for context conditions here: OCL for context conditions, as defined in the previous section, is to be evaluated when models are processed, and such are present at runtime of the tool. Relating the abstract syntax of the model with the execution domain is a requirement specification for the development of the tooling infrastructure. Ideally they are used for testing the correctness, but it should not be necessary to check these OCL conditions anymore at runtime.

4.3.3 Conjunct Use of MOF and OCL

The metamodel in Figure 4.3.3 specifies the concepts and relationships of the Petri net domain structure, expressed in MOF. A **PetriNet** is composed of several **Arcs** and several **Nodes**. **Arcs** have a source and a target **Node**, while **Nodes** can have several incoming and outgoing **Arcs**. The model distinguishes between two different types of **Nodes**: **Places** or **Transitions**.

The metamodel in Figure 4.3.3 accurately captures all the concepts that are necessary to build Petri nets, as well as all the valid relationships that can exist between these concepts in a net. However, there can also exist valid instances of this structure that are not valid Petri nets. For example, the model does not prevent the construction of a Petri net in which an arc's source and target are only places (instead of linking a place and a transition). Thus, the sole metamodel

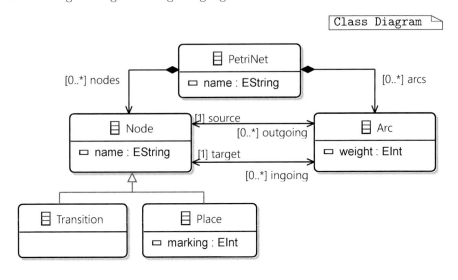

Figure 4.8 MOF-based domain structure for Petri nets.

of Figure 4.3.3 is not sufficient to precisely model the specific domain of Petri nets, since it still allows the construction of conforming models that are not valid in this domain.

The domain structure needs to be enhanced with additional properties to capture the domain more precisely. The following well-formedness rules, expressed in OCL, show some mandatory properties of Petri nets.

*PN*1: Two nodes cannot have the same name.

```
context PetriNet inv : self.nodes->forAll(n1, n2 | n1 <> n2
  implies n1.name <> n2.name)
```

*PN*2: No arc can connect two places or two transitions.

```
context Transition t,v, Place p,q inv:
  not t.outgoing.target == v and not p.outgoing.target == q
```

*PN*3: A place's marking must be positive.

```
context Place inv: self.marking >= 0
```

*PN*4: An arc's weight must be strictly positive.

```
context Arc inv: self.weight > 0
```

One can notice that *PN*2 could have been modeled with MOF by choosing another structure for concepts and relationships. However, the number of concepts and relationships would have increased, hampering

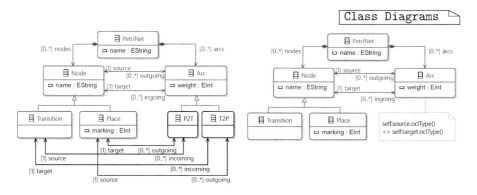

Figure 4.9   *PN2* expressed in MOF.   Figure 4.10   *PN2* expressed in OCL.

the understandability of the metamodel and increasing the distance between the metamodel and a straightforward representation of domain concepts (see Figures 4.9 and 4.10).

We learn from this example that the construction of a precise metamodel that accurately captures a domain requires: (i) mastering two formalisms: MOF for concepts and relationships and OCL for additional properties; (ii) building two complimentary views on the domain model; (iii) finding a balance between what is expressed in one or the other formalism; (iv) keeping the views, expressed in different formalisms, consistent. This last point is particularly challenging in case of evolution of one or the other view. One notable case from the OMG and the evolution of the UML standard is that the `AssociationEnd` class disappeared after Version 1.4 in 2003, but as late as Version 2.2, released in 2009, there were still OCL expressions referring to this meta-class [132, 17]. In the same manner, the OCL 2.2 specification depends on MOF 2.0, however a particular section of the specification defining the binding between MOF and OCL [111, p.169] makes use of the class `ModelElement`, which only existed until MOF 1.4.

Figure 4.11 illustrates how OCL and MOF formalisms are bound to each other [111, p.169]. This figure specifies that it is possible to define `Constraint`s on `Element`s (everything in MOF is an `Element`, cf. Figure 3.5). They can be defined as `Expression`s, and one particular type of expression is `ExpressionInOCL`, an expression whose body is defined with OCL. The existence of this binding between formalisms is essential for metamodeling: this is how two different formalisms can be smoothly integrated in the construction of a metamodel. Notice that

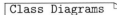

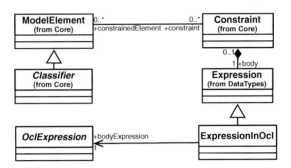

Figure 4.11 OCL Expression language bound to MOF expressions as subclass.

the `ModelElement` class in Figure 4.11 refers to the `Element` meta-class in Figure 3.5.

4.4 EXERCISES

Exercise 4.1 Context Condition for the CAER Language

Define the OCL constraints necessary to ensure that evolution rules don't have undesired language elements from the initialization language embedded.

Exercise 4.2 Collecting Objects of a Hierarchy

- Introduce a new function `getExpressionObjects` of class `IntegerExpression` that delivers the set of all its expression objects.

- Specify this function using OCL contracts on the subclasses of `IntegerExpression`.

- Ensure that no CAER model has an illegal `PositionLiteral` object.

Exercise 4.3 Evaluating Expressions

Complete the specification for `evaluate()` defined in Section 4.3.2 for the core language.

Exercise 4.4 n-Dimensional Geometries

In Section 4.3.2, when expanding the regularity check to n dimensions, the variability of the dimensions need to be taken into account, e.g., by encoding coordinates as sequences of indices instead of fixed x- and y-coordinates.

- Introduce a class `Coordinate` that uses dimensionality `n` and a sequence of integers of length `n` to specify n-dimensional coordinates.

- Introduce helper functions, e.g., to check whether cells of two coordinates should be related according to the RegularGeometry definition.

- Add a coordinate object to each cell of the universe (instead of x, y).

- Now specify that the cells of a universe have a regular geometry as defined by a CAIR model.

Building Editors and Viewers

CONTENTS

THE aim of this chapter is to describe and demonstrate a range of mechanisms that allow us to represent models for use by humans concretely. This includes the construction of viewers and editors for the previously discussed kinds of concrete syntax: tree based, diagrammatic, textual, and tabular, including both generic syntaxes that work for any modeling languages, or specific syntaxes customized for the domain. After reading this chapter, the user will be able to build tools for rendering and/or manipulating concrete representations of models.

5.1 INTRODUCTION

The core of modeling is the identification of the essential syntactic concepts, and relationships between those concepts, to express the view of reality that we need for our cognitive purpose. However, to make productive use of our models, they need a concrete syntactic form. We thus distinguish the *model essence* and its concrete *syntactic representation*.

As we discussed in Section 2.2, there are many concrete forms we can choose for our models. Some modeling languages are better represented by textual syntax, others in graphical syntax, table/form-based views, tree-based views, hybrid views incorporating combinations of these, or even multiple views at one time.

The optimal form of a model presentation also varies according to the purpose at hand. If we need to be able to store our models for later use, then we might be interested in defining a file format into which they can be serialized, or a database schema into which they can be stockpiled. If, however, human users need to be able to see, understand, and modify their models, we might require understandable languages, such as perhaps graphical languages, with supporting software tools. In this latter case, the specific user groups who will be accessing the models must also be considered: specific syntaxes are often appropriate for users with differing levels of domain knowledge, technical expertise, or experience in using the modeling language in question.

The tasks we wish to perform with our models will also determine the way we go about designing these concrete syntaxes of our models. File transmission raises concerns other than human readability or adaptability.

Some syntaxes are intended to be inspected and modified by the user. For example, textual syntaxes typically allow the user to make modifications which are then reflected back into the model's abstract representation. In these cases, the tools we are interested in building are *editors*. Sometimes representations are only intended to be read. For example, the printed tabular view of the CAIR language shown in Figure 2.2 is intended to be read but not modified. In these cases, we are interested in building *viewers*, rather than editors. This distinction clearly makes a big difference in the way we go about constructing tools.

When applying a specific concrete syntax, this can necessitate extra information that is not directly part of the model. For example, in the case of a graphical syntax, the positioning of the model elements must be captured. This is usually done in an additional model, called a *diagram*. Different diagrams can be defined for the same model, supporting the definition of different viewpoints for the same model.

In this chapter we will investigate a variety of mechanisms we can use in order to make the concrete syntax of a model accessible for use.

5.2 GENERIC VERSUS SPECIFIC CONCRETE SYNTAX

Through the use of metamodels, as presented in Chapter 3, the modeling languages we are building are all based on a common internal representation. Because of this, it is not always possible for tools supporting concrete syntax—be they textual, graphical, tabular or other styles—to be generated without consideration for concrete syntax choices which are specific to the modeling language. We term these *generic tools* resulting in a *generic syntax*.

Commonly, however, it is necessary either to customize these generic editors to reflect language-specific choices about syntax. And sometimes editors are constructed from scratch in order to best meet the needs both of a specific syntax and of the specific interactions by which the user engages with the syntax for viewing or editing. We term these *specific* tools.

Most forms can or must be combined with other forms. For example, a box-and-line diagram will often use some textual forms, included within the diagram, for some information in the model in order to present all the data from the underlying model. In other cases, different concrete syntaxes can be used side-by-side. For example, in some cases it is useful to have a textual and graphical editor in parallel, combining the benefits of both (for example, search-and-replace functionality in the text editor with the easier navigability of the graphical editor).

We will start by presenting the representations dedicated to human use and finish with representations intended for machine consumption. In doing so, we will start with the generic versions of a representation form, which require little or no human design or customization, then describe how we can build versions with more significant decisions to be made about the appearance of the models to the people who will use them.

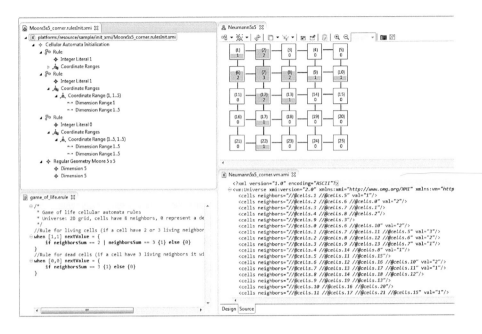

Figure 5.1 Various editor types applied to cellular automata.

Figure 5.1 shows some types of editors that have been designed for the cellular automata example. It presents a generic textual editor (bottom right), a custom textual editor (bottom left), a customized tree editor (bottom left), and a graphical editor (top right).

5.3 VISUAL REPRESENTATIONS FOR HUMAN READING

When we are editing a model using a concrete syntax, there are actually two models involved. On the one hand is the *domain model*, which had been in focus of the earlier Chapters. But within the editor, there is another model, the *representation model*, which stores additional information.

In most cases, this will include extra information not necessarily present in the domain model. The representation model will include details related to the presentation of the model within the editor, such as indentation or comments in a textual representation, or details about the size, position, or ordering of elements in a graphical presentation.

There may also be missing information. In a lot of cases, a concrete syntax is only intended to capture a visible subset of the domain model. These relevant parts will be present in (or referred to by) the representation model, but the other parts of the model, which are not of interest to the current syntactic representation, will not.

In some cases, it is necessary for the representation model to include multiple redundant representations of a single object from the domain model. This can be useful in cases such as graphical diagrams where having a node appear multiple times can simplify the layout of the graph (for example, by avoiding having a lot of connecting lines which overlap each other). By having separate models for the domain and the representation, we can even have different syntactic representations for the same domain object.

The process of building an editor, then, generally follows the same principle regardless of what language we are building, or for what metamodel: the domain model is mapped to a representation model. Having accomplished this mapping, it is possible to obtain an editor that allows the presentation and/or manipulation of the model using the specified concrete syntax. In order to simplify the process, some tools can reduce the work of specifying some of these representation models and their mapping from the domain model. They accomplish this either by using some implicit rules, or by automatically generating the representation model from the domain model.

For example, if we are defining a graphical editor, then rather than requiring a mapping from each kind of object to a representation shape, we might allow the developer to work under the assumption that, unless otherwise specified, all objects in the model will be shown as boxes. This makes the process of getting a "version zero" editor much simpler.

Figure 5.2 shows how the abstract syntax is connected to the concrete syntax and how these models are used to build an editor.

In addition, if the editor is generated (in contrast to editors that are interpreted like the one produced by Obeo Designer), it is sometimes possible to customize the generated code provided that the generator is able to keep track of the manual changes (using the approach described in Chapter 9).

5.4 TREE VIEW

For a lot of modeling languages, the user tends to think about the information in the form of a tree. This is particularly true when there is a strong natural decomposition or containment hierarchy to the information being modeled. Even for models where this is not the case,

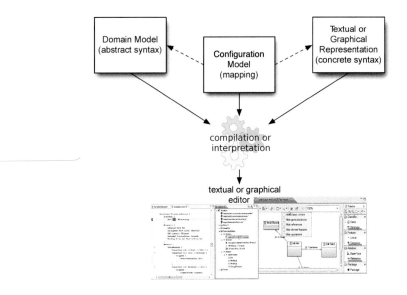

Figure 5.2 Elements of an editor generator.

a tree-based editor is often a useful tool to start with editing models, as it tends to be the easiest editor to generate.

Tree-based editors have a range of common functionality which can be automatically generated regardless of the content being edited. Individual branches of the tree can be collapsed and expanded to show more or less of the model, which is useful for managing information overload. Through knowledge of the objects permitted by the metamodel, the editor can allow the user to add a new child or sibling elements into the tree, and view or modify properties of the objects in the tree using a table-based properties form. Cut/copy/paste functionality on subtrees is provided either by click activation or by drag-and-drop. In some cases, the tree can be exported into a textual form or an image, for inclusion in other documents.

5.4.1 Generic Tree View

A default tree view will use one of the internal characteristics of every model: its containment relationships. Many frameworks, including EMF, include either a generic tree-based editor for modifying models, or a simple code generator for producing such an editor.

This generic view is often a very useful early step when creating a modeling language, because it allows the modeler to quickly construct example models from a metamodel without having to spend time designing or developing a specific editor or viewer.

Using the EMF framework, a generic tree editor such as this can be created for any Ecore model by selecting the *Generate Editor* command. Such an editor is not only a convenient tool for the early development steps, it can also be a valuable base for building an outline view for more sophisticated editors. Although its operation is simple, and the presentation of the model elements is somewhat crude, it includes a lot of editor features which prove very useful later on. For example, editors like this one often have support for resource management actions such as open/save/save as, for multi-level undo and redo commands, for cut/copy/paste operations, and for managing the elements which are selected (and sharing these selections between editors). For this reason, it can often make sense to build custom editors by starting with generic editors, rather than starting from scratch.

5.4.2   Customization of the Tree View

Having generated an initial implementation as source code, it is often quite easy to customize a tree view editor to reflect specific syntactic choices for a modeling language. For example, EMF allows generating the code for the tree editor. Once generated, annotations can be added to the code. These annotations allow for manual code modifications which are preserved even if we regenerate the editor after a metamodel modification.

By doing this, the language designer can customize how some parts of the model are presented. In the simple case, this might be custom icons for certain model elements or icons which vary depending on certain properties of the model. Another easy modification is to customize the text of the labels in the tree view to present a more informative view of the model object in question without having to delve deeper into its contents or its properties.

The intrinsic hierarchy given by containment is always available for any model, but depending on the domain and its semantics, there may be other trees (or graphs) available in the model. For example a class model can have both a containment hierarchy and an inheritance hierarchy. A model of a company's workforce can use trees for reporting relationships or for budget structures. These alternative hierarchies can also be displayed in a tree, but as they are domain specific, they require the developer to configure them explicitly. All that is needed to define such a hierarchy is a function that takes an element of the model and returns a list of child nodes, according to whatever notion of "child" is appropriate.

When customizing tree-based editors to use a domain-specific hierarchy, or even just when building an editor for large models, a common technique is to use *lazy loading*. Rather than loading the entire model when the editor is first started, using lazy loading, the children of a node are only calculated and retrieved from the domain model when the node is expanded.

Using custom hierarchies, e.g., to refer to other model parts and lazy loading, construct editors which unfold potentially indefinitely deep structures.

5.4.3 Illustrative Example: Tree Editor for CAIR

Figure 5.3 shows a generic tree view for a model in the CAIR language. The editor is generated by the EMF infrastructure. In this kind of view it is reasonably easy to see the structure of the model, in terms of the metamodel classes which are being used. Clearly, this is not the kind of editor that would be used for viewing or editing these models in a final production system.

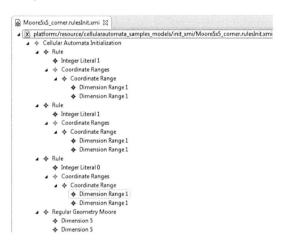

Figure 5.3 Generic tree editor for CAIR initialization rules.

This editor is obviously not particularly effective at displaying all the information in the model. For example, the upper range isn't displayed directly in the tree and the user needs to open an additional property view to display this information. Fortunately, the EMF generator used for this editor makes it fairly easy to make enhancements to the editor. Once generated, the editor code can be edited, for example to indicate how the labels are computed. Listing 5.1 shows how the **getText** operation is changed for DimensionRange objects to obtain an editor such as the one in Figure 5.4, in which the labels provide more useful information. This figure also shows that replacing some of the image files used in the generated code of the editor to represent nodes in the tree can improve its general expressivity and look and feel.

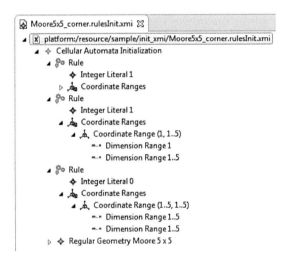

Figure 5.4 Customized tree editor for CAIR initialization rules.

Java

```java
/**
 * This returns DimensionRange.gif.
 * <!-- begin-user-doc -->
 * <!-- end-user-doc -->
 * @generated
 */
@Override
public Object getImage(Object o) {
  return overlayImage(o, getResourceLocator().getImage("full/obj16/
      DimensionRange"));
}
/**
```

```
 * This returns the label text for the adapted class.
 * <!-- begin-user-doc -->
 * <!-- end-user-doc -->
 * @generated NOT
 */
@Override
public String getText(Object o) {
  DimensionRange dimensionRange = (DimensionRange)object;
  String dimensionRangeString;
  if(dimensionRange.getLower() == dimensionRange.getUpper()){
    dimensionRangeString = getString("_UI_DimensionRange_type")+" "+
      dimensionRange.getLower();
  }
  else {
    dimensionRangeString = getString("_UI_DimensionRange_type")+" "+
      dimensionRange.getLower() + ".." + dimensionRange.getUpper();
  }
  return dimensionRangeString;
}
```

Listing 5.1 Customized editor code for CAIR.

Note the use of the *@generated NOT* tag in the code in order to tell the generator that this operation should not be overridden in case of regeneration (for example, after an enhancement of the CAIR metamodel).

5.5 DIAGRAM VIEW (BOX AND LINE)

Today the most popular syntax for representing models is the use of diagrams in which various shapes, different types of connectors between shapes, and the relative position of these elements on a canvas are used to represent the objects and relationships of a model as an ordinary graph. This kind of representation is often a very natural representation for object-based models, since they closely resemble the structures contained in the models. They are particularly useful in getting a sense of the relationship between different parts of the model, since they present the information so that many objects can be seen at once.

Diagram-style representations are rather well supported by tools. Frameworks such as GMF, Eugenia, and Sirius allow the user a high degree of control over the presentation of models as diagrams. This is definitely also necessary, because a good layout for a given graph is often hard to achieve. Experiences have shown that layout of diagrams very much depends on the kind of the diagram as well as on user and project-specific desires. Technically these tools frequently use the idea of two separately stored models, the domain model itself and the representation information related to the model's presentation, e.g., the position or size of elements within the diagram.

Like the tree editors described above, diagram editors can be used either in a generic way or by customizing the editor to incorporate the syntax choices of the language designer.

5.5.1 Generic Diagram View

It is possible to build a generic diagram which presents all the objects of the model and their relationships. In the simplest form, this can be done by representing the model as a graph in which each object appears as a shape and each reference between the objects as a line. This approach yields a formalism similar to the UML Object Diagram, and which is a close analogy to the generic tree editor presented in Section 5.4.1 or the generic text editor presented in Section 5.6.1. Thus generic graph editors are essentially like UML object diagram editors.

This generic representation is usually convenient for understanding the underlying objects and their relationships in small models. However, generic diagram editors generally don't scale up very well for complex models, since they lack the ability to collapse or hide parts of the model in the way that tree editors and some textual editors can and are inefficient in presenting relevant information.

5.5.2 Customization of the Diagram View

The use of unmodified generic diagram editors is rare in industrially used tools. In most cases, language designers will give careful consideration to the syntax they desire for their models, and reflect these choices by customizing the editor. There is a wide variety of customizations possible. These can be simple, such as assigning specific shapes to different kinds of model elements, or different line styles to the connectors associated with inter-object relationships. It is possible to omit certain model elements or represent them implicitly through the relative position of other elements. For example, in a cell universe, where links are all bidirectional, it may be sufficient to show only one link instead of both. If all objects shown are cells, the object type as well as the attribute name and type can be omitted.

For example, a series of boxes placed directly adjacent to one another might reflect that the objects they represent exist within an

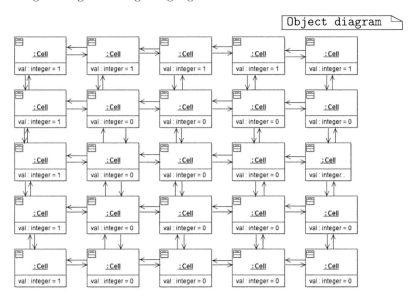

Figure 5.5 Generic diagram representation of a two-dimensional universe (as a UML object diagram).

implicit container object in the abstract model.

5.5.3 Illustrative Example: Graphical Editor for Universe Models

As an example of such a custom editor, the left part of Figure 5.6 shows the specification of an editor for the cell universe. It maps the concept of Cell to a square node and the concept of neighbors to lines. Cell labels are computed from the position in the universe and the value of the cell. Additionally, the color is a gauge that fills the square if the cell value is at the maximum value present in the model. The right part of the figure is a sample of the resulting editor opened on a 2-dimensional regular Von Neumann universe.

5.6 TEXTUAL VIEW

In many situations, a textual syntax for a modeling language offers a quite expressive language allowing efficient editing of the model. For example, a well-chosen textual syntax can be manipulated by whatever text editor the user is most comfortable using, without having to reimplement standard editor features. Also, by using a mapping

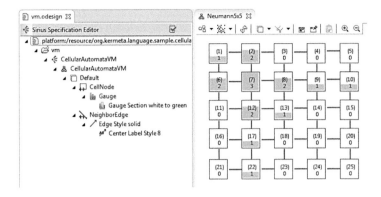

Figure 5.6 Sirius editor specification and sample Universe model.

Tool 5.1 Sirius

Eclipse Sirius enables the creation of multi-view modeling workbenches through graphical, table, or tree modeling editors. Based on a viewpoint approach, Sirius makes it possible to equip teams who have to deal with complex architectures on specific domains. The Sirius runtime natively provides mechanisms for managing model complexity: layers, filters, style customization, validation rules, among others.

Using Sirius a modeling workbench is specified using declarative descriptions (a Viewpoint Specification Model) in which all the shape properties and behaviors are easily configured with a minimum of technical knowledge. This description is then dynamically interpreted to materialize the workbench within the Eclipse IDE. In contrast with other technologies, no code generation is involved, and the specifier of the workbench can have instant feedback while adapting the description. Once completed, the modeling workbench is deployed as a classic Eclipse plugin.

Sirius is an open-source software project which is part of the yearly Eclipse release since 2014. More information, including documentation and tutorials, can be found on the website http://www.eclipse.org/sirius.

between syntax and domain model concepts, tools like Xtext [33], EMFText [62], Monticore [94, 53, 80], or Sintaks [98] can automatically generate the code of the various parts of a language-specific textual editor. These tools generally offer to generate the parser and "pretty printer" that respectively allow the transformation of text into a model and of a model into text. The generated editor usually supports syntax highlighting and code (respectively model) completion while editing the text, and other tools such as error detection/location and documentation tools. Moreover, these tools automatically integrate into the IDE (in these cases Eclipse) by generating the glue code for buttons and menus to be included in the IDE and thus leveraging all the functionalities of the platform, such as printing service, logging, cut/copy/paste, multi-level undo/redo, selection services, etc. One of the most intriguing advantages for an explicitly textual language is that version control comes for free, while for graphical languages, even today, versioning of graph structures is not easily achievable.

A popular rule of thumb for concrete syntax is that the structure of the model being represented should be reasonably close to the structure of the syntax. It is much easier to design parsers where this is the case, and trying to bridge the structural gap using parsers can lead to problems with ambiguities in the parser, or to difficulties maintaining the mapping. If the situation arises that the intended structure of the syntax differs significantly from the structure of the model, it is often worth investigating the possibility of using model-to-model transformations (see Chapter 6) to map the model to/from a structure more closely resembling the syntax, then defining parsers/printers relative to that model.

There are two mainstream approaches to define a textual language. One starts by defining the metamodel, capturing the core language concepts, and then tries to derive a grammar from there. Some tools offer to generate a basic generic grammar such as that given by the HUTN (Human-Usable Textual Notation) specification [109] from the OMG. At least for the prototyping step, it is acceptable to start from such regular grammar then incrementally adapt it to the intended syntax.

The other popular approach is to start with a concrete language example that has been discussed with the users of a language and to reuse pieces of existing languages, such as expressions, statements, etc., and derive a grammar for those. The grammar can then be used to automatically derive the metamodel (e.g., done by MontiCore [80]) and include imported metamodels of already existing language extracts by including their grammars, and as a consequence, also tooling. The advantage is that the grammar leads to a more user-friendly and effective language, but usually a less language-developer-friendly metamodel.

5.6.1   Generic Textual View

As discussed, it is possible to generate a generic textual syntax for any modeling language that is defined by a metamodel only. One way of doing this is by using the Human-Usable Textual Syntax [109], which defines a mapping from any MOF metamodel to a grammar representing a concrete syntax. This mapping represents each object in the model using a simple block structure (in the style of object-oriented programming languages). Objects linked by containment are represented as nested blocks, while other relationships are represented using nominated or default identifiers.

Implementations of this kind of textual language often work by generating a parser and pretty-printer for converting text to model and vice versa. As mentioned above, these can often be used to bootstrap into a specific editor. Other implementations, such as the one provided by the Epsilon framework [126], are generic, in that they can work immediately to transform to/from any model without the need to generate code.

5.6.2   Customization of the Textual View

Like tree-based and graphical editors, it is rare to see a generic textual syntax used with any regularity in a production environment. Although systems such as HUTN provide for some limited forms of customization (such as using certain attributes as identifiers to link between objects), it is usually necessary to select more sophisticated tools in order to specify the textual appearance of models with more precision.

In some cases this can be done using existing language processing tools, typically based on grammars and/or templates, then linking these to model management systems through programming APIs. This can be an attractive option particularly in the case where a grammar already exists for the language.

The other way to achieve this is to use one of the many tools available expressly for the purpose of linking models to textual syntax tools, such as Xtext (cf. sidebar Tool 5.2). These tools also require the user to specify their language in a grammar-like formalism, but include notations for detailing the links with modeling constructs, as well as substantial code-generation facilities for producing integrated editors and associated tools for managing the link in a way more comfortable for users.

5.6.3 Illustrative Example: A Textual Editor for Cellular Automation Evolution Rules

Listing 5.2 is an excerpt of an Xtext grammar defined for the evolution language of our cellular automaton. Thanks to that, it is able to generate an editor with syntax highlighting and basic completion support as illustrated in Figure 5.7.

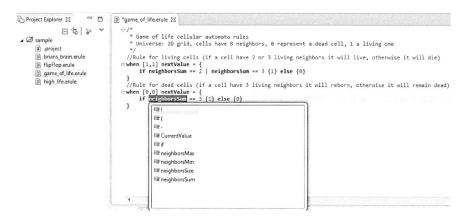

Figure 5.7 Text editor for CAER generated with Xtext.

Xtext

```
grammar org.kermeta.language.sample.cellularautomata.rules.Evol with
    org.kermeta.language.sample.cellularautomata.rules.Core

import "platform:/resource/org.kermeta.language.sample.
    cellularautomata.rules.evolution.model/metamodel/rules_evol.ecore"
import "http://www.eclipse.org/emf/2002/Ecore" as ecore
import "platform:/resource/org.kermeta.language.sample.
    cellularautomata.rules.core.model/metamodel/rules_core.ecore" as
    core

/* Root rule for Evolution Metamodel */
CellularAutomata returns CellularAutomata:
```

```
{CellularAutomata}
rules+=Rule (rules+=Rule)*;

Rule returns core::Rule:
  'when' (filter=PopulationRange)? 'nextValue' '=' '{' evaluatedVal=
    Conditional '}';

PopulationRange returns PopulationRange:
  {PopulationRange}
  '[' (lowerRange=EInt)? ',' (upperRange=EInt)? ']';

LiteralsExpression returns core::IntegerExpression:
  '(' Conditional ')' | Max | Min | Sum | Size | CurrentCellPopulation
    | IntegerLiteral;

/* Rules for Neighbors expressions */
Max returns Max:
  {Max}
  'neighborsMax' (neighborsFilter=PopulationRange)?;

Min returns Min:
  {Min}
  'neighborsMax' (neighborsFilter=PopulationRange)?;

Sum returns Sum:
  {Sum}
  'neighborsSum' (neighborsFilter=PopulationRange)?;

Size returns Size:
  {Size}
  'neighborsSize' (neighborsFilter=PopulationRange)?;

CurrentCellPopulation returns core::IntegerExpression:
  {CurrentCellPopulation} 'currentValue';
```

Listing 5.2 Evolution language textual grammar.

5.7 TABULAR VIEW

There are certain languages where models are naturally represented using a table metaphor. For example, tables often make sense for languages where all objects in the model share a common set of attributes, which can therefore be represented as columns, with each row in the table representing an object. An example of this is ledgers or journals used for representing costs or financial information (for an example of this, see the quantity takeoff example in Chapter 15, which

---

Tool 5.2 Xtext

Xtext is a framework that enables the creation of rich text editors for DSLs. It supports features such as syntax coloring, code completion, static analysis, outline view, hovers, code folding, or rename refactoring.

Xtext uses a declarative grammar to describe how an Ecore model is derived from a textual notation. This grammar is used to generate the tooling code such as lexer, parser, prettyprinter, checker, etc. used to obtain the editor. The framework provides mechanisms for customizing the default components and adapting the generated tools to a wide range of needs.

Several development scenarios are supported: writing the grammar first and then deriving the Ecore from it; or use an existing Ecore and obtain a grammar for it.

Started in 2006, this open source framework was initially targeting Eclipse IDE by deploying the tools as classic Eclipse plugins. It is now also able to target IntelliJ IDEA and web browsers.

More information, including documentation and tutorials can be found on the website `http://eclipse.org/Xtext/`.

---

combines a tree view with a table view).

One of the most commonly seen examples of table-based editors is the properties view used to complement many of the other editors presented above, which presents a table containing property names in one column and their values in another. The property view at the bottom of Figure 5.8 is an example of such a table-based representation.

Other languages which lend themselves to this kind of view are calendars or other models where the two dimensions can be used to represent two simultaneous grouping mechanisms (all cells in the first column are Mondays, all cells in a row are in the same week).

In our illustrative example, we can use a table representation as an alternative to our CAIR language to initialize regular two-dimensional cellular automatons. A simple language represented as a table such as the one in Figure 5.9 can have its rows and columns mapped to the dimensions in the cellular automata universe model.

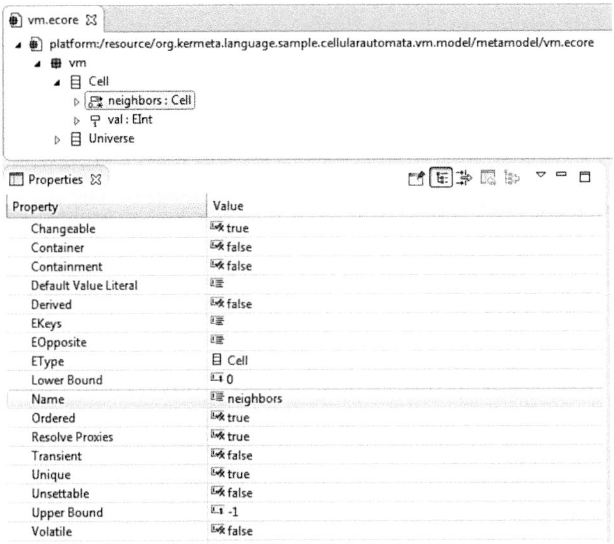

Figure 5.8 Property view of an Ecore editor as a tabular representation example.

1	1	1	1	1
1	0	0	0	0
1	0	0	0	0
1	0	0	0	0
1	0	0	0	0

Figure 5.9 Model initialization from a table.

5.8 OTHER VIEWS

Often there exist other and more appropriate model representations. Some domains have classical representations that can be used in modeling. They usually tend to closely look like the physical world, incorporate time as a special dimension, or are used by experts in the domain and thus have a user-specific appearance. In these cases where a domain has a customary form of syntax for representing models, it is often worth spending the effort to create editors that reproduce an interface familiar to the intended audience.

In this category, we can list, for example:

- **3D models:** used in games, cinema, building and construction

- **Maps:** used in cartography, urban planning, meteorology, air traffic control

- **Statistical graphs and charts:** used in mathematics, physics and more generally in sciences and economics

- **Timing diagrams and UML sequence diagrams:** used in system development and analysis

- **Gauges and meters:** often used for example in the automotive domain, avionics, chemical engineering

Due to their possibly close relationship with a domain, it is more difficult to directly reuse or adapt generic representations like those presented before. In most cases, those views are built by reusing visualization libraries. However, they can still be used as models as exposed in this book and be combined with the other kind of view or benefits from being included in a modeling process. For an example of how this is done, see the Building and Construction example in Chapter 15. Another example is the use of gauges in the diagram presented in Figure 5.6.

Model Transformation: from Contemplative to Productive Models

THIS chapter presents how to define the tooling of a given DSML to automate the manipulation of the conforming models.

The chapter starts by motivating the need for model manipulation, including model transformation. It then roughly classifies the various existing approaches, and further develops one of them, Kermeta, a model-oriented language that is going to be used in many examples in the rest of this book. Kermeta will be illustrated with the definition of explicit transformations on cellular automata examples. However, this is only an introduction to these techniques, since more advanced and dedicated transformations will be detailed in the next chapters.

6.1 MOTIVATION

Creating models is all very well, but the real value of models is in what they do or what we do with them. It is in defining this purpose of a modeling language where the real value of a model-based approach is brought to bear. Potential uses for model transformations include the following:

- Simulation or execution of a model (e.g., run the game of life).

- Generation and implementation of editors and views. When these tool are generated, the generator uses model manipulation techniques. The implementations of the editors and views also manipulate models.

- Refinement of a given model by adding information or restructuring given elements of the model. This typically happens for requirement models, where uncertainty (also called underspecification) is reflected within the model and has to be successively reduced, when the necessary information becomes available.

- Refactoring as a mechanism to retain desired externally observable properties while restructuring the internal architecture, and other internal structures.

- Mapping an abstract model into a more implementation oriented model in another language. The target language may have different natures. It may be an executable programming language (the mapping is then also known as *code generation* or *model-to-model transformation*), or another modeling language, which is more concrete and closer to the implementation.

- Extracting essential information, like architectural dependencies, behavioral interaction patterns, metrics, and other useful information that allows developers to understand a complex model and possibly identify errors and other deficiencies. The resulting information may be as simple as metric values, or complex models at a more abstract level.

- Deriving technology-specific commands or expressions that will be used in the product, for example, when interacting with frameworks, components, or foreign technologies. SQL statements from requirements models is a good example of this.

- When a model is present at runtime, for example describing a grid of a cellular automaton, adapting the state of that grid can be described through a transformation, which is a so-called "transformation at runtime."

There are many ways we can do this, depending on the nature of the models and modeling language we are dealing with. For some modeling languages, models can be directly interpreted and executed, or compiled into some other form which can then be executed. For others, the models can be transformed into one or more artifacts, which can then be used as parts of a larger system. In other cases, models can be passed off to analysis tools, or combined with other models to provide insights or predictions about the domain.

In this chapter we outline a number of ways that modeling languages can be equipped with tools which make them a productive part of a software system.

6.2   OVERVIEW OF MODEL TRANSFORMATIONS

In the broadest definition, a model transformation can be interpreted as simply any operation which is performed on a model —whether it is a modification of the model, the carrying out of some actions based on the model, or the creation of some data, or another model. However, a more commonly used definition for model transformation is that it involves the transformation or mapping of some models (*source* models) into some other models (the *target* models), whatever the form of the target models. Thus, a very general definition of model transformation could be:

Definition 6.1 (Model Transformation) *A model transformation applies on one or more source models and transforms them into one or more target models.*

In the following, we review the different kinds of model transformations and the way to express them.

6.2.1 Model-to-Text vs. Model-to-Model

A distinction is often drawn between transformations where the target is text (including code or other programmatic artefacts)—*model-to-text* transformations—or those where the target is a model or a set of models—*model-to-model* transformations. However, the general term is usually taken to imply model-to-model transformations. Model-to-text transformations are discussed in Chapter 9.

6.2.2 Homogeneous vs. Heterogeneous

The source and target metamodels may or may not be the same. If they are the same, the transformation is called *endogenous* (also called *homogeneous*). Conversely, transformations in which the target model/s belong to a different modeling language are called *exogenous* (also called *heterogeneous*) transformations. It is also important to note that this definition of model transformation does not rule out the possibility of the source model/s and target model/s being the same. These cases, where models are effectively being modified directly, are characterized as *in-place* transformations. A common example of these in-place transformations are the refactoring transformations discussed in Chapter 8. Of course, in-place transformations are *endogenous.*

6.2.3 Declarative vs. Imperative

There is a wide variety of languages and tools available for defining and executing model-to-model transformations, as much as there is in languages and tools for programming. These languages have different strengths in terms of the kinds of transformation problems they are capable of, or suited to, solving.

One of the chief distinctions drawn between transformation languages is whether they are "declarative" or "imperative." In reality, the distinction between these kinds of languages is vague, and many languages cannot easily be classified as one or the other. However, they do give some indication as to the style in which the language permits a developer to express their transformations.

The broad (and sometimes vague) category of *declarative* transformation languages focuses on allowing the transformation developer to concentrate on the "what" of the transformation rather than the how, by expressing rules describing how objects in the source model/s correspond to objects in the target model/s, but without explicitly controlling how the correspondences will be established, or in what order the rules will be evaluated. In particular, declarative languages often automate the process of searching for the source model patterns which need to be transformed. They tend to offer few constructs for controlling the evaluation of the rules or modification of the models, leaving the details of this control to the engine responsible for executing the transformations. This abstraction makes this style of transformations convenient in the cases when they are applicable, but does mean that some transformation problems are awkward to solve. Examples of declarative model transformation languages include Tefkat, ATL, ETL, and the languages based on graph transformation, such as Viatra, GReAT, and GrGen.

On the other hand, *imperative* transformations leave the control of the transformation process in the hands of the transformation developer, much in the way that imperative programming languages do. They offer more familiar control constructs and are often applicable to a wider range of problems, although they are sometimes more verbose for simple transformation problems. The most interesting of these languages, for us, is Kermeta, since this is the language we will principally use for our examples. It is described in the next section.

In order to compare the two approaches, let's consider the creation of the copy of a `Cell` in a new model. In ATL, the creation of the new model element is defined in rules that can be broken up using guards. Rules in Listing 6.1 will create a new `Cell` in a new model for any `Cell` that matches their guard condition. It will also take care of linking the copies of neighbors.

ATL

```
rule copyDeadCells {
  from s : CURRENT!Cell (s.val = 0)
  to   t : NEXTSTEP!Cell (
      val <- if(s.neighbors->select(n | n.val = 1)->size() = 3)
          then 1 else 0 endif,
      neighbors <- s.neighbors
    )
}
rule copyLiveCells {
  from s : CURRENT!Cell (s.val = 1 )
  to   t : NEXTSTEP!Cell (
      val <- if(  s.neighbors->select(n | n.val = 1)->size() = 2
            or s.neighbors->select(n | n.val = 1)->size() = 3)
          then 1 else 0 endif,
      neighbors <- s.neighbors
```

```
    )
}
```

Listing 6.1 Declarative way to create a new model element.

In an imperative language such as Kermeta, the programmer has more control over the creation and must explicitly create and link the model elements. In Listing 6.2, the main logic has been placed in a single method; a temporary copy `cellCopy` is used to maintain the traceability between the source and target `Cells` and allows the copying of the neighboring references.

Kermeta ⬎

```
@Aspect(className=Cell)
class CellAspect{
  public Cell cellCopy
  public def void copyCell(){
    _self.cellCopy = VmPackage.eINSTANCE.vmFactory.createCell
    val liveNgbCount = _self.neighbors.filter[n | n.^val == 1].size
    if(_self.^val == 0){
      if(liveNgbCount == 3) _self.cellCopy.^val = 1
      else _self.cellCopy.^val = 0
    } else {
      if(liveNgbCount == 2 || liveNgbCount == 3)
        _self.cellCopy.^val = 1
      else _self.cellCopy.^val = 0
    }
  }
  public def void linkNeigbours(){
    _self.neighbors.forEach[n | _self.cellCopy.neighbors.addAll(n.
      cellCopy)]
  }
}
@Aspect(className=Universe)
class UniverseAspect{
  public Universe universeCopy
  public def Universe copyUniverse(){
    _self.cells.forEach[cell | cell.copyCell]
    _self.cells.forEach[cell | cell.linkNeigbours]
    _self.universeCopy = VmPackage.eINSTANCE.vmFactory.createUniverse
    _self.universeCopy.cells.addAll(_self.cells.map[c | c.cellCopy])
    return _self.universeCopy
  }
}
```

Listing 6.2 Imperative way to create a model element.

6.2.4 Unidirectional vs. Bidirectional

An unidirectional model transformation always takes as input the same type of model, and produces the output models (e.g., code generation). In the case of a bidirectional model transformation, the same type of model can sometimes be input and other times be output (e.g., to keep a set of models consistent).

Foundation 6.1 Transformation

Mathematically, a transformation for a single model is denoted with this signature:

$$\Re : \mathbb{L}_1 \to \mathbb{L}_2$$

where $\mathbb{L}_1$ and $\mathbb{L}_2$ are modeling languages.

For endogenous transformations $\mathbb{L}_1 = \mathbb{L}_2$ holds.

For bidirectional transformations $\Re$ and inverse $\Re^{-1}$ must exist and effectively be executable.

The definition of $\Re$ may be extended to accept several models from different starting languages as well as produce several models of different languages.

6.2.5 Traceability

One of the problems that becomes very significant when writing transformations that link together a number of models is keeping track of the provenance of the objects that are created, or the reasons why values where changed. This information, capturing the history of the transformations that are carried out, is known as *traceability*.

The process of storing traceability is actually relatively simple. In the general case, a trace link between objects consists of a simple functional dependency pointing to the source object(s) upon which the mapping depends, the target object(s) that depend upon them, and sometimes a link to the transformation rule which was responsible. It is possible to store these using a generic language for storing traces, although in some applications it is preferable to create a specific trace language capable of storing extra information or to persist it in a specific way.

Some transformation languages make use of traceability as a central part of the transformation execution. In the Tefkat language, for example, the implicit links between, and ordering of, transformation rules is based on which traces they either depend upon or establish. When using languages such as this, traceability is stored implicitly.

6.3 KERMETA: AN EXECUTABLE METAMODELING APPROACH

Among the many possible ways to implement the DSML tooling with model transformation, we concentrate in this book on an approach called *executable metamodeling*. To obtain a complete environment for a modeling language, including interpreters and compilers, the DSML metamodel must be complemented with other aspects capturing its behavioral semantics.

This is precisely the goal of Kermeta[1], a kernel metamodeling language and environment, that we are going to use in several examples of this book as an example of an executable metamodeling platform. The next subsections explain how and why.

6.3.1 Kermeta as an Ecore Extension

Kermeta is a Model Driven Engineering platform for building rich development environments around metamodels using an aspect-oriented paradigm [99, 68, 69]. Kermeta has been designed to easily extend metamodels with many different concerns (such as syntactic correctness including context information, execution information, model transformations, tracing information, connection to concrete syntax, etc.) expressed in heterogeneous languages. A meta-language such as Ecore (resp. the Meta Object Facility (MOF) standard [112]) indeed already supports an object-oriented definition of metamodels in terms of packages, classes, properties, and operation signatures, as well as model-specific constructions such as containments and associations between classes. However, Ecore does not include concepts for the definition of constraints or operational semantics (operations in Ecore do not contain bodies). Instead, EMF proposes a code generator to generate the Java code corresponding to the metamodel, which can be complemented by operations directly written in Java.

Kermeta can thus be conceptually seen as an extension of Ecore with an imperative action language for specifying constraints and

---

[1] Cf. `http://www.kermeta.org` and `http://diverse-project.github.io/k3/`

operation bodies at the metamodel level. This allows engineers to abstract away from the gory details of the generation schema of EMF and to be able to inject the code of the operations directly into the generated code.

6.3.2 Kermeta as an Xtend Extension

In practice, Kermeta relies on the Xtend programming language[2] supplemented with annotations to specify the operational semantics through the definition of aspects weaved into the metamodels. The action language provided by Xtend includes classical control structures (e.g., blocks, conditional and loops), is statically typed with generics, and also provides reflection and an exception handling mechanism, and modern language features such as powerful macros, lambdas, and operator overloading. Xtend compiles into Java 5–compatible source code, and Kermeta ensures a seamless integration with other artifacts generated using EMF (e.g., Java code corresponding to the Ecore metamodel).

It also provides an extension mechanism through active annotation that we use to complement the action language with model-specific constructions such as containment and associations. These elements require a specific semantics of the action languages in order to maintain the integrity of associations and containment relations. For example, in Kermeta, the assignment of a property must handle the other end of the association if the property is part of an association and the object containers if the property is a composition.

6.3.3 Kermeta as an OCL Extension

Expressions are also very similar to Object Constraint Language (OCL) expressions. In particular, the action language includes operations similar to OCL iterators on collections such as *each, collect, select* or *detect*, and most of the operations that are defined in the OCL standard framework. This alignment allows OCL constraints to be directly specified and evaluated. Pre-conditions and post-conditions can be defined for operations and invariants can be defined for classes thanks to specific active annotations.

---

[2]Cf. `http://www.eclipse.org/xtend/`

6.3.4 Kermeta as a Metamodel Integration Platform

Since Kermeta is an extension of Ecore, an Ecore metamodel can conversely be seen as a valid Kermeta program that just declares packages, classes and so on but *does* nothing. Kermeta can then be used to *breath life* into this metamodel by incrementally introducing aspects for handling concerns of static semantics, dynamic semantics, or model transformations [99].

One of the key features of Kermeta is the static composition operator introduced by the active annotation *@Aspect*. This annotation allows an Xtend program to extend an existing metamodel with new elements such as properties, operations, constraints, or classes. This operator allows defining these various aspects in separate units and integrating them automatically into the metamodel. The composition is done statically and the composed model is typed-checked to ensure the safe integration of all units. This mechanism makes it easy to reuse existing metamodels or to split metamodels into reusable pieces. It can be compared to the open class paradigm [24], or the static introduction concept found in aspect-oriented programming.

A simple example of aspects used to weave behavior in the `Universe` meta-class of the Universe language defined in Figure 2.4 is given in Listing 6.3. The `_self` variable refers to the element on which the aspect is ultimately woven (a Universe object in this case) and allows the aspect to access all its features (the list of cells from the base object and the new `populationCount` attribute from the aspect in this case). The *@Aspect* annotation specifies the pointcut of the aspect, while the rest of the class definition defines its advice (new methods and attributes to be inserted). The ˆ character is used to make sure to access the `val` attribute in the cell meta-class and distinguish it from the `val` keyword of Xtend.

Consequently, a meta-class that identifies a domain concept can be extended without editing the metamodel directly. Open classes in Kermeta are used to organize "cross-cutting" concerns separately from the metamodel to which they belong, a key feature of aspect-oriented programming [73]. With this mechanism, Kermeta can support the addition of new meta-classes, new subclasses, new methods, new properties, and new contracts to an existing metamodel. The *@Aspect* mechanism also provides flexibility. For example, several semantics could be defined in separate units for a single metamodel and then alternatively composed depending on particular needs. This is the case

```
                                              ┌─────────────┐
                                              │ Kermeta     │
                                              └─────────────┘
@Aspect(className=Universe)
class UniverseAspect{
  public Integer populationCount

  public def void countPopulation(){
    _self.populationCount = 0
    _self.cells.forEach[cell |
      _self.populationCount = _self.populationCount + cell.^val
    ]
  }
}
```

Listing 6.3 Aspect weaving in a metaclass and use of `_self`.

for instance in the UML metamodel when several semantics variation points are defined.

Thanks to this composition operator, Kermeta can remain a kernel platform to safely integrate all the concerns around a metamodel. As detailed in the previous chapters, metamodels can be expressed in Ecore and constraints in OCL. Model transformations can be expressed using Xtend and the model-based features provided by the additional active annotations. Finally, Kermeta also allows importing Java classes in order to use services such as file input/output or network communications during a transformation or a simulation.

Once all the language concerns have been defined using the different meta-languages (i.e., Ecore, OCL and Xtend), Kermeta provides a compilation chain to generate the language runtime. To generate the runtime code, Kermeta relies on the EMF compiler (a *genmodel* generating Java code from an Ecore file) and the Xtend compiler (generating Java code from the aspects file), and then ensures a seamless integration between both using the extension method mechanism offered by Xtend.

6.3.5 Examples with Kermeta

In this section, we illustrate how to write simple imperative transformations by solving some problems within the context of the cellular automata example that we presented earlier.

First we will try to write a very simple example. Let us consider the most common automata evolution rule—Conway's Game of Life, as described in Section 1.4. To recall, cells that are white can become black if they have 3 black neighbors, and black cells can remain black if they have 2 or 3 black neighbors.

According to the classifications above, this is an endogenous, in-place transformation, since it is modifying the universe model where it stands. It is a fairly simple matter to write a transformation that executes a single generation of this heuristic. The example below shows this transformation written in Kermeta.

Kermeta

```
@Aspect(className=Universe)
class UniverseAspect{
  public def void playOneStep(){
    _self.cells.forEach[cell | cell.computeGameOfLifeFutureValue]
    _self.cells.forEach[ cell | cell.^val = cell.futureValue]
  }
}
@Aspect(className=Cell)
class CellAspect{
  public Integer futureValue

  public def void computeGameOfLifeFutureValue(){
    var count = _self.^val
    for(neighborCell : _self.neighbors) { count = count +neighborCell.
        ^val}
      if (count <= 2 || count >= 5){ // dead
          _self.futureValue = 0
      }
      else if (count == 3){ // life
          _self.futureValue = 1
      }
      else _self.futureValue = _self.^val
  }
}
```

Listing 6.4 In-place transformation example: hard coded Game of Life.

This shows how to change the values in a model. The next example shows how to change the structure of the model, by creating new objects and links between objects. Imagine we have a universe in which the cells can have a wide range of states; the values can be any integer. We would like a transformation which takes situations where neighboring cells differ in value by 10 or more, and introduces an intermediate cell with a value halfway between the two original values.

Kermeta

```
@Aspect(className=Universe)
class UniverseAspect{
  public def void insertNeighbors(){
    _self.cells.forall[cell | cell.insertNeighbors()]
  }
}
@Aspect(className=Cell)
class CellAspect{
  public def boolean insertNeighbors(){
    val hasInsertedNeighbor = _self.neighborsWithHighValDifference().
        size > 0
    _self.neighborsWithHighValDifference().forEach[ neighborCell |
      _self.neighbors.remove(neighborCell)
      neighborCell.neighbors.remove(_self)
      val intermediateCell = VmPackage.eINSTANCE.vmFactory.createCell
      intermediateCell.^val = _self.intermediateVal(neighborCell)
      _self.neighbors.add(intermediateCell)
      neighborCell.neighbors.add(intermediateCell)
      intermediateCell.neighbors.addAll(newArrayList(_self,neighborCell
          ))
    ]
    return hasInsertedNeighbor
  }
  public def HashSet<Cell> neighborsWithHighValDifference(){
    val commonNeighbors = new HashSet<Cell>
    commonNeighbors.addAll(_self.neighbors.filter[otherCell |
      Math.abs(_self.^val - otherCell.^val) > 10
    ])
    return commonNeighbors
  }

  public def int intermediateVal(Cell otherCell){
    val min = Math.min(_self.^val, otherCell.^val)
    val max = Math.max(_self.^val, otherCell.^val)
    return min+((max-min)/2)
  }
}
```

Listing 6.5 Insert node transformation example.

Of course, doing this once does no guarantee that there are no neighbors still separated by 10 or more. To avoid this, we make our transformation run until there are no such cases:

Kermeta

```
while(_self.cells.forall[cell | cell.insertNeighbors()]){}
```

Already we see that we are starting to break up our transformation into a more structured form: the transformation which inserts the intermediate node is defined in its own operation, which can be reused. The way this is done in Kermeta resembles the way it is done in Java or other object-oriented languages. Behavior can be structured using parameterized operations, or organized into classes using inheritance and other abstraction mechanisms.

In Section 1.4 we introduced some of the different kinds of neighborhood topologies; von Neumann neighborhoods have the north, south, east, and west adjacent cells, while Moore neighborhoods also have the four diagonal neighbors. For our next example we would like to convert universes with a von Neumann neighborhood into universes with a Moore neighborhood. This can be done using the following transformation:

Kermeta

```
@Aspect(className=Universe)
class UniverseAspect{
  public def void vonNeumann2Moore(){
    _self.cells.forEach[cell | cell.vonNeumann2Moore]
  }
}
@Aspect(className=Cell)
class CellAspect{
  public def void vonNeumann2Moore(){
    val neighborsToAdd = new HashSet<Cell>
    _self.neighbors.forEach[neighborCell1|
      _self.neighbors.forEach[neighborCell2|
       if(neighborCell1 != neighborCell2){
         neighborsToAdd.addAll(neighborCell1.commonNeighborsWith(
             neighborCell2).filter[possibleCommonNeighbor |
           possibleCommonNeighbor != _self
         ])
       }
      ]
    ]
    _self.neighbors.addAll(neighborsToAdd)
  }
  public def HashSet<Cell> commonNeighborsWith(Cell otherCell){
    val commonNeighbors = new HashSet<Cell>
    commonNeighbors.addAll(_self.neighbors.filter[neighbor | otherCell.
        neighbors.contains(neighbor)])
    return commonNeighbors
  }
}
```

Listing 6.6 In-place transformation example: von Neumann to Moore.

We can see in this example that the pattern we are looking for—a node with two distinct neighboring cells who share a common (fourth) neighbor—is starting to be more complicated, and we can see that, as a result, the control structures we are using are starting to also become more complex. This is where declarative languages with powerful pattern matching support starts to be helpful.

6.3.6 Scaling Up Transformations in Kermeta

When writing programs in a given programming language, the passage from simple examples to more complex problems necessitates the use of patterns which improve the structure of the program in terms of readability, conciseness, and sometimes performance.

The same is true of writing transformations in Kermeta. As problems necessitate the identification of more numerous and more sophisticated patterns of objects in the source model(s), design patterns such as the visitor pattern [38] become particularly valuable in structuring the transformation. The same is true for a number of other patterns; since Kermeta offers a very similar set of constructs to classical object-oriented programming languages such as Java, the patterns that have been developed in those languages are frequently useful in Kermeta.

6.4 EXERCISES

Exercise 6.1 Roman Numbers to Decimal

Write a transformation going from Roman numbers (e.g., XLII) to arabic (e.g., 42) and vice versa in both Kermeta and ATL. What do you conclude?

Exercise 6.2 Populate an Empty Universe with a Pattern

Use the cellular automata universe metamodel provided in the book companion website.

Write a transformation populating an empty universe with a specific pattern, e.g., (1001)* given as a parameter.

Interpreter

CONTENTS

T HIS chapter discusses how to use model transformations to implement an interpreter for a given DSML that supports the execution of the DSML models. After reading this chapter, you will be able to implement an interpreter based on the definition of the abstract syntax of the DSML according to state-of-the-art design practices (e.g., based on the visitor pattern in the case of an imperative model transformation language). The chapter is illustrated by the definition of an interpreter for cellular automata evolution rules. Several variants of the interpreter are provided in order to highlight the pros and cons of the possible designs.

7.1 INGREDIENTS FOR INTERPRETATION

The creation of an interpreter can be useful to validate and verify models early in the development process, before their refinements toward more concrete implementations. Sometimes the interpretation of models is also useful by itself. In this case the interpreter becomes part of the product. This is, for example, the case when models act as *configurations* of an adaptive product that can be changed by the users themselves.

In any case, defining an interpreter in an operational way consists of describing the effect of the execution of the language elements over a model of the world, which is called a semantic domain. Conversely, this semantic domain can be seen as the execution state of the running model, i.e., the runtime data storing its changeable values, also often called a virtual machine (VM). This model can be either an extension of the domain model captured in the abstract syntax, or can be completely separated.

The concrete definition of an interpreter consists of complementing the abstract syntax with execution functions (aka computational steps). These are defined as operations over the abstract syntax and the runtime data. By convention, these operations are usually called `evaluate` or `interpret`. They materialize the operational semantics of the language as a mapping between the abstract syntax (i.e., the domain model) and the runtime data model (i.e., the semantic domain). The interpretation operations traverse through the execution flow of the abstract syntax and their effects are captured and stored in the runtime data model.

7.1.1 Runtime Data

The runtime data model is an essential part of an interpreter. It captures the current state of the running model. It is important to conceptually distinguish the runtime data from the structural data of the interpreted model. The runtime data is defined on its own (either separately or by extension of the domain model), while the running model is defined by the abstract syntax of the language (i.e., the domain model). The interpreter and its operations need both and thus the runtime data is made accessible and can be changed from every part of the interpreter. We call this the `Context` of the execution.

In our cellular automata example, the state of the system is

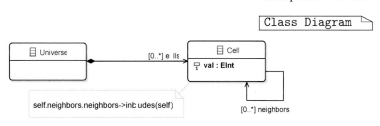

Figure 7.1 Virtual machine metamodel of the universe of cellular automata.

represented as a runtime data model called `Universe`. It is composed of cells, neighbors, and population (see class diagram in Figure 7.1). The links between the `Cells` representing the neighborhood allow us to store any N-dimensional grid conforming to the game board geometry.

When evaluating a `Rule` for a given `Cell`, the evaluation of the expressions related to this rule requires knowing this `Cell`. Therefore the necessary `Context` contains the two kinds of information depicted in Listing 7.1.

Java

```java
public class SimulatorContext {
  public Universe currentUniverse;
  public Cell currentCell;
...
}
```

Listing 7.1 Cellular automata visitor context.

Note that the definition of the runtime data can also benefit from the application of design patterns or the use of specific features for modularity or extension (cf. Section 7.4.3 and Section 7.4.4).

7.1.2 Computational Steps

The computational steps are implemented as operations in the classes of the domain model and thus manipulate the runtime data. This is the approach used by the design pattern *Interpreter* (see Section 7.2). However, this design pattern directly adapts the domain model and thus potentially interferes with possible other usages of the domain model. Therefore it would not necessarily scale well when adding many new concerns to the language.

Adding a design pattern *Visitor* to the design pattern *Interpreter*

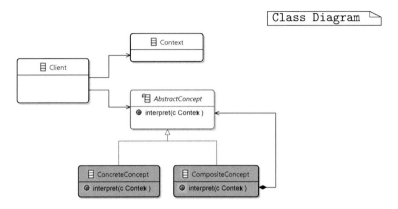

Figure 7.2 Interpreter design pattern.

allows us to minimize the impact on the domain model. The visitor is defined in a generic way and thus may be used to fulfill other purposes than only implement the interpreter. The actual interpreter is thus factored out into a visitor class and may therefore be changed at will.

As described in Section 7.4.1, programming languages with static introduction capabilities no longer require explicit addition of the visitor structure since the operations can seamlessly be woven into the domain classes.

7.2 DESIGN PATTERN INTERPRETER

The basic idea of the Interpreter design pattern is to implement one class for each concept of the language and a method **interpret** in each of these classes. In Figure 7.2, we assume the language has one root abstract concept **AbstractConcept** and two concrete concepts **ConcreteConcept** and **CompositeConcept**. When implementing this design pattern for a concrete language, these classes are replaced by all the classes of the language metamodel.

The **interpret** method uses a **Context** class to store intermediate values and at the end the result of the execution. As described above, this **Context** constitutes the interpreter runtime data that is passed and modified from call to call to the **interpret** method. This strategy is quite intuitive and straightforward since it directly maps to the structure of the metamodel classes used to define the language.

Its drawback is that for its implementation we need to directly modify the classes implementing the concepts. This doesn't encourage reuse.

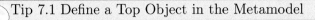

> **Tip 7.1 Define a Top Object in the Metamodel**
>
> Applying the Interpreter design pattern can be applied at best if there is one single abstract concept in the language that acts as a super type for all concepts of this specific language.
>
> If there is no such top concept, one possibility is to split the interpreter into several smaller collaborative interpreters (one for each local top concept). Another alternative is to use the general `Object` class of the modeling framework that is the super class for all concepts (e.g., `EModelElement` in Ecore). However, in this second case, the typing is less controlled and needs more attention to prevent errors during use.

7.3 COMBINING THE INTERPRETER AND VISITOR DESIGN PATTERNS

7.3.1 Approach Overview

Object-oriented programming languages allow us to use a better approach to attach behavioral operations by applying the design pattern *Visitor*. This pattern enables separation of concerns by allowing us to virtually or dynamically add new operations to existing object structures without modifying those structures. In this pattern, a *Visitor* defines an `accept` method that is in charge of calling the appropriate `visit` method depending on the type of the visited element (see Figure 7.3). Then, the interpreter in a visitor is implemented by putting the code of the `interpret` methods proposed by the previous section into the `visit` methods of the Visitor.

This approach combines these two design patterns. Its achievements are: (1) The interpreter is factored out of the metamodel and thus several interpreters can be defined independently. (2) The structure and especially the traversal of the metamodel is part of the visitor and factored out of the interpreter. Thus, the interpreter is relatively robust against structural changes of the models. According to [63], the Visitor design pattern generally improves maintainability while not having substantial performance differences compared to a pure

Interpreter design pattern. (3) The only prerequisite to this approach is to tool the domain classes with an `accept` operation. This minimizes the impact on the domain model implementation while enabling various usages for the domain model classes.

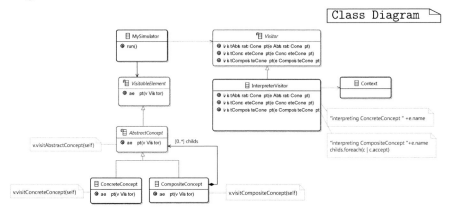

Figure 7.3 Interpreter and Visitor design pattern integration.

Once introduced in the concept structure, the Visitor pattern isn't restricted to implementing interpreters, it can be the support for other usages such as analysis, compilation, documentation generation, or model transformation, which are presented in Chapter 6 and Chapter 9. Adding a new tool for a language simply consists of adding a new concrete implementation of the `Visitor`.

While the Visitor design pattern helps in reusing domain classes for several uses, in case of a large domain with a lot of classes, the basic structure may not be enough to keep the code readable and maintainable. For example, adding the code directly into the `visit` methods may produce a huge class. More sophisticated approaches split these into smaller chunks, e.g., using delegation or a composition design pattern.

7.3.2 Illustrative Example: Interpreter for Cellular Automaton Using a Visitor

The variant of the visitor developed in our example follows the standard Visitor pattern. However, in order to simplify the writing of the concrete visitor, we have changed the return type to `int` so we can directly send these frequent data to the caller instead of going through a dedicated stack structure in the `Context`. The visitor has the following signature:

Java

```java
interface CAERVisitor {
    //from Core
  int visitIntegerExpression(IntegerExpression s);
  int visitBinaryExpression(BinaryExpression s);
  int visitUnaryExpression(UnaryExpression s);
  int visitAnd(And s);
  int visitAdd(Add s);
  int visitConditional(Conditional s);
  int visitDiv(Div s);
  int visitEqual(Equal s);
  int visitFilter(Filter filter);
  int visitGreater(Greater s);
  int visitIntegerLiteral(IntegerLiteral s);
  int visitLower(Lower s);
  int visitMinus(Minus s);
  int visitMod(Mod s);
  int visitMult(Mult s);
  int visitNot(Not s);
  int visitOr(Or s);
  int visitRule(Rule rule);
  int visitUMinus(UMinus s);
    // from Evol
  int visitCellularAutomata(CellularAutomata automata);
  int visitCurrentCellPopulation(CurrentCellPopulation s);
  int visitMax(Max s);
  int visitMin(Min s);
  int visitNeighborsExpression(NeighborsExpression s);
  int visitPopulationRange(PopulationRange popRange);
  int visitSize(Size s);
  int visitSum(Sum s);
}
```

Listing 7.2 CAER visitor interface.

In addition, all the implementation classes of the CAER metamodel have been modified to implement the `accept` method, which dispatches the call to the correct `visit*` method. For example, the `AddImpl` class defines the following accept method:

Java

```java
@Override
public int accept(final CAERVisitor visitor) {
  return visitor.visitAdd(this);
}
```

Please note that in the visitor interface, methods for abstract concepts such as IntegerExpression or Filter are also included. While they are not used in our interpreter, they are still present because they might be useful when reusing this visitor for other purposes.

A concrete visitor can now implement a specific method for each subclass that can occur in an `IntegerExpression`. We only show the implementation for some representative classes:

Java

```java
class SimulatorVisitor implements CAERVisitor{
  public SimulatorContext context;

  public SimulatorVisitor(SimulatorContext context) {
    super();
    this.context = context;
  }
  @Override
  public int visitCellularAutomata(CellularAutomata automata) {
    HashMap<Cell, Integer> futureCellValues = new HashMap<Cell,
        Integer>();
    for (Cell cell : context.currentUniverse.getCells()) {
      context.currentCell = cell;
      Optional<Rule> rule = automata.getRules().stream().filter(r ->
          isRuleApplicableForCell(r, cell)).findFirst();
      if(!rule.isPresent()){
        // no rule applicable, report the current value as the future
        futureCellValues.put(cell, cell.getVal());
      } else {
        futureCellValues.put(cell, rule.get().accept(this));
      }
    }
    for (Cell cell : context.currentUniverse.getCells()) {
      cell.setVal(futureCellValues.get(cell));
    }
    return 0;
  }
  @Override
  public int visitRule(Rule rule) {
    return rule.getEvaluatedVal().accept(this);
  }
  @Override
  public int visitIntegerLiteral(IntegerLiteral expression) {
    return expression.getVal();
  }
  @Override
  public int visitAdd(Add expression) {
    return expression.getLeft().accept(this) + expression.getRight().
        accept(this);
```

```
  }
  @Override
  public int visitConditional(Conditional expression) {
    if (expression.getCondition().accept(this) != 0) {
      return expression.getIfTrueExpression().accept(this);
    } else {
      return expression.getIfFalseExpression().accept(this);
    }
  }
  @Override
  public int visitGreater(Greater expression) {
    int left = expression.getLeft().accept(this);
    int right = expression.getRight().accept(this);
    return left > right ? 1 : 0;
  }
...
  @Override
  public int visitCurrentCellPopulation(CurrentCellPopulation
      expression) {
    return context.currentCell.getVal();
  }
  @Override
  public int visitSum(Sum expression) {
    if (expression.getNeighborsFilter() == null) {
      return context.currentCell.getNeighbors().stream()
        .mapToInt(cell -> cell.getVal()).sum();
    } else {
      Filter filter = expression.getNeighborsFilter();
      return context.currentCell.getNeighbors().stream()
        .filter(cell -> isFilterApplicableForCell(filter, cell))
        .mapToInt(cell -> cell.getVal())
        .sum();
    }
  }
...
}
```

Listing 7.3 Cellular automata operational semantics as visitor.

The visitor declares a `Context` class that stores the current state of the grid of `Cells`. It also contains the currently evaluated `Cell`. This contextual data is used for example in `CurrentCellPopulation` or `Min`.

For simple cases such as the `CurrentCellPopulation` instruction, the mapping to the virtual machine is straightforward: it boils down to calling the relevant virtual machine instruction, i.e., `context.currentCell.getVal()` (see method `visitCurrentCell-Population` in Listing 7.3).

Note 7.2 Use Implementation Language Features to Ease Coding of the Semantic

When coding the behavior of some concepts such as the Add instruction, there are two possible choices. The first one, illustrated in method visitAdd of Listing 7.3, makes the assumption that the semantics of the cellular automata Add can be directly mapped to the semantics of "+" in the hosting language: Java for this example. The interest of this first solution is that it provides a quick and straightforward way of defining the semantics of that kind of operator. If however the semantics we want for the cellular automata Add is not the one that is built into Java for whatever reason (e.g., we want it to handle 8-bits integers only), we can define the wanted Add operation semantics in the cellular automata virtual machine and change the visitAdd method so that it first calls accept on the left-hand side, stores the results then calls accept on the right-hand side, and finally delegates the process by calling the Add operation offered by the VM.

In our example, the visit of the CellularAutomata (see method visitCellularAutomata in Listing 7.3) will take care of computing the first applicable Rule for each Cell and then apply the result to the whole Universe.

Once the operational semantics for the cellular automata has been defined as described above, defining an interpreter is pretty straightforward: we first load the cellular automata "program" (see call to loadRule in Listing 7.4), instantiate a Context (that contains the cellular automata universe chosen as the initial state) and then call evaluate(Context) on the root element of the CellularAutomata.

Java

```java
import evol.CellularAutomata;
import evol.EvolPackage;
import vm.Universe;
import vm.VmPackage;
...
public class Simulator {
  public void simulateWithAsciiArt2Dvisualizer(String ruleFile, String
      gridFile, Integer universeLength) {
    Universe grid = loadGrid(gridFile);
```

```
CellularAutomata automata = loadRule(ruleFile);

SimpleAsciiArt2DVisualizer visualizer = new
    SimpleAsciiArt2DVisualizer();
visualizer.visualizeRegular2DUniverse(universeLength,grid);

SimulatorContext context = new SimulatorContext(grid);
SimulatorVisitor simVisitor = new SimulatorVisitor(context);
for(int i = 0; i<3; i++) {
  automata.accept(simVisitor);
  visualizer.visualizeRegular2DUniverse(universeLength, grid);
}
}
public CellularAutomata loadRule(String ruleFile) {
  XMIResourceFactoryImpl fact = new XMIResourceFactoryImpl();
  if (!EPackage.Registry.INSTANCE.containsKey(EvolPackage.eNS_URI)) {
    EPackage.Registry.INSTANCE.put(EvolPackage.eNS_URI, EvolPackage.
      eINSTANCE);
  }
  Resource.Factory.Registry.INSTANCE.getExtensionToFactoryMap().put("
    *", fact);
  ResourceSet rs = new ResourceSetImpl();
  URI uri = URI.createURI(ruleFile);
  Resource res = rs.getResource(uri, true);
  return (CellularAutomata)(res.getContents().get(0));
}
public Universe loadGrid(String gridFile) {
...
  URI uri = URI.createURI(gridFile);
  Resource res = rs.getResource(uri, true);
  return (Universe)(res.getContents().get(0));
}
}
```

Listing 7.4 Cellular automata interpreter main.

Loading an instance of a cellular automaton and executing it this way will change the state of the model of its universe. Upon execution, the population of the universe of cells would evolve according to the chosen rules.

Often users want to see a visualization of the execution on the screen. For that purpose, the visualization only has to traverse the VM model to print a simple ASCII art representation in text of 2D universes (Figure 7.4). For a more sophisticated interface, the implementation could use the Observer design pattern. During the execution, the interpreter calls the relevant methods to notify the screen that something has changed; the user interface will be in

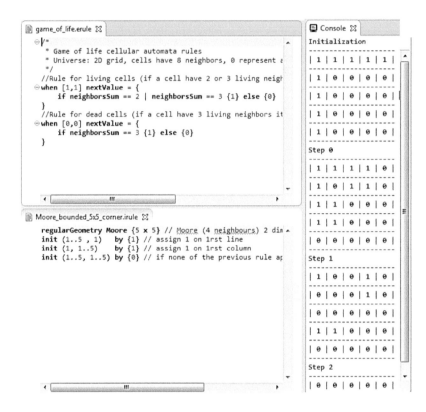

Figure 7.4 Interpreter console result using ASCIIART textual representation.

charge of reading the relevant part of the VM memory and create the representation.

7.4 ASPECT WEAVING WITH STATIC INTRODUCTION

7.4.1 Approach Overview

With their static introduction mechanism, aspect-oriented languages render the use of the Visitor design pattern somehow obsolete. Since new methods can now be added into existing classes, we no longer need an accept operation in the domain model anymore. The static introduction mechanism allows us to directly weave the operations required by the Interpreter design pattern into the relevant classes.

This mechanism takes advantage of the Interpreter design pattern

---

Foundation 7.3 Visitor Modularization Limitation

Since the CAER metamodel is a specialization of the CORE metamodel, the attentive reader might have expected a similar modularity on the visitor side, i.e., a visitor for the CORE metamodel (CORE visitor) that is specialized by the visitor for the CAER metamodel (CAER visitor). However, this is impossible with the object-oriented paradigm. The methods `accept` in the CAER metamodel indeed cannot restrict the accept methods of the CORE metamodel to only accept the CAER visitor (because this would lead to a covariant redefinition of the parameter of the methods `accept`). Consequently, we have chosen to not modularize the visitor, i.e., there is no CORE visitor and all the content is defined into the CAER visitor (see Listing 7.2). Note that another possibility would have been to modularize the visitor but not the metamodels. This problem is well-known in the research literature as the *expression problem*. Cf. https://en.wikipedia.org/wiki/Expression_problem.

---

without the structure overhead of the Visitor design pattern and without giving up the separation of concerns requirement. Moreover, the methods do not need to follow a strict convention and can be named according to their purpose. This produces an intuitive, more compact, and often more maintainable code, even though Aspect Oriented Programming (AOP) often increases implicit (and therefore ugly) code dependencies.

7.4.2 Illustrative Example: Operational Semantics for Cellular Automaton Using Static Introduction

When using static introduction in our CAER example, we chose to implement the mapping between the abstract syntax of the rules and the virtual machine as a set of `evaluate` functions woven into the relevant classes of the rules metamodel.

A context is provided as a parameter of the `evaluate` operation. This context contains an instance of the `Universe` class of the runtime metamodel (see Listing 7.1). Listing 7.5 presents how the operations `evaluate` are woven into the abstract syntax of the rules. An abstract operation `evaluate` is defined on class `IntegerExpressionAspect`

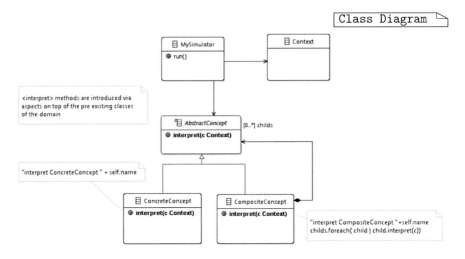

Figure 7.5 Interpreter using static introduction.

and implemented in every subclass to handle the execution of all constructions.

Kermeta

```
@Aspect(className=typeof(IntegerExpression))
abstract class IntegerExpressionAspect
{
  def abstract public Integer evaluate(Context context)
}
...
@Aspect(className=typeof(Lower))
class LowerAspect extends BinaryExpressionAspect{
  def public Integer evaluate(Context context) {
    if ( _self.left.evaluate(context) < _self.right.evaluate(context))
        return 1
    else return 0
  }
}

@Aspect(className=typeof(Minus))
class MinusAspect extends BinaryExpressionAspect {
  def public Integer evaluate(Context context) {
    return _self.left.evaluate(context) - _self.right.evaluate(context)
  }
}

@Aspect(className=typeof(Mod))
class ModAspect extends BinaryExpressionAspect {
```

```
  def public Integer evaluate(Context context) {
    var leftVal = _self.left.evaluate(context)
    var rightVal = _self.right.evaluate(context)
    return leftVal % (rightVal)
  }
}
...
@Aspect(className=typeof(Size))
class SizeAspect extends NeighborsExpressionAspect {
  def public Integer evaluate(Context context) {
    var result = 0
    var List<Cell> selectedCells = new ArrayList<Cell>()
    if ( _self.neighborsFilter == null) {
      selectedCells = context.currentCell.neighbors
    } else {
      selectedCells = context.currentCell.neighbors.filter[cell | _self
          .neighborsFilter.matchesValue(cell.^val)] as List<Cell>
    }
    if (selectedCells != null) {
      result = selectedCells.size
    }
    return result
  }
}

@Aspect(className=typeof(Sum))
class SumAspect extends NeighborsExpressionAspect {
  def public Integer evaluate(Context context) {
    var List<Integer> selectedCellValues = new ArrayList<Integer>()
    if ( _self.neighborsFilter == null) {
      selectedCellValues = context.currentCell.neighbors.map[cellValue
          | cellValue.^val]
    } else {
      selectedCellValues = context.currentCell.neighbors.filter[cell |
          _self.neighborsFilter.matchesValue(cell.^val)].map[cellValue
          | cellValue.^val] as List<Integer>
    }
    return selectedCellValues.reduce[p1, p2| p1 + p2]
  }
}
```

Listing 7.5 Cellular automata operational semantics using AOP.

7.4.3 Adding Runtime Data Using Static Introduction

In some cases, the runtime data can be built as an extension of the
domain model. For example, Figure 7.6 shows the metamodel of a
Finite State Machine(FSM). When creating an interpreter for a FSM,

the `Context` for such an interpreter needs to store the current state of each state machine in the system. Rather than creating an external data structure for this (like a hashmap), it will result in a simpler data structure to directly reuse the domain model structure itself and extend it. Figure 7.7 shows that a simple `currentState` attribute added on the `FSM` class will be enough. Each instance of `FSM` will store its own current state.

In that case, the general interpreter pattern proposed in previous sections can be simplified even more since both the static and dynamic data can be manipulated together. The `interpret`/`evaluate` method will not need an explicit context parameter since everything is accessible directly from the model itself.

Luckily, some languages like Kermeta have a static introduction mechanism that allows such extension.

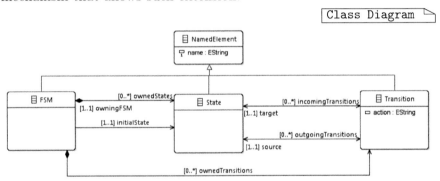

Figure 7.6 Finite State Machine metamodel.

This optimization should be considered when the runtime data structure is close enough to the domain model structure so the data can be efficiently modularized this way.

7.4.4 Modeling the Interpreter Runtime Data

In the Interpreter design pattern, the `Context` that is passed from call to call can take advantage of modeling techniques. Actually, the `Context` is usually an object structure that can itself be defined using modeling techniques.

This has several advantages. For example, it clarifies the structure by providing an explicit class diagram for the runtime data. Also

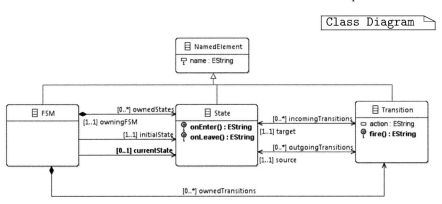

Figure 7.7   Finite State Machine metamodel extended by runtime data.

metamodels come with some predefined tools that may be helpful when creating the interpreter tooling. Expressed as a model, the runtime data obtains observable capabilities and serialization capabilities.

With these capabilities, it is straightforward to implement a concrete visualization that can be used to observe the internal work of the interpreter. For example, the interpreter can periodically save the current runtime data model to create snapshots. These snapshots can be used to analyze the behavior or be the base to create some trace mechanism. Since the navigation and representation are easy to establish, the creation of a debugger on top of the interpreter is simplified.

Thanks to the observable capabilities of models, an animation view can be built using the runtime data model. Even better, an animation view can be seen as a kind of concrete representation as discussed in Chapter 5 but with restricted edition capabilities. Built similarly to a standard editor, the animation view will normally discourage changes on the model or model runtime data except if the interpreter runs in debug mode. The screenshot in Figure 7.8 shows a view created with Sirius that is connected to the VM model of a running cellular automata. During the execution, thanks to EMF notification, the view is refreshed, changing the labels and highlighting the boxes depending on the cell values.

Having the runtime data represented as model makes it relatively easy to create a full-fledged animator based on an interpreter.

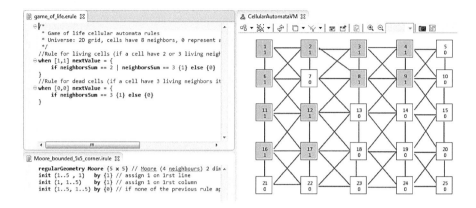

Figure 7.8 Sirius editor displaying the VM model of a CA simulation.

7.5 EXERCISES

Exercise 7.1 Evaluation in Sequential, Nonstrict Order

In the illustrative example of Section 7.3.2, implement a version of the **visitAnd** and **visitOr** operations that evaluate the right part of the expression in a sequential, nonstrict order (like in C).

Exercise 7.2 Fixed Point Detection

In the illustrative example of Section 7.3.2, implement a stop condition that detects that the model has reached a fixed point, i.e., the evolution rules have no effect anymore.

Exercise 7.3 Loop Detection

In the illustrative example of Section 7.3.2, implement a stop condition that detects that the model has reached a repeating loop. How can you do this efficiently?

Refactoring and Refinement

I N Chapter 6, we've already learned about transformations in general. We now focus on applying transformation techniques to restructure models. Restructuring of models may have different purposes. In this chapter, we consider two main purposes:

- It is helpful to *refactor* a model when the content is essentially correct, but its representational structure should be improved. This is quite similar to code refactoring and allows, for example, to improve one or several non-functional properties of the model such as readability, maintainability, extensibility, etc.

– During an iterative development process, the information available about the system to develop becomes more and more detailed. Iterative extension of models is called *refinement* and allows us to transform abstract, incomplete, and problem-oriented models into solution-oriented, complete and finally executable models.

Both forms of transformations are homogeneous, i.e., they transform models within the same language. During a development process it may however also happen that models of a problem-oriented DSML are mapped to another more solution-oriented DSML.

8.1 FOUNDATIONS

8.1.1 Refactorings

Developers almost never get a model right from the beginning. Models of interesting systems are typically complex and error-prone. So during a development project, a model needs to be adapted according to identified misconceptions, badly structured representation, new information that developers got from users and, of course also according to newly identified requirements. It is always possible to manually adapt a model and all the related implementation artifacts and see whether the result fits the new requirements, for example, by intensive testing.

However, testing efforts can be considerably reduced when we are able to use specific transformation tools with carefully engineered transformations that allow us to systematically modify a model only in such a way that we know by definition that we do not do anything harmful.

Definition 8.1 (Refactoring) *Refactoring is a relation between two models. Model B is a refactoring of model A, if all information that model A describes about the modeled system can also be derived from model B, but not more.*

The relational definition gives us a clear understanding of what refactoring is, but doesn't help us much in performing refactoring. Thus, the relational definition needs to be realized by operational and thus practically usable transformations. In Section 8.3, we will discuss how to build refactoring transformations during a development process using our CA example.

Foundation 8.1 Refactoring Operator

Mathematically, a refactoring operator is denoted with this signature:

$$\Re : \mathbb{L} \to \mathbb{L}$$

For a refactoring operator it must hold that its application leads to a semantically equivalent model that might exhibit a better internal structure and representation of its information. Thus, the following must hold:

$$\forall m \in \mathbb{L} : \mathbb{M}(\Re(m)) = \mathbb{M}(m)$$

Refactoring is a horizontal transformation that stays on the same level of detail. For example, the removal of unreachable states in an automaton, or the removal of a method that cannot be called in a class diagram can be such refactorings.

In real projects, however, many models are used and a model transformation only becomes a refactoring if the context restricts the usage in a certain way. For example, if it can be deduced from the context that a class is not instantiated or otherwise used anymore in a class diagram, its removal is a refactoring.

Foundation 8.2 Refactoring Equivalence

A context $C \subseteq \mathbb{L}$ is a set of given models that is composed with a refactored model and thus together establishes the equivalence:

$$\forall m \in \mathbb{L} : \mathbb{M}(C \otimes \Re(m)) = \mathbb{M}(C \otimes m)$$

While refactoring a model usually stays in the same language, in practice it may be interesting to use additional language concepts and thus the underlying metamodel may also be modified.

For cellular automata models, we can for example refine the map that is being used as underlying data structure from a very general n-dimensional map to two dimensions, and constrain the layout and the size. We can also constrain the applicability of rules in case there are situations where there are choices between several rules.

Foundation 8.3 Heterogeneous Refactoring

The refactoring definition above covers heterogeneous refactoring by understanding $\mathbb{L}$ as a super-language that contains all involved languages as sub-languages.

For programming languages, there have been many *refactoring* techniques defined. These by definition [44, 114] modify the structure of the program, while retaining the externally observable behavior. If we look into Fowler's book [44], we see that refactoring techniques are applied on Java while they are explained using class diagrams. Therefore, many of these refactoring techniques can be straightforwardly used for class diagrams too. In general, refactoring on models is even more promising than on cluttered, detailed code, where data structures, architectures, sequences of correct behavior, etc., are much more visible and explicit.

8.1.2 Refinement

In contrast to refactoring, a *refinement* is a transformation on a given model that by its application not only retains all information about the system under development, but also adds more information and details to the model. Prominent examples of refinement on class diagrams are adding new attributes, associations, or classes. Refinement on behavioral models typically completes behavioral descriptions or reduces underspecification, e.g., by selection of one out of several alternative behaviors.

Definition 8.2 (Refinement) *Refinement is a relation between two models. Model B is a refinement of model A, if all information that can be derived from model A can also be derived from model B.*

For each refinement operator, it must hold that its application leads to a more detailed, refined model. The more details a model incorporates, the less possible implementations it has.

While refactoring and refinement are different in their intention, there may be transformations that are both at the same time, e.g. if a refinement is intended, but actually doesn't add new information and thus equality holds in the above equation.

> **Foundation 8.4 Refinement Operator**
>
> Thus, the following must hold for a refinement operator $\Re$ (that has essentially the same signature as a refactoring):
>
> $$\forall m \in \mathbb{L} : \mathbb{M}(\Re(m)) \subseteq \mathbb{M}(m)$$

Please also observe that an empty model embodies no information and thus does not constrain the set of implementations at all. Adding information thus always imposes new constraints and therefore always reduces the number of implementations.

There may be quite a number of refinement operators that can be defined for a language $\mathbb{L}$, in particular when the language consists of many syntactic concepts. It of course depends on the chosen semantics, e.g., the view semantics $\mathbb{M}_{view}$ on class diagrams allows us to freely add attributes and associations as refinement, whereas $\mathbb{M}_{impl}$ doesn't. The former just gives semantics to what is explicitly denoted in the model, but does not enforce completeness, while the latter assumes that the implementation corresponds exactly to the model and no additional surprises exist. Thus, generally a specification-oriented semantics is better for a modeling language when used together with refinement, because it allows more freedom of adding information.

Refinement, refactoring, and *composition* are especially helpful when they fit together.

8.1.3 Refinements, Refactorings, and Compositions

It is worth noting that according to our definition, refinement as well as refactoring transformations can be chained: the sequential application of several transformations (refinements, resp. refactorings) in a chain is a refinement, resp. a refactoring.

Chaining of transformations together with compatibility of these transformations with composition is an extremely powerful mechanism to decompose system development and parallelize the workload.

Using compatible refinement, refactoring, and composition, we can indeed decompose the system into components and subcomponents. We can develop them individually by iteratively applying refinement and compose the resulting system at the end. If we are sure that the

---

Foundation 8.5 Refinement and Composition

It is important and should be a must that refinement, refactoring, and composition are compatible. This means that replacing the original component by a refined component leads to a refinement of the overall composition:

$$\forall m_1, m_2 \in \mathbb{L}: \quad \mathbb{M}(\Re(m_1)) \subseteq \mathbb{M}(m_1) \quad \Rightarrow$$
$$\mathbb{M}(\Re(m_1) \otimes m_2) \subseteq \mathbb{M}(m_1 \otimes m_2)$$

Sometimes however, the transformed model m_1 does not lead to refinement in general, but it may be considered as a refinement only in a given context. For example, modifying the transition structure of an automaton may be a safe refinement when the context ensures that certain paths are not taken away.

We call it *refinement in a given context* $C \subseteq \mathbb{L}$, when the context C contains enough additional information, such that the transformation is a refinement of the composition in this context:

$$\mathbb{M}(C) \cap \mathbb{M}(\Re(m_1)) \subseteq \mathbb{M}(C) \cap \mathbb{M}(m_1)$$

or alternatively:

$$\mathbb{M}(\Re(m_1) \otimes C) \subseteq \mathbb{M}(m_1 \otimes C)$$

Foundation 8.6 Chain of Refinements (Refactorings)

Given several refining (resp. refactoring) transformations $\Re_1, \ldots, \Re_n$ their chaining $\Re_1 \circ \cdots \circ \Re_n$ is a refinement (respectively, behavior preserving refactoring) iff

$$\forall m \in \mathbb{L}: \mathbb{M}((\Re_1 \circ \cdots \circ \Re_n)(m)) \subseteq \mathbb{M}(m)$$

initial decomposition is correct, for example by rigorous analysis as an early development activity, we will have much less integration testing to execute.

For programming languages, these refinement and composition operations cooperate quite well: composition is done by the compiler and refinement is done informally when applying certain refactoring steps that are correct by application.

For modeling languages, composition and refinement are not so well elaborated and may often depend on the language. That is the reason why we have a relatively hard time in decomposing models into independent models that are then implemented in a parallel process by independent developers. When the modeling language does not explicitly support composition, we may use techniques like model merging and weaving. This form of composition is described in Section 11.2.

8.1.4   Testing Refactorings and Refinements

Both refactorings and refinements are specialized forms of *transformations* applied on models. To ensure the correctness of such a transformation, which typically can grow quite complex, we can apply the same concepts as for any quality challenge, namely we can define tests. The test setting in this case typically consists of source models, a driver that applies the transformation, and the prescription of the desired result. These are standard black box tests. However, as we are normally talking about refinement and refactoring transformations on models that describe an executable system, it is also possible to take a two-step test process with *target execution*. Instead of an examination of the resulting model, we can compile executable models into a piece of code and write tests that examine the behavior of this code. This especially has the advantage that we can use the original model as an oracle for these tests: We translate both models into code and let them run against each other. If behavioral differences occur, the applied transformation cannot be a refactoring.

8.2   APPLYING MODEL REFACTORING

We do not refactor models without a reason. Usually the model has some flaw in its representation and could be represented in a more compact form, or we want to add additional information during the development process, which can be added more easily when we have first refactored the model.

8.2.1 Illustrative Example: CAIR-Lite Refactoring

Let us examine the CAIR-Lite model first shown in Figure 2.1. What are possible refactorings that do not affect the semantics of the model? Obviously, we can rearrange the layout and add or remove comments without any semantic effect, because neither comments nor whitespaces have semantics in CAIR.

For additional possible refactorings, we can refer to the semantic definition given in Foundation 2.5. Adapting the geometry (5 x 5) to any other kind of grid would obviously change the semantics of the model; this would not be a refactoring in the strict sense.

However, we can adapt the order of the rules, potentially repeat or split them or introduce overlapping rules that have consistently the same value on the overlapping part. An example is given in Listing 8.1 that contains useful and some less useful refactorings of the original CAIR model in Listing 2.1.

CAIR

```
regularGeometry {5 x 5}
init {[2..5] x [2..5] } = { 0 }
init { 1      x 1      } = { 1 }
init {[2..5] x 1      } = { 1 }
init { 1      x [2..5] } = { 1 }
init { 1      x [2..5] } = { 1 }
```

Listing 8.1 Refactored CAIR model.

To derive the model in Listing 8.1, we applied several semantics preserving refactorings. The last clause has been duplicated, one has been split, and the order of clauses has been altered. This is all fine, because even if the semantic definition uses the order of **init** clauses, it wouldn't be a problem because the clauses in this model refer to disjoined sets of positions.

However, the possibilities to refactor a CAIR model are limited to examples like the ones we have seen above. If our semantics would be more abstract respectively from our context, we could infer that the size of the universe doesn't matter. For example, we could adapt the height from 5 to another size while at the same time adapting the initialization clauses. In Listing 8.2, we show a Kermeta transformation executing this refactoring.

Kermeta

```
@Aspect(className=CellularAutomataInitialization)
class CellularAutomataInitializationAspect{
  def public void extendDimension( int dimIndex, int incr){
    if(_self.geometry instanceof RegularGeometry){
      val dimension = (_self.geometry as RegularGeometry).dimensions.get
          (dimIndex)
      val int dimPrevSize = dimension.extent
      dimension.extent = dimPrevSize + incr

      _self.seedRules.forEach[rule|
        rule.extendDimension(dimIndex, dimPrevSize, incr)
      ]
}}}

@Aspect(className=Rule)
class RuleAspect {
  def public void extendDimension( int dimension, int dimPrevSize, int
      incr){
    if(_self.filter instanceof AreaFilter){
      (_self.filter as AreaFilter).areas.forEach[area |
        val DimensionRange dimRangeToExtend = area.dimensionRanges.get(
            dimension)
        if (dimRangeToExtend.upper == dimPrevSize){
          dimRangeToExtend.upper = dimPrevSize + incr
        }
      ]
}}}
```

Listing 8.2 Refactoring that extends a dimension of a CAIR model by an increment.

The main rule in this transformation enlarges a dimension (identified by its index) by the parameter increment. It also adapts all rules that use the limit of this dimension and increases them too. If automata in the following code is a variable referencing our original CAIR model of Figure 2.1,

```
automata.extendDimension(1, 5)
```

then the resulting model will be:

CAIR

```
regularGeometry Moore {5 x 10}
init {[1..5] x 1     } by {1}
init { 1     x [1..10] } by {1}
init {[1..5] x [1..10] } by {0}
```

8.2.2 Illustrative Example: CAER Refactoring

Refactoring becomes more interesting when applied to syntactically complex languages or language components, such as an expression sublanguage or a statement language that we know from typical programming languages.

Expression languages, for example, typically allow us to apply many small adaptations of their expressions based on algebraic laws such as commutativity $(a + b = b + a)$, associativity, logical laws, such as idempotence $(a \wedge a = a)$, numeric laws $(a + a = 2 * a)$, or laws of underlying data types (e.g., in a set a, $a.add(b).add(b) = a.add(b)$. Similarly, there are quite a few possibilities to adapt algorithmic statements.

As an example, we define refactorings for the cellular automaton evolution language (CAER). Since we have several ways to write evaluations equivalently, we may provide a transformation that refactors an evaluation from one form to another. The standard rules for Game of Life are represented in Listing 8.3: If a living cell has two or three living neighbors, it will live in the next step, otherwise it will die. A dead cell will revive if it has exactly three living neighbors, otherwise it will remain dead.

CAER ⌐

```
/* Standard Game of life (CAER rule) */
when [0,1] nextValue = {
  if currentValue == 1 {
    if neighborsSum == 2 | neighborsSum == 3 {1} else {0}
  }
  else {
    if neighborsSum == 3 {1} else {0}
  }
}
```

Listing 8.3 Game of Life before refactoring.

Listing 8.3 uses a hierarchy of two levels of conditional expressions. However, CAER also provides filters that can replace the conditionals. Therefore we can refactor this rule into the following rules given in Listing 8.4. Both individual rules use a more selective filter. The first applied on the range of the current value being 1, representing the then-case, while the second rule represents the else-case. The transformation decouples a larger clause into two smaller ones while fully preserving the operational semantics. This kind of refactoring can have quite a significant impact on the understanding of the rules if applied properly.

CAER ⬑

```
/* Standard Game of life (CAER rule) */
when [1,1] nextValue = { // when cells live:
  if neighborsSum == 2 | neighborsSum == 3 {1} else {0}
}
when [0,0] nextValue = { // when cells are dead:
  if neighborsSum == 3 {1} else {0}
}
```

Listing 8.4 Game of Life after refactoring.

Like any other transformation, a refactoring transformation typically consists of two *search-and-apply* phases: an identification phase that looks for places in the model where the refactoring can apply and an application phase that removes the identified part and replaces it by new model elements.

The operation `refactorCondition` in Listing 8.5 shows these two phases, which are done recursively in case the basic refactoring operation might have created another applicable place in the model. The concrete detection and refactoring transformation operations can be directly woven in the metamodel concepts as shown in Listing 8.6.

Kermeta ⬑

```
import static extension caer.refactoring.RuleAspect.*

class EvolutionRuleRefactoring {
  def public refactorCondition(String ruleFile, String ruleOutFile){
    initEMFRegistry()
    val CellularAutomata automata = loadRules(ruleFile)
    var splittableRules = detectSplittableRules(automata.rules)
    while(!splittableRules.empty){
      splittableRules.forEach[rule |
        automata.rules.remove(rule)
        automata.rules.addAll(rule.splitEqual())
      ]
      splittableRules = detectSplittableRules(automata.rules)
    }
    saveRules(automata, ruleOutFile)
  }

  def public List<Rule> detectSplittableRules(List<Rule> rules){
    val result = new ArrayList<Rule>()
    rules.forEach[rule|
      if(rule.isEqualSplittable) {
        result.add(rule)
      }
    ]
```

```
    return result
  }

  public def CellularAutomata loadRules(String rulesFile) {
    var rs = new ResourceSetImpl()
    var res = rs.getResource(URI.createURI(rulesFile), true)
    return res.getContents.get(0) as CellularAutomata
  }
  public def saveRules(CellularAutomata automata, String rulesFile) {
    var rs = new ResourceSetImpl()
    var res = rs.createResource(URI.createURI(rulesFile))
    res.getContents.add(automata)
    res.save(null)
  }

  public def initEMFRegistry(){
...
  }
}
```

Listing 8.5 Starting part of the refactoring transformation of conditions in evolution rules.

Kermeta

```
import static extension caer.refactoring.EqualAspect.*
import static extension caer.refactoring.PopulationRangeAspect.*

@Aspect(className=typeof(Rule))
class RuleAspect {
  def public Boolean isEqualSplittable() {
    if(_self.filter instanceof PopulationRange){
      val lower = (_self.filter as PopulationRange).lowerRange
      val upper = (_self.filter as PopulationRange).upperRange
      if (lower != upper){
        if(_self.evaluatedVal instanceof Conditional){
          val conditional = (_self.evaluatedVal as Conditional)
          if(conditional.condition instanceof Equal){
            val equal = conditional.condition as Equal
            if(equal.isOperandCurrentCellPopulation && equal.
                isOperandIntegerLitOnRangeBorder(lower, upper)){
              return true
    } } } } }
    return false
  }

  def public List<Rule> splitEqual() {
    val result = new ArrayList<Rule>
    val lower = (_self.filter as PopulationRange).lowerRange
    val upper = (_self.filter as PopulationRange).upperRange
```

```
    val evaluatedValCond = _self.evaluatedVal as Conditional
    val equalcondition = evaluatedValCond.condition as Equal

    var Integer literalValue
    if (equalcondition.left instanceof IntegerLiteral)
      literalValue = (equalcondition.left as IntegerLiteral).^val
    if (equalcondition.right instanceof IntegerLiteral)
      literalValue= (equalcondition.right as IntegerLiteral).^val

    val lowerRule = CoreFactory.eINSTANCE.createRule
    val upperRule = CoreFactory.eINSTANCE.createRule
    if(literalValue == lower){
    lowerRule.filter = EvolFactory.eINSTANCE.createPopulationRange.
        init(lower, lower)
    lowerRule.evaluatedVal = evaluatedValCond.ifTrueExpression
    upperRule.filter = EvolFactory.eINSTANCE.createPopulationRange.
        init(lower+1, upper)
    upperRule.evaluatedVal = evaluatedValCond.ifFalseExpression
    }
    else{
    lowerRule.filter = EvolFactory.eINSTANCE.createPopulationRange.
        init(lower, upper-1)
    lowerRule.evaluatedVal = evaluatedValCond.ifFalseExpression
    upperRule.filter = EvolFactory.eINSTANCE.createPopulationRange.
        init(upper, upper)
    upperRule.evaluatedVal = evaluatedValCond.ifTrueExpression
    }

    result.add(lowerRule)
    result.add(upperRule)
    return result
}}

@Aspect(className=typeof(Equal))
class EqualAspect {
  def public boolean isOperandCurrentCellPopulation() {
    return _self.left instanceof CurrentCellPopulation || _self.right
        instanceof CurrentCellPopulation
  }

  def public boolean isOperandIntegerLitOnRangeBorder(int lower, int
      upper) {
    return (_self.left instanceof IntegerLiteral && ((_self.left as
        IntegerLiteral).^val == lower || (_self.left as IntegerLiteral)
        .^val == upper))
      || (_self.right instanceof IntegerLiteral && ((_self.right as
        IntegerLiteral).^val == lower || (_self.right as
        IntegerLiteral).^val == upper))
}}
```

```
@Aspect(className=PopulationRange)
class PopulationRangeAspect {
  def public PopulationRange init(int lowerRange, int upperRange){
    _self.lowerRange = lowerRange
    _self.upperRange = upperRange
    return _self
  }
}
```

Listing 8.6 Aspect part of the refactoring transformation of conditions in evolution rules.

While the refactoring itself seems to be relatively intuitive and easy to understand, defining the refactoring rule as an explicit transformation rule is typically more complicated. However, if the rule is correctly designed, we can reuse the rule in different contexts and therefore speed up the development process. Furthermore, if the rule is validated, its application is correct by construction and thus eases refactoring quite a lot. Please note that the rule can be applied in more general contexts, such that there is a good chance for reuse.

8.3   APPLYING MODEL REFINEMENT

We refine models in order to add additional information. This is quite common for data structure models, most typically class diagrams, when we add new classes, new attributes, and associations. However, we can also refine behavioral or interaction models, and in particular, we can refine domain-specific models when we know what their semantics actually is.

8.3.1   Example and Caveats: Data Structure Refinement

Let us assume that we have a library application, which is partially given in Figure 8.1. Obviously, the information about books is not complete and thus we add authors, information about whether the book

Figure 8.1 Class diagram describing a library application.

is rented, the proposed day of return, and so on. Figure 8.2 shows the resulting extension. It is a true refinement, because all we knew about our library application from the first figure is still true. However, now we have more information available.

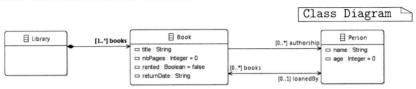

Figure 8.2 Refined class diagram through extension.

Introducing a new, abstract superclass Item in Figure 8.3 to contain all information about the rental and making Book a subclass of it is also a refinement because we can still use the original information e.g., that all Books have return dates, etc., even though this information is not explicitly presented in the class Book anymore. We see that refinement of class diagrams is to a large extent based on extending the available information. To some extent it also allows us to restrict given information and restructure elements especially along the inheritance hierarchy. This is always possible, if we know from the context of the model that the new version of the developed system will behave like the old one plus provide the refined extra elements.

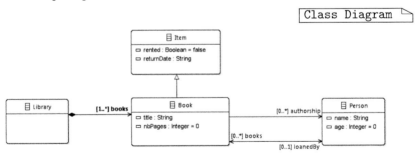

Figure 8.3 Second refinement of the class diagram.

It would be a natural adaptation to migrate the Book-end of the loaned association to the superclass Item as well. In practice this is done quite often, however formally speaking, it is not a strict refinement. This is because after the adaptation, a Person object that accesses its links to books can suddenly be confronted with the more general objects of class items. However, a good programming or modeling language uses the typing to check these possible problems and thus imposes the appropriate constraints to our model. If the transformation is syntactically correct and the result well typed, it can also be regarded as a refinement.

There are other subtle problems with refinement, especially if we not only want to read the data structure, but also want to modify its elements. For example, when an association is accessible for reading and writing, its multiplicities may not be changed anymore. To explain this, let us examine the `books` association. If we replace the multiplicity `1..*` on the right end by a more relaxed `0..*`, then algorithms relying on the existence of at least one book could come into trouble. On the other hand, if we restrict the multiplicity, e.g., to `1..2`, then algorithms that expect to be able to assign more than two authors to a book, can fail. Relaxing is dangerous to reading access and strengthening is dangerous to writing access. So if both are allowed by the context that has access to such a model or the data described by the model, no adaptation of multiplicity is allowed.

In practice, it is very often the case that a transformation is only a refinement in the context of additionally existing models, e.g., if we know that we do not rely on certain multiplicity constraints, or we know from other models that certain restrictions apply anyway, then we can much more easily refine a model. So in practice, the introduced context plays an important role. It is therefore necessary to distinguish an open or a closed world of development. In an *open world of development*, a model is published to a set of external potential users, who develop their parts of the system with the knowledge that everything that is present in that model still holds in a later implementation. So any kind of adaptation of the model has to reflect that you cannot control what kind of information is being used outside and who is relying on this information. The context is basically unknown and adaptation is therefore very much restricted because otherwise incompatibilities may occur.

In a *closed world of development*, adapting a model only has to ensure that the currently existing context does not rely on the changed part (or that it can be adapted together with the model). As said, the context contains all other models and pieces of code currently existing in that closed world. In practice, many projects allow a closed world assumption, especially if they share the repository and have common artifact ownership. Agile development projects typically have this assumption. Framework projects, in contrast, or subprojects that develop individual components, have a rather restricted possibility to adapt things, like APIs and data structures that have been published, because they don't know the (potentially future) context in which they are used.

8.3.2 Example: Data Structure Refinement with OCL

In Chapter 4 we discussed the use of OCL constraints for the specification of invariants and behavior. A typical use case for OCL is to constrain a data structure in specific ways to ensure correctness of the overall application. This is a typical form of refinement too. Each additional OCL constraint adds information to the model, thus giving additional information about the data contents and their relations. We might for example have adult readers only:

OCL ⬑

```
context Person p inv AdultReaders:
    p.books->notEmpty implies p.age >= 18
```

Or we might disallow authors to rent their own books (for whatever reason):

OCL ⬑

```
context Book b inv AuthorsDontLoan:
    not b.authorship.contains(b.loanedBy)
```

As a refinement, it is also possible to strengthen an existing OCL constraint, e.g.,

OCL ⬑

```
context Person p inv 21YearReaders:
    p.books->notEmpty implies p.age >= 21
```

is a strengthening of **AdultReaders** and thus may be added to the existing constraints or replace the **AdultReaders** constraint. OCL has an expression sublanguage embedded; therefore it allows us to apply all the algebraic and data type manipulations that expression languages typically have. We can also translate the representation of the OCL constraints in different forms, for example, replacing the context by a quantifier, such as in the following:

OCL ⬑

```
inv AdultReaders:
    Person->forall( p: p.books->notEmpty implies p.age >= 18 )
```

This transformation is information preserving but not a true refinement; it is a refactoring.

8.3.3 Example: Behavioral Refinement with OCL

A good modeling language should allow developers to constrain potential behavior of the system according to the known knowledge about what the system should do, but not enforce developers to choose specific behavior, without knowing customer requirements yet. However, all programming languages and unfortunately many modeling languages only allow two possibilities: They either fully define (resp. implement) behavior in a deterministic form (method body exists), or leave the implementation completely open (abstract method, no body). Refinement of behavior then boils down to implementing a method body that has not been defined before.

> ### Note 8.7 Overwriting Method
>
> Technically, overwriting a method in a subclass is not a refinement, but only a modification, but logically we regard this as a refinement if we know that the superclass implementation is just a default.

If, however, the language provides explicit mechanisms for underspecification, then behavioral refinement suddenly becomes an interesting option. We investigate two examples: OCL and state machines. As discussed in Chapter 4, OCL is perfect for specifying desired behavior of a method and leaving open several potential implementations for subclasses, because it explicitly provides underspecification.

For the OCL example, let us reuse the universe of cells and examine a specification that executes one step on a cell.

```
context Universe::oneSteponCell(Cell c)
  pre: c.val >= 0 and c.val <= 1
  post: c.val >= 0 and c.val <= 1
```

The specification is highly underspecified, and it basically only says that when the input is valid, namely a cell has a valid value, it will afterward also have a valid value. We can now strengthen the postcondition to refine the specification. For example, the following would be a rather empty universe, where revival is not possible:

```
context Universe::oneSteponCell(Cell c)
  pre: c.val >= 0 and c.val <= 1
  post: c.val <= c.val@pre
       and c.val >= 0 and c.val <= 1
```

Another form of refinement of OCL would be to relax the precondition, for example by making the function completely robust on positive numbers and delivering a valid universe even though the input might contain arbitrary positive numbers:

```
context Universe::oneSteponCell(Cell c)
  pre: c.val >= 0
  post: (c.val@pre==0 implies c.val=0)
       and c.val >= 0 and c.val <= 1
```

The correctness of a refinement on OCL is, however, typically shown by verifying mathematical properties. However, testing is possible as well. Even so, test design can be tricky. We refer to the appropriate literature for testing of behavior evolution, refactoring, and refinement [14].

8.3.4 Example: Behavioral Refinement with State Machines

A number of state machine dialects allow nondeterministic descriptions of their behavior. Nondeterminism means that the state machine offers several alternative transitions with differing behavior or differing target states. In the execution of the state machine, only one transition is taken. We can interpret this availability of alternatives at runtime, which amounts to nondeterminism of the running system or as available alternatives that can be decided by the developer during design time. Developers can thus remove one or several of the alternatives, if at least one alternative is still available. Figure 8.4 shows a nondeterministic

Statemachine, where we can remove some of the conditions, but also select a subset of the available initial states only. Please note that users of the developed system cannot distinguish between a nondeterministic choice at runtime or a predefined deterministic implementation (except with statistical arguments).

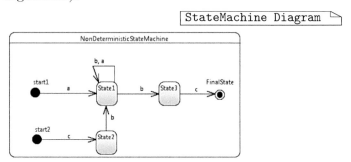

StateMachine Diagram

Figure 8.4   Refinable nondeterministic state machine.

The state machine in Figure 8.4 exhibits incompleteness, which can be handled in different semantic forms. If the underlying assumption is that there will be an error when running the state machine, then the semantics can be considered as relatively deterministic and does not need further refinement. If on the other hand, the semantics does not say anything about incomplete behavior, we are fully free to add additional transitions to complete the state machine and make it more informative. Again, we see that whether a transformation of a model is a refinement depends both on the syntax of the model and on its intended semantics.

For behavioral models, we explicitly need underspecification to be able to refine them by making them more detailed and more deterministic. The CAER rule language of our cellular automata is fully deterministic and thus does not really allow us to make semantic refinements, but only semantic-preserving refactorings as discussed in the previous section.

8.4   EXERCISES

Exercise 8.1 Defining Refactoring Transformations on CAIR Models

In the illustrative example of Section 8.2.1.

- Write a Kermeta transformation that duplicates all init clauses.

- Write a Kermeta transformation that inverts a CAIR model such that when it is evaluated, each value is inverted. Is that a refactoring?

Exercise 8.2 Refinement of OCL

The examples is Section 8.3.3 show several forms of OCL specifications for the `oneSteponCell` method.

- If you had to mathematically prove the refinement relation, what would your argument be?

- How can you use an OCL specification for testing implementations?

- Can you also test correctness of refinements between OCL constraints?

- Develop another refinement of the initial OCL specification such that after a step, a certain pattern cell is always visible in the universe (e.g., 0 at cell [1,1] and 1 at cell [1,2]). Can you still implement this?

Generators

CONTENTS

T HIS chapter discusses the design of generators. It demonstrates what kinds of transformations can be used to generate concrete artifacts from models, including implementation code, documentation, and test cases.

Since these target artifacts end up as a textual representations, we will first focus on *model-to-text* transformations. We will learn how to use and modify existing generators, as well as how to construct your own using template-based or visitor-based techniques.

Next, we will see how *model-to-model* approaches can also be used to pre-process a model in order to simplify a further model-to-text transformation. Finally, we will detail a test generation scenario.

9.1 USEFULNESS OF TEXT AND CODE GENERATION

In the preceding sections we looked at how we can use transformations to make changes on a model, or generate a model with a different form, by writing transformations that work at the abstract syntax level, i.e., by manipulating models.

However, there are often cases where language tooling does not expose APIs for manipulation at the abstract syntax level. Then, working with the concrete textual syntax may be the only choice. In other cases, it is simply more convenient to target the concrete syntax. This is frequently the case when generating code for a general purpose programming language such as C or Java, in particular when a large part of the result can directly be written in the programming language, with only specific elements inserted from the model.

The generation of artifacts (code, tests, documentation, etc.) is one of the cornerstones of Model Driven Engineering. Actually, many people even identify MDE with code generation. While we take a much broader view in this book, we still acknowledge the central role played by artifact generation in MDE and we now discuss its interest.

We already explained in detail that a model is an abstraction of an aspect of the reality it describes. As a side effect of abstraction, the model should be smaller, more comprehensible to understand, and easier to maintain and evolve than the reality it represents. Abstraction is one key to efficiency in model-based software development.

The second key is that code can often be systematically, and thus automatically, derived from models. There are situations where the derivation happens repeatedly within the project, e.g., when we need a factory class for each domain class. Some code may also be tightly coupled, and thus vulnerable to evolutionary changes, e.g., procedures for encoding, transmitting, storing, and decoding of data must be kept consistent, because they are different aspects of the same "thing." Also, similar code will occur in forthcoming projects in a product line, e.g., like the GUI. Then, code generation is a key for developer efficiency as well as code quality.

Generating code from a model means that all necessary and interesting details need to be present to be able to generate a complete running program. As an abstraction of the system, the model will by definition not contain all these details. There are basically the following possibilities to handle this:

1. The model has a one-to-one mapping to code. Then it is not really an abstraction, but still might be useful to give an alternative representation of the code, e.g., graphical.

2. We use several models of different kinds to describe different aspects of the system, such that each model abstracts away from certain details, but altogether we describe a complete system.

3. Missing details are added by writing several parts of the system directly by hand within the target programming language. This will allow us to fill in omitted details, but needs a good understanding of how to integrate generated and handwritten code.

4. The generator exhibits intelligence to fill out missing details so that the developer and the user are satisfied with omitted details. This *intelligence* can start with *defaults* that for example generate additional code in a standard way, when no explicit information about omitted details are given.

While these four approaches can be combined, each of them has several consequences that are worth discussing. Only then are we able to choose and design generators appropriately.

Approach (1) does not allow abstraction and therefore would not result in the desired improvement in development efficiency. Some compactification would be possible, but would have limited effects.

Approach (2) in some cases also expects that every detail is described using some model elements. However, thanks to the different viewpoints that each of the models may have, certain correlations can be understood and examined more easily. The complete system becomes easier to develop. The consequences of this approach are typically a better quality of the product and, to a lesser extent, an efficiency improvement. Additionally, as a side effect, individual viewpoints (modeled in individual artifacts) might become reusable in a better way than was possible when all aspects of the system were interwoven in one big program or model.

Approach (3) uses some kind of integration of generated and handwritten code. For this purpose, several forms of integrations are possible [52]. Some of them have consequences on the MDE process. We highlight a few:

(a) Changing a generated class by hand is catastrophic, because the code cannot be regenerated. We get a "one shot" process, where the model becomes obsolete as soon as the generation has been executed and evolution on the model level is not possible.

(b) Round-trip engineering would try to extract hand-coded changes. It works only on models which provide some structure to capture and store all the changes. The best results are obtained when the model abstraction is close to the syntax abstraction. For example, a class diagram model may store any object-oriented program but this is not optimal since the actual instructions in the operations are usually stored in the model only as simple strings. An improvement that allows us to reverse engineer more code to the model is to add constraints on the handwritten code so the user can only write structures that can be round-tripped.

(c) Pieces of handwritten code are stored within or adjunct to the model and are integrated by the generator. This is in fact an easy way to implement Approach (2) from above, but without much control over the result.

(d) The code is generated in the form of a framework and anticipates the injection of handwritten code through various plug-ins, delegation and inheritance mechanisms that ensure the handwritten code is clearly separated from the generated code. Once again, it is a way of implementing Approach (2) from above, in a more controlled way.

In the last Approach (4), neither the model nor the handwritten code is necessary to fill out the details, because the generator encapsulates the know-how to do that in a systematic way. Prominent examples are the systematic generation of getters and setters from attributes, factories, or builders for classes, etc. While these prominent examples deal with small extensions in the application core, there are examples of intelligent generators that could also derive a complete graphical user interface, with lots of generated code. However when the generation does not work the same for all cases, the generator may need some parameters that tune the result. If these parameters are complex, they can be considered as a model. Thus, this approach can again be considered as a variant of Approach (2) where some models are implicitly used by the generator.

As a conclusion, Approach (2) is the more general one, and we could even pretend that it subsumes the others [68], or put another way, that the others are degraded forms of Approach (2). However, from the practical point of view, it is often easier to implement and understand the other approaches.

9.2 MODEL-TO-TEXT TRANSFORMATIONS

One of the simplest ways of making models useful is to allow the generation of arbitrary pieces of text. Many of the commonly used representations that we need to generate can indeed be expressed using plain text. The way it is done in MDE is through the use of *model-to-text* transformations.

Because they are used to generate artifacts that can generally be plugged straightforwardly into other tools, model-to-text transformations represent highly valuable tools. Interestingly, there are also situations where model-to-text transformations can be implemented more easily than, for example, model-to-model transformations. Indeed, for the generation of simple documents, model-to-text transformations are fairly easy to implement using basic MDE techniques. However, in larger use cases, with multiple models contributing to the same documents and other more complex relationships between them, there are practices that can aid in managing the complexity of these transformations.

The interest in such transformations is actually well understood by the programmer community, which is accustomed to writing data in files or using compilers. For this reason, most existing DSLs propose model-to-text transformations to complement their tooling.

As for the model-to-model transformation tools in Chapter 6, model-to-text transformation tools can benefit from the source or from the target structure. This will help in organizing the transformation code. Let's now introduce the three major model-to-text transformation techniques used in MDE for text generation.

– General purpose transformation languages that offer string and file manipulation operators

– Template-based languages

– Pretty printing, as a special case of both

There also exist techniques like text-to-text tools (e.g., Unix awk), that work at the syntactic level without leveraging the underlying model concepts. But these are not within the scope of this book.

9.2.1 General Purpose Transformation Languages for Text Generation

Since `String` is a basic type present in almost all modeling languages, all model transformation languages need to offer to manipulate them. This includes simple or qualified names, adding prefixes, or manipulating method bodies. Many transformation languages also provide some mechanisms to write down those strings into files. Given an appropriate transformation structuring, these languages can be used to produce complex text, e.g., complete classes with all their attributes and methods.

Due to the ordered nature of text, a complex and structured transformation usually needs to control the data and control flow within the transformation. It often needs to control the order in which the generation operation occurs, because different orders may lead to different results. This implies that transformation languages need to incorporate imperative abilities to scale up for such tasks. Therefore, sometimes general purpose programming languages are used for that kind of transformation.

The typical structure for these transformations is using a Visitor, which will ensure the traversal order. Acting similarly to the Visitor used for interpreters seen in Chapter 7, the result of the traversal will typically populate one large or several string buffers that would be saved to the artifact at the end of the process.

9.2.2 Illustrative Example: Straightforward Approach

As an illustrative example, we reuse our cellular automata example. The starting point is that we do have models and behavior for cellular automata at hand, and we want to run them efficiently while at the same time getting a useful visualization of the runs.

A generator is not only dependent on the source model (language), but also on the target language and the technological components that it has to address.

Therefore, we first need to choose a target programming language and to understand whether we can reuse some components, libraries, or frameworks of that language. For example, we can chose Java and the Mason framework [89] as the target for our system. It is a simulation framework that offers the notion of system runs as well as stepwise execution. It is able to visualize its system runs, and has a documented guidance on how to implement cellular automata. Therefore, it suits our requirements. However, often, there are some issues with its offered API that prevent a straightforward connection to our own abstractions. This will allow us to demonstrate how the MDE flexible generation technology can address these issues.

We start with a small example that we are going to extend later. Here, we concentrate on the mapping of the `IntegerExpression` sublanguage on expressions to Java. That sublanguage was defined in Figures 3.9, 3.10, and 3.11. This kind of translation is quite well suited for a visitor-based approach, since the source model and the target language do exhibit rather similar structures. The main task of the visitors in this example is to add concrete syntax to the output. As we stay within one expression, we do not care about the layout of the result.

The visitor developed in this example follows the typical Visitor pattern, defined in [38] and already presented in Section 7.3. For the sake of simplifying the example code in this book, the visitor signature has been modified to return a string and has the following signature:

Java

```
interface ModelToTextVisitor {
    //from Core
    String visitIntegerExpression(IntegerExpression s);
    String visitBinaryExpression(BinaryExpression s);
    String visitUnaryExpression(UnaryExpression s);
    String visitAnd(And s);
    String visitAdd(Add s);
```

```
String visitConditional(Conditional s);
String visitDiv(Div s);
String visitEqual(Equal s);
String visitFilter(Filter filter);
String visitGreater(Greater s);
String visitIntegerLiteral(IntegerLiteral s);
String visitLower(Lower s);
String visitMinus(Minus s);
String visitMod(Mod s);
String visitMult(Mult s);
String visitNot(Not s);
String visitOr(Or s);
String visitRule(Rule rule);
String visitUMinus(UMinus s);
  // from Evol
String visitCellularAutomata(CellularAutomata automata);
String visitCurrentCellPopulation(CurrentCellPopulation s);
String visitMax(Max s);
String visitMin(Min s);
String visitNeighborsExpression(NeighborsExpression s);
String visitPopulationRange(PopulationRange popRange);
String visitSize(Size s);
String visitSum(Sum s);
}
```

A concrete visitor can now implement the specific method for each subclass that can occur in an `IntegerExpression`. We only show the implementation methods for some representative classes, since the others are very similar:

Java

```
class ExpressionVisitor implements ModelToTextVisitor {
  public String visitUMinus(UMinus s) {
    return "(-" + s.getTarget().accept(this) + ")";
  }
  public String visitIntegerLiteral(IntegerLiteral s) {
    return Integer.toString(s.getVal());
  }
  public String visitCurrentCellPopulation(CurrentCellPopulation
      expression) {
    return "currentVal";
  }
  public String visitGreater(Greater s) {
    return "("+ s.getLeft().accept(this) + " > "
            + s.getRight().accept(this) + "? 1 : 0)";
  }

  public String visitSum(Sum expression) {
    if(expression.getNeighborsFilter() != null){
```

```
    return "Utils.neighborSum(tempGrid, x, y, new RangeFilter("
        + expression.getNeighborsFilter().getLowerRange()+","
        +expression.getNeighborsFilter().getUpperRange()+"))";
  }
  else{
    return "Utils.neighborSum(tempGrid, x, y)";
  }
 }
}
```

In order to simplify the code generator, we deliberately chose that the resulting code does not need to be formatted, supposing the user would not have to read it. Therefore, we create lots of parentheses, even if some of them are useless. Also we resort to the Java string concatenation operator (+) instead of using a StringBuilder shared among the visit methods. Fortunately, a modern compiler will optimize most of that automatically.

In the generator code below that applies to the Conditional expression, the source code has been formatted, but not the resulting code. This allows easier reading of the program:

Java

```
// ... part of class ExpressionVisitor:
  public String visitConditional(Conditional s) {
    return s.getCondition().accept(this) + " == 1 ?"
      + s.getIfTrueExpression().accept(this)+":"
      + s.getIfFalseExpression().accept(this);
  }
```

Given the model (i.e., an IntegerExpression) in Figure 9.1, we get as a result of the generation:

Java

```
// Result of visitor execution:
(currentVal > 0? 1 : 0)== 1 ?(Utils.neighborMax(tempGrid, x, y) - 1):1
```

Note 9.1 Optimizing the Generated Code

In this implementation, we didn't optimize the generated code and mapped every IntegerExpression to a Java expression returning an int. However, by adding some context, a code generator would be able to detect if the IntegerExpression is used in a Boolean context and thus generate a more compact and efficient code.

CAER Model

```
▲ X platform:/resource/cellularautomata_samples_models/evol_xmi/sampleIntegerExpression.evol.xmi
  ▲ ✧ Conditional
     ▲ ✧ Greater
          ✧ Current Cell Population
          ✧ Integer Literal 0
     ▲ ✧ Minus
          ✧ Sum
          ✧ Integer Literal 1
       ✧ Integer Literal 1
```

Figure 9.1 Sample IntegerExpression to be compiled.

9.2.3 Template-Based Languages

Templates can be seen as raw pieces of code (or documentation or other kinds of artifacts), where specific information from the source model still has to be inserted. A template is usually "executed" by a template engine that executes the macros and inserts the result in order to transform the raw piece of code into a complete artifact.

Definition 9.1 (Template) *Is a raw piece of an artifact with explicitly marked expressions that are evaluated relative to a model and whose results are inserted to complete the artifact.*

A template-based language actually involves three languages, namely the target language, the template expression language, and an explicit control language. While the template engine is often rather agnostic to the target language, by considering this as a sequence of characters, it explicitly reacts to the macros that evaluate to strings or control further actions.

The expression language used by a template engine will slightly impact the ease of writing the macros. For example, the Freemarker template engine [43] uses a variant of Java expressions as its expression language, thus allowing a deep integration into the internal model representation when this representation is written in Java. This is especially useful when complex calculations are needed, because they can directly be written in Java and used in the templates. Other template engines use a language with native model manipulation primitives. For example, Acceleo [100] uses a variant of OCL as its expression language. This makes the model navigation easier with more compact queries.

The third sub-language that a template language usually offers allows us to control repetition (e.g., for a list of model elements), conditionals, case statements, and inclusion of sub-templates. In general, template languages therefore comprise a kind of programming language with full procedural capabilities (but the specific purpose of producing text).

This technique is very efficient when most of the generated text is part of the template so that a template will contain more final text than expression and control code. Otherwise the visitor-based approach has advantages.

Tool 9.2 Acceleo

Acceleo is an environment to create, run, and package model-to-text transformations and code generators. It supports incremental generation, which can be launched in Eclipse but also through continuous integration using Maven or ANT. The templates authoring environment offers syntax highlighting, code completion, refactoring, a debugger, and a profiler. The template language of Acceleo is an implementation of the Object Management Group (OMG) MOF Model-to-Text Language (MTL) standard and model navigation is specified using OCL expressions. Once defined for a given metamodel, a set of templates definition can be applied on a model instance to generate any text-based format being code, HTML, or something else.

Acceleo is an open-source software project which is part of the yearly release of Eclipse. More information, including documentation and tutorials, can be found on the website `http://www.eclipse.org/acceleo`.

9.2.4 Illustrative Example: Template Approach

As a second illustrative example, we demonstrate the use of templates for the generation of the class code to initialize a cellular automaton simulation. While code generation of the expression sublanguage was rather agnostic to the target frameworks, but only dependent on the target language, here, we need to incorporate knowledge about the framework we use.

For this example we use Acceleo. In this template language, the control language is expressed using tags having a syntax similar to

XML but replacing the < and > signs by [and] signs.

In Listing 9.1 we see the main template that is responsible for the construction of the Java class file that embodies the cell behavior in the simulation:

```
                                                              Acceleo
[module generate('http://rules/core/1.0', 'http://rules/evol/1.0')]
[import cellularautomata::acceleo::compiler4mason::generateSubTemplates
    /]
[template public generateMasonAutomata(anAutomata : CellularAutomata )]
[ file ('MyGeneratedMasonAutomata.java', false, 'UTF-8')]
package generated_ca;

import cellularautomata.mason.utils.*;
import sim.engine.*;
import sim.field.grid.*;

public class MyGeneratedMasonAutomata implements Steppable{
  // the width and height will change later
    public IntGrid2D tempGrid = new IntGrid2D(0,0);

   @Override
   public void step(SimState state){
      CA_SimulationState tut = (CA_SimulationState)state;
      // first copy the grid into tempGrid
      tempGrid.setTo(tut.grid);

      // now apply the CA rules for each cell...
      int width = tempGrid.getWidth();
      int height = tempGrid.getHeight();
      for(int x=0;x<width;x++){
    for(int y=0;y<height;y++){
      int currentVal = tempGrid.field['['/]tempGrid.stx(x)[']['/]
         tempGrid.sty(y)[']'/];
[for (aRule : Rule | anAutomata.rules)]
  [aRule.generateRule()/]
[/for]
      }
    }
  }
}
[/ file ]
[/template]
```

Listing 9.1 Main template of the Acceleo code generator.

Acceleo ⬑

```
[template public generateRule(aRule : Rule)]
      if([aRule.filter.generateFilter()/]){
          tut.grid.field['['/]x[']['/]y[']'/] = [aRule.evaluatedVal.
              generateExpression()/];
      }
[/template]
...
[template public generateFilter(aFilter : PopulationRange)]
  [aFilter.lowerRange/] <= currentVal && currentVal <= [aFilter.
      upperRange/]
[/template]
...
[template public generateExpression(aLiteral : IntegerLiteral)]
[aLiteral.val/]
[/template]
[template public generateExpression(aCurrentCellPopulation :
      CurrentCellPopulation)]
currentVal
[/template]
[template public generateExpression(aGreater : Greater)]
([aGreater.left.generateExpression()/] > [aGreater.right.
      generateExpression()/] ? 1 : 0)
[/template]
```

Listing 9.2 Subtemplates of the Acceleo code generator.

The first template, `generateMasonAutomata`, exhibits several concepts present in such a template language: It shows its ability to generate a file on the disk. It embodies large parts of the target Java code including code for calling the Mason API, etc. It also embodies control structures, such as a `for` loop that navigates the model and gets the Rules out of the CelullarAutomata. From these Rules, it calls a subtemplate `generateRule` which in turn calls other templates. Listing 9.2 shows some of these subtemplates.

CAER ⬑

```
when [1,1] nextValue = {
  if neighborsSum == 2 | neighborsSum == 3 {1} else {0} }
when [0,0] nextValue = {
  if neighborsSum == 3 {1} else {0} }
```

Listing 9.3 Example model of evolution rules to be generated.

When the template is interpreted on a concrete model, such as the one in Listing 9.3, then it results in a complete Java class shown in Figure 9.2.

Java

```
MyGeneratedMasonAutomata.java ☒
1  package generated_ca;
2
3  import cellularautomata.mason.utils.*;
4  import sim.engine.*;
5  import sim.field.grid.*;
6
7  public class MyGeneratedMasonAutomata implements Steppable{
8      public IntGrid2D tempGrid = new IntGrid2D(0,0);
9
10     @Override
11     public void step(SimState state){
12         CA_SimulationState tut = (CA_SimulationState)state;
13         // first copy the grid into tempGrid
14         tempGrid.setTo(tut.grid);
15
16         // now apply the CA rules for each cell...
17         int width = tempGrid.getWidth();
18         int height = tempGrid.getHeight();
19         for(int x=0;x<width;x++){
20             for(int y=0;y<height;y++){
21                 int currentVal = tempGrid.field[tempGrid.stx(x)][tempGrid.sty(y)];
22                 if(1 <= currentVal && currentVal <= 1){
23                     tut.grid.field[x][y] = ((((2 == Utils.neighborSum(tempGrid, x, y)? 1 : 0) != 0) || ((3 == Utils.neighborSum(tempGrid, x, y)? 1 : 0)) != 0))? 1: 0;
24                 }
25
26                 if(0 <= currentVal && currentVal <= 0){
27                     tut.grid.field[x][y] = (3 == Utils.neighborSum(tempGrid, x, y)? 1 : 0)== 1 ? 1 : currentVal;
28                 }
29             }
30         }
31     }
32 }
```

Figure 9.2   Java class resulting from template generation of Listing 9.1.

9.2.5   Pretty Printing

Pretty printing is a rather simple form of generating code into a target language. A pretty printer exactly generates a textual version of a given internal representation of the very same model. For code generation purposes, pretty printing only works when the internal "model" directly represents the program. This usually means that before a pretty printer can be used, internal model-to-model transformations are necessary to transform the original source model into an internal representation of the target programming language. The task of a model-to-text transformation is therefore split into a first phase of model-to-model transformations and a standard pretty printing phase.

It can be argued that pretty printing tries to combine the best of both worlds. However, the second phase, namely the pretty printing, is relatively dull and thus has not much abstraction built into it. Therefore all the intelligence of the transformation needs to be part of the internal transformation. This, however, exhibits almost the same problems as the first approach, which becomes inconvenient when lots of code from the target language is added.

It is noteworthy that pretty printing can be implemented using both previously seen techniques, namely a fixed set of templates, as well as a closed program in a general purpose language.

> **Tip 9.3 Exploit Print API of Generated Editors**
>
> In many cases, a pretty printer can be obtained almost for free when using the tools dedicated to building a textual editor as seen in Section 5.6. Indeed, these tools usually generate both a parser and a pretty printer in order to implement the editor. Most of the time the parser and pretty printer can be used thanks to a public API.

9.2.6 Mixing All Approaches

Each of the approaches for code generation we described above has its pro and cons. Experience shows that for components like the GUI, a template-based approach works pretty well, while for the definition of an application core, templates would be rather cluttered, comprising lots of hard-to-express logic and calls to subtemplates. The data structure of an application core could, therefore, best be generated through a model-to-model transformation followed with a pretty printing. Finally, when the target structure is roughly isomorphic to the structure of the original model, a visitor-based approach is often appropriate.

In most complex situations however, we need to mix all these approaches. On a coarse-grained level, we should be able to decide individually for each artifact which approach to take. On a fine-grained level, we should be able to mix these approaches within one artifact, for example using a visitor to define the shape of an attribute and a template or a pretty printer to put it in the right place within Java files.

9.3 CODE GENERATION

We already know that code generation helps very much when repetitive, systematic tasks are to be carried out. This may be within a project at several places, or several times during evolution of the product, or repeatedly within a product line.

Generation could also assist optimization purposes. For example, complex code from a state machine can be better optimized on the state machine level, even though the compiler also does lots of efficient optimizations and should be used as well for that purpose.

Tip 9.4 How to Decide Which Language to Use for M2T Transformation?

The decision to use one or another transformation language will mainly depend on the content and nature of the resulting text. If it contains a large amount of static text that should be easily read and modified, then a template-based language should be considered first. If the final document structure closely maps to the model structure with little extra text or if it contains data that need complex computation, then general purpose transformation combined with pretty printing techniques should be considered first.

Once the first main language is selected, there are usually many ways to call and insert the result of subtransformations written using another approach. The reason is that in a given technological space, e.g., Eclipse/Ecore, all transformation languages are compatible because they work on the same data structure: the metamodel that is defined in, e.g., Ecore.

The generated code may be generated in order to be read by a human. For example, the code may be used or extended by a human or is subject to certification. The minimal requirement will be to provide clean interfaces. However, in the extension and certification case, it will be necessary to produce readable code for human readers to understand its internal mechanisms. This constraint forces the generator to not optimize too much. Furthermore, the code needs to be formatted in a proper form, such that humans can really read it.

Code completely generated and especially those with optimization goals will often take human readability as a minor requirement. An extreme example of non-readable code generation is obfuscation, which deliberately generates non-human-readable artifacts to protect the resulting program.

9.3.1 Illustrative Example: Code Generation

Let us now complete the code generation for the simulation of cellular automata. The Mason simulation framework actually needs three classes to be able to execute a simulation: A subclass of `SimState` to model the state and its initial state, a subclass of `Steppable` to

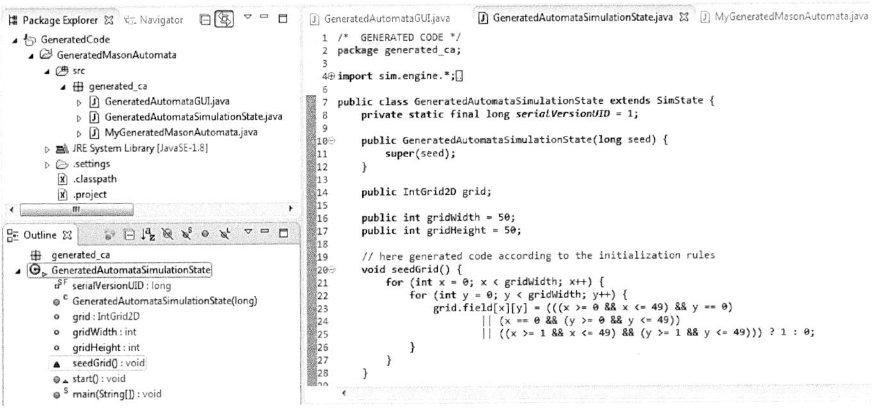

Figure 9.3 Generated project using Mason framework.

advance the situation in steps, and a subclass of GUIState to initialize a graphical interface. In Figure 9.3, we have completed the previous piece of generated code by generating the next two parts in a project. On the right part of the figure, we can see that the CAIR language has been processed in the same way as the CAER language was. It allows us to create the grid with the correct size and initialize it via the seedGrid method.

This finally leads to a running simulation that produces, e.g., the screen shots in Figure 9.4.

We also used a pretty printer when generating the GUIState class. It provides the *About* text that is embedded in the generated application, which is visible on the right part of the figure.

9.4   DOCUMENTATION GENERATION

Keeping documentation up to date with a project is a tedious job. It helps when the documentation can either be directly generated from source artifacts, such as JavaDoc for interfaces of Java classes. It is a well-known best practice to write and store comments and documentation very close to the model/code that is being documented, ideally in the same artifact. For example, Java comments are carried over to the JavaDoc documents. While this is well established for programming, it is also very helpful for other kinds of models, such as state machines, architectural models, as well as any domain-specific

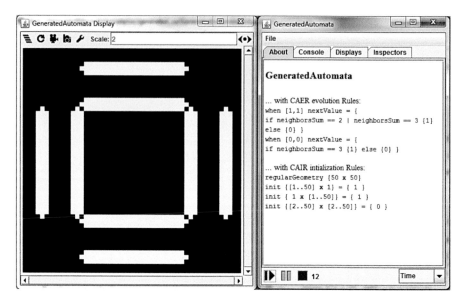

Figure 9.4 Generated code running using Mason framework.

models.

We might also be interested in documenting system runs, snapshots, or results of tests. In these cases, the document would contain data from the execution. In principle, however, the generation of documentation from the model, from static analysis of the model and from executions of the model/program does not differ much.

Documentation can be generated about the model or program itself as well as about a careful analysis of the statically available information and also about the system executions. For example, we might generate an HTML document that contains the initial models for defining a cellular automaton, i.e., the CAIR and CAER models. We might also do an analysis of the models to understand their quality and prevent errors. In the cellular automaton example, that could be questions such as: Does the CAIR initialization cover all cells? We can, e.g., generate a map with red markers for uncovered cells. In the modeling and programming domains, that very much corresponds to a careful analysis of code smells [35] and various other guidelines, such as useful names, not too deep nesting of inheritance or loops, analysis for unreachable codes or unreachable states in state machines, etc.

Again, we have to understand what the target language will be. The first intuitive approach is to consider documentation as unstructured text. In that case, all the transformation languages proposed in Section 9.2 can apply. As discussed in Section 9.2.6, the decision to use one or another transformation language would mainly depend on the content and nature of the resulting text and how it is going to be used.

If the document needs to be manually modified in some places, then we need to be able to isolate the modified text, either by being able to split the document or using a transformation language that offers to insert user text.

A second approach is helpful when the target document is not pure unstructured text, or when its internal structure is complex and not well documented. Usually, the target language is assisted by an appropriate tool. Microsoft's Word, Excel, and PowerPoint are of that form. If the tool offers a useful and well-documented API, then the document can be filled through this API. This method however starts to look like a model-to-model transformation and should thus be handled with those techniques.

As a third approach, we might use specialized template editors that offer a GUI for a certain document format. For example, we could write the template with WYSIWYG support for the text formatting and style dedicated to the target format. This is just offering MDE techniques with an end-user domain look and feel. An example of such a template tool can be Sodius MDWorkbench, which presents the templates in the Word application.

9.4.1 Illustrative Example: Documentation Generation for a Universe Model

This cellular automata example illustrates the use of a template-based transformation for generating documentation out of a Universe model together with its populated information. The template in Listing 9.4 generates a LaTex document that gives some simple statistics about the cells in the model. This example also illustrates the use of *protected* tags. These blocks delimit portions of text that are generated only once, and are preserved in subsequent generations. This is very useful in order to allow users to add or customize text in some areas of the generated files while keeping the rest of the file under the control of the generator. In the sample, the template allows the addition of LaTex configuration commands, the modification of the authors, and of the

Tip 9.5 Take Advantage of Documentation System Capabilities

Some documentation systems can provide complex processing support. For example, LaTex [85] provides a rich framework of commands that can be extended by the user, Word can be used with macros and VisualBasic, and even HTML provides JavaScript support. In that case, the documentation generator can make the most of the opportunity to use this additional processing phase.

When using such additional processing supports the documentation generation looks like code generation as discussed in the previous section. As such, other techniques seen in this book will also apply. For example, it may help to use some model-to-model transformation to correctly model some intermediate data that should be displayed using the document processor.

Objective section content. The *protected* tags must be placed in the comments of the target language (i.e., after a % sign in LaTex).

It also shows the use of the *query* definition, which is a way to enable calls to some standard programming language in the template. In the sample, it invokes some Java utility that retrieves the name of the model file.

Acceleo

```
[module generateLatex('http://vm/1.0')]
[query public getBaseFilename(u : Universe) : String = invoke(
  'cellularautomata.acceleo.generateLatex.Utility',
  'getBaseFilename(vm.Universe)', Sequence{u}) /]
[template public generateElement(anUniverse : Universe)]
[comment @main/]
[ file (anUniverse.getBaseFilename().concat('.tex'), false, 'UTF-8')]
\documentclass{article}
\usepackage{graphicx} % Required for the inclusion of images
% [protected ('additional configurations')]
%\usepackage{times} % Uncomment to use the Times New Roman font
% [/protected]

\title{Basic statistics about [anUniverse.getBaseFilename()/] Universe}

\author{
% [protected ('authors')]
  John \textsc{Smith}
```

```
% [/protected]
}
\date{\today} % Date for the report

\begin{document}
\maketitle % Insert the title, author and date

\section{Objective}
The goal of this document is to present a small overview of [anUniverse
    .getBaseFilename()/] Universe.
% [protected ('Objective')]
%\subsection{Definitions}
% [/protected]

\section{Statistics}
\begin{tabular}{ll}
Number of cells: & [cells->size()/]\\
Number of dead cells: & [cells->select(val = 0)->size()/]\\
Number of cells with value higher than 1: & [cells->select(val > 1)->
    size()/]
\end{tabular}

List of live cells:
[for (aCell : Cell | anUniverse.cells->select(val <> 0)) separator (',
    ')]
[anUniverse.cells->indexOf(aCell)/][/for]

\section{Details about live cells}
[for (aCell : Cell | anUniverse.cells->select(val <> 0)) ]
\subsection{Live cell [anUniverse.cells->indexOf(aCell)/]}
\begin{tabular}{ll}
Cell value: & [aCell.val/]\\
Numbers of neighbors alive: & [aCell.neighbors->select(val <> 0)->size
    ()/]
\end{tabular}

[/for]
\end{document}
[/file]
[/template]
```

Listing 9.4 Templates producing documentation in LaTex.

9.5 MODEL GENERATION

Code or text generation is quite well adopted by the programming community because in many cases the programmer can directly see the resulting text and thus the benefit. In the MDE context, the activity of defining generators is actually much broader than using only model-to-text techniques. Depending on the nature of the generated artifact, there are several scenarios where the result is better handled when combining several of the techniques previously seen.

Designing and maintaining a generator as a combination of model-to-model techniques seen in Chapter 6 with model-to-text techniques can be much easier than using model-to-text techniques alone.

MDE helps in the tooling of complex creation processes, while using the most appropriate format for a given artifact. This helps focussing on the user of the artifact (human or program), providing a point of view suitable to ease the creation, the use, and the maintenance of the artifact.

For example, many of the results of a generator are not intended to be read by humans and may use some compact encoding. In that case, manipulating the abstract syntax (i.e., the model) will be easier than manipulating the concrete textual syntax. This is the case for generated artifacts that are primarily intended to be used in a transformation chain. The possibility to read such artifacts may become a minor requirement versus having an efficient transformation or supporting optimization.

Sometimes the source models and the target artifacts have a structure that does not share similar concepts and does not have a straightforward mapping. For example, this is the case when the computation of the result depends on a model with a lot of cross references. It might be possible in theory to write the generator using a single model-to-text transformation but it would feature overly complex mapping rules. Breaking the transformation into smaller pieces would help in designing and understanding it. This is similar to compiler techniques, where the compilation is split in steps. Each step may compute and add some data. It may also adapt the structure; create temporary data in order to be more efficient. The last step will finally clean the data when writing the final artifact.

9.5.1 Illustrative Example: Generation of VM Model from Initialization Rules

In this example, we combine several of the previously seen techniques. A generator can be written as an interpreter. This is the case for the VM generator. This transformation uses the initialization rule language (CAIR) to create virtual machine models suitable as an entry point for simulators based on the interpreter seen in Chapter 7. The operation `generateInitialUniverseForAutomata` in Listing 9.5 basically creates a grid according to the specified geometry, then on each `Cell` it will search for the first applicable rule to calculate the value of the cell. The computation of the applicable rules and the cell value are simplified by adding the appropriate operations directly on the language classes by aspects (see Listing 9.6). In this case, the initialization rules language (CAIR) acts as a configuration language for the generator.

Kermeta

```
def public Universe generateInitialUniverseForAutomata(
    CellularAutomataInitialization automata) {
  var Universe result
  val geometry = automata.geometry
  switch geometry{
    RegularGeometry case (geometry.neighbors == Neighborhood.NEUMANN)
            && (geometry.dimensions.size == 2)
            && (!geometry.dimensions.exists[ d | d.isCircular]): {
      result = genVNeumannRectBoundedUniverse(geometry.dimensions.get
          (0).extent, geometry.dimensions.get(1).extent)
    }
    RegularGeometry case (geometry.neighbors == Neighborhood.MOORE)
            && (geometry.dimensions.size == 2)
            && (!geometry.dimensions.exists[d | d.isCircular]): {
      result = genVNeumannRectangleBoundedUniverse(geometry.dimensions
          .get(0).extent, geometry.dimensions.get(1).extent)
    }
    default: {
      println("Configuration not supported yet.")
      return null;
    }
  }
  // compute initial values for cells
  result.cells.forEach[cell |
    // select the rule that applies (there must be maximum one)
    val rules = automata.seedRules.filter[r |
      r.isApplicableForCell(cell)].toList
    var Rule rule = null
    if (!rules.empty){
      rule = rules.get(0)
    }
    if (rule != null) {
      var Context context = new Context
      context.initialize(getResult, cell)
      cell.^val = rule.evaluatedVal.evaluate(context)
    }
```

```
  ]
...
  return result
}
...
def public Universe genVNeumannRectBoundedUniverse(Integer
     universeLength, Integer universeWidth) {
  println("Generate a square Universe using von Neumann neighborhood")
  var Universe g = new VmFactoryImpl().createUniverse
  val Integer cellNumber = universeLength * universeWidth
  println("Generate "+cellNumber.toString+" Cells")
  for (int i : 0..cellNumber-1) {
    var Cell cell = new VmFactoryImpl().createCell
    cell.init
    cell.globalPosition = i
    cell.coordinates.add(i / universeWidth) // x
    cell.coordinates.add(i % universeWidth) // y
    g.cells.add(cell)
  }
  println("Generate bounded VonNeumann neighborhood for "+cellNumber.
     toString+" Cells")
  for (int i : 0..cellNumber-1) {
    val Cell currentCell = g.cells.get(i)
    val Integer currentLine = i / universeWidth
    val Integer currentColumn = i % universeWidth
    var Integer maxCol = universeWidth - 1
    switch currentLine{
      case currentLine > 0 :    // add north
        currentCell.neighbors.add(g.cells.get(i-universeWidth))
      case currentColumn < maxCol:  // add east
        currentCell.neighbors.add(g.cells.get(i+1))
      case currentLine < maxCol:  // add south
        currentCell.neighbors.add(g.cells.get(i+universeWidth))
      case currentColumn > 0:    // add west
        currentCell.neighbors.add(g.cells.get(i-1))
    }
    currentCell.^val = 0
  }
  return g
}
```

Listing 9.5 Main operations of the VM generator.

Kermeta ▷

```
@Aspect(className=AreaFilter)
class AreaFilterAspect extends FilterAspect {
  def public Boolean isApplicableForCell(Cell cell) {
    var Boolean result = true
    for (Area area: _self.areas){
```

```
      result = area.isInRange(cell)
      if(result) return result
    }
    return false // no range have matched the cell
  }
}
...
@Aspect(className=DimensionRange)
class DimensionRangeAspect {
  def public Boolean isInRange(Integer i) {
    return ((_self.lower <= i) && (i <= _self.upper))
  }
}


@Aspect(className=PositionLiteral)
class PositionLiteralAspect extends IntegerExpressionAspect {
  def public Integer evaluate(Context context) {
    return context.currentCell.coordinates.get(_self.dimensionIndex)
  }
}
```

Listing 9.6 Aspect part of the VM generator.

9.6 TEST GENERATION: MODEL-BASED VALIDATION AND VERIFICATION

While an important part of software development, testing is still often neglected because of its cost. Actually, MDE techniques can help in being more productive and cost effective by proposing generators that cover the test generation activity.

9.6.1 Introduction

The IEEE defines validation and verification (V&V) as:

Validation The assurance that a product, service, or system meets the needs of the customer and other identified stakeholders. It often involves acceptance and suitability with external customers.

Verification The evaluation of whether or not a product, service, or system complies with a regulation, requirement, specification, or imposed condition. It is often an internal process.

As Barry Boehm put it, validation is checking that you are building the right thing, while verification is checking that you are building it right [15]. *Building the right thing* refers to the user's needs, while *building it right* checks that the specifications are correctly implemented by the system.

In any case, the important point is that the system needs to be assessed with respect to something else, either the *user's needs* or the *specifications*. Model-based V&V can then be defined as capturing this *something else* in the form of a model, and using MDE technologies to automate either validation or verification. That of course encompasses quite a number of possible approaches that we cannot fully cover in this book. We are only going to briefly discuss one possible approach at model-based testing for our cellular automaton example (Section 9.6.2), and then give a more advanced example from the broader scope of using UML use cases and scenarios to generate test cases for a system (Section 9.6.3).

9.6.2 Model-Based Testing

Dating from the 1980s with the Specification and Description Language (SDL) that became quite popular in the telecom industry, one of the first applications of the modeling of software systems has been formal validation. As soon as a modeling language is equipped with a precise operational semantics, a model can be seen as a transition system on which many state-based validation techniques can be applied.

Model-based V&V techniques vary widely in their forms and their abilities, but they all have the goal of assessing properties of the system under consideration, with some confidence level. The designer may attack her software by three complementary techniques. We list their advantages and major drawbacks in the following subsections.

9.6.2.1 Formal Verification of Properties

Formal verification gives a definite answer about validity by formally checking that all possible executions of the model of the software respect some properties (e.g., no deadlock). But existing methods, such as *model checking*, which is examining the states the system could reach, can only be easily applied to the analysis of very simplified models of the considered problem. Otherwise there is a combinatory explosion of the number of states that forbids such a brute force verification. This forces the model to be described at a high abstraction level, but introduces the problem of property preservation during its refinement course.

Our cellular automata example is probably too simple to have model checking give any interesting result. However, if we consider an extension of our basic metamodel with the notion of randomly adding a neighbor, then the execution of the cellular automata would become non-deterministic: the same initial configuration would possibly lead to many different outcomes. Let's call that extension a stochastic cellular automata. Then model checking could be applied to check that some properties always hold on all the possible execution paths.

9.6.2.2 Intensive Simulation

Simulation can deal with more refined models of the problem and can efficiently detect errors (even tricky or unexpected ones) on a reasonable subset of the possible system behaviors. Formally, it consists of a random walk through the reachability graph of the model. The main difficulty is to formally describe and simulate the execution environment. This is generally quite simplified, because it would not be realistic (nor interesting) to take into account all the parameters of a real system. Simulating our stochastic cellular automata would simply consist of modifying the interpreter we have defined for the cellular automata to use a random choice of the next step from the available steps. As with model checking, we could check along the way that some properties hold on all the explored execution paths, and end up with the computation of a probability that this property is true. This is why this technique is often also called statistical model-checking.

9.6.2.3 Testing

In testing, the execution environment is a real one. But as E.W. Dijkstra already put it in 1972 [31],

Testing shows the presence, not the absence of bugs.

Still it is one of the few techniques that actually works in practice for raising the level of confidence one can get in a real piece of software. Testing consists of providing the System Under Test (SUT) with some input data, and then comparing the state of the SUT against *oracles*. An oracle is a way of checking an assertion about the SUT, based on, e.g., specifications, contracts, related products, or simply user expectations.

Model-based testing of a cellular automata consists of using the model as the oracle to tell if the implementation is correct. Of course, if the implementation is automatically obtained from the model, we only check the consistency of our tool chain! So it is only interesting when the implementation has been done manually (or with another technique). Then we can use the cellular automata model for both

- computing some valid initial configuration and giving it as input data to the SUT, and

- computing the expected outcome after a given number of simulation steps (the oracle), and compare the result with the result computed by the SUT.

Even if the principle of model-based testing can fully be applied with this cellular automata example, it is still too simple to be able to grasp the power of this technique. So in the next section we outline a richer example model-based testing, using UML use cases and scenarios to generate test cases for a real system.

9.6.3 Automatic Test Generation: A Use Case–Driven Approach

9.6.3.1 Principle of the Approach

In [102] we presented a method-based on user defined use cases enhanced with contracts (based on pre- and post-conditions of use cases) as they are defined in [25]. Lifting up B. Meyer's Design by Contract [92] idea to the requirement level, they propose to make these contracts executable by writing them in the form of requirement-level logical expressions. Those more formalized, but still high-level, requirements can then be interactively "played" to check their consistency and correctness. They can also be used to explicitly build a model of all the valid sequences of use cases, and from it to extract relevant paths using some coverage criteria. These paths are called *test objectives*. Once these test objectives are generated, the second phase aims at generating test scenarios from these test objectives. In typical development processes based on the UML, each use case is documented with several sequence diagrams. Building on these existing sequence diagrams, test scenarios are generated by replacing each use case with a sequence diagram that is compatible in terms of static contract matching. As a result, we obtain test scenarios that are close to the implementation. Figure 9.5 summarizes this two-phase method to automatically generate functional test scenarios from requirement artifacts.

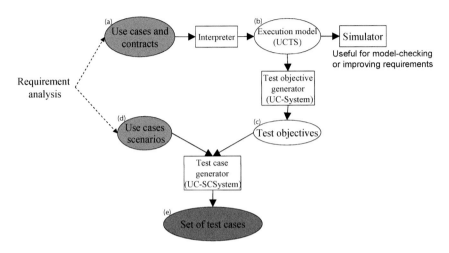

Figure 9.5 Global methodology for requirement-based testing.

The first phase of the method (steps (a) to (c) in Figure 9.5) aims at generating test objectives from a use case view of the system. The use cases diagram is a global view describing the system's main functions, without any notion of ordering. These use cases can however be annotated with pre- and post-conditions, as proposed in Catalysis in a form of the *requirement-by-contract* approach, inspired by the *design-by-contract* approach. These contracts are used to infer the correct partial orders of functionalities that the system should offer.

From the use cases and their contracts, an MDE tool called *UC-System* builds a simulation model (step (b) of Figure 9.5) and generates correct sequences of use cases (step (c) of Figure 9.5).

In the following, such a correct sequence of use cases is called a *test objective*. As shown in Figure 9.5, the use cases model can be simulated. This simulation phase allows the requirement engineer to check and possibly correct the requirements before tests are generated from them.

The second phase (steps (c) to (e) of Figure 9.5) aims at generating *test scenarios* from the test objectives. A test scenario may be directly used as an executable test case, or may need some additions from the tester, if some messages or parameters are still missing. To go from the test objectives to the test scenarios, additional information is needed, specifying the exchanges of messages involved between the environment and the system. Such information can be attached to a given use case in the form of several artifacts: sequence diagrams, state machines, or activity diagrams. All these artifacts describe the scenarios that correspond to a use case. For the sake of simplicity, we only deal here with sequence diagrams, which are called *use case scenarios*. The principle of the transformation from test objectives to test scenarios consists of replacing each use case of the test objective by one of its use case scenarios, using the *UC-SCSystem* tool.

This approach is designed to be integrated in a typical UML-based software engineering process. The functional requirements are expressed using use cases with contracts for which a dedicated editor has been developed. At the requirement level, a use case mainly depends on the specific actors to which it is connected, and to the business level concepts it has to handle. Actors involved in a use case can be considered as parameters of this use case. When the parameters have been specified for a use case, contracts are expressed in the form of pre- and post-conditions involving these parameters. The use case contracts are first-order logical expressions combining predicates with logical operators. A predicate has a name, an arity, and a set of (potentially empty) typed formal parameters. The predicates are used to describe facts in the system (on actors state, on main concepts states, or on roles).

Since Boolean logic is used, a predicate is either true or false, but never undefined. A system of use cases with pre and post conditions thus needs an initial state setting in which predicates are true at the initial state of the system.

Classical Boolean logic operators are used: conjunction (**and**), disjunction (**or**), negation (**not**), and implication (**implies**) (implication is used to guard a new assertion with an expression). Quantifiers can also be used in order to increase the expressiveness of the contracts: these quantifiers are **forall** and **exists**.

The precondition expression is the guard of the use case execution. The post-condition specifies the new values of the predicates after the execution of the use case. When a post-condition does not explicitly modify a predicate value, it is left unchanged. The declarative definition of such contract expressions forces the requirement analyst to be precise and rigorous in the semantics given to each use case, being at the same time flexible and easy to maintain and to modify. The set of used predicates can be seen as the vocabulary to describe the requirements, and it is thus necessary to keep the predicate names consistent.

9.6.3.2 Simulating the Use Cases

To check the correctness of the requirements, we propose to simulate the requirements: using the contracts, we are able to decide which use cases with which parameters can be applied from a given simulation state. In fact, starting from an *initial state* and the *enumeration of all the business entities* present in the system, the idea is to "instantiate" the use cases with a set of values (the actual parameters, i.e., the actual actors and business concepts) replacing their formal parameters to get to a new state, from which the same process can be repeated. This simulation tool allows the requirement analyst to check her requirements: the simulator is an interactive tool that proposes to the user the list of all the instantiated use cases that can be applied from the current simulation state (starting from the initial state). It simulates the execution of a selected instantiated use case, thus producing a new current state. Using such a tool, the requirement analyst can check whether the requirements she has specified are conform to the ones she had in mind, comparing the obtained behavior with the expected behavior. Inconsistencies between predicates and contracts can be identified, as well as under-specification or errors in the requirements.

9.6.3.3 Exhaustive Simulation and Transition System

Defining contracts for each use case allows ordering of dependencies among use cases to be inferred. In our model, if there is no explicit dependency between two use cases, then these use cases can be executed in parallel. A representation of the valid sequences of the use cases is built by exhaustively simulating the system. It results in a transition system called the Use Case Transition System (UCTS).

The states of the UCTS represent an abstraction of the states of the system: a state of the UCTS is a reachable combination of values of predicates. Each transition, labeled with an instantiated use case, represents the execution of an instantiated use case. A path in the UCTS is thus a valid sequence of use cases.

Such a UCTS is built from the simulation model using algorithm of Listing 9.7, which successively tries to apply each instantiated use

Foundation 9.6 Use Case Simulation Tool Limitations

Since there is no predicate calculus in the simulation tool used in Section 9.6.3.2, its main limitation relates to predicate dependencies. When a use case U has "a and b" as preconditions, while the predicate c is true in the current state, if it happens that c=a and b, then our simulator would not propose to apply U. This is because we do not provide ways to define relations among predicates (here that c=a and b). On the other hand, the same contract can be formulated in several different ways (e.g., "A implies B" or "not A and B") without any impact on the simulation because a state is defined as a set of values for predicates.

The requirements that can be expressed with contracts on the use cases are high-level ones, e.g., they are not suitable to handle complex data types (including arithmetic calculus for example). Only in simple cases of requirements including numeric, we can use a simple kind of abstract interpretation, abstracting a number by a set of intervals.

Foundation 9.7 Use Case Transition System (UCTS)

Formally, the UCTS is defined by a quadruple $(Q, q_0, A, \hookrightarrow)$ where:

- Q is a finite and non-empty set of states, each state being defined as a set of instantiated predicates;

- q_0 is the initial state;

- A is the alphabet of actions, an action being an instantiated use case;

- $\hookrightarrow \subseteq Q \times A \times Q$ is the transition function.

Note 9.8 UCTS Parallelism Is Implemented Using Interleaving

Note that we use an interleaving semantics to represent the potential parallelism between use cases.

case from the current state (initially from the initial state). Applying a use case is possible when its precondition is implied by the set of true predicates contained in the label of the current state, and leads to creating an edge from the current state to the state representing the system after the post-condition is applied. The algorithm stops when all the reachable states have been explored.

Algorithm

```
algorithm buildUCTS
param initState: STATE ; useCases: SET[INSTANTIATEDUSECASE]
var
  result : UCTS
  to_visit : STACK[STATE]
  currentState : STATE
  newState : STATE
init
  result.initialState←initState
  to_visit.push(initState)
body
  while (to_visit≠∅) do
    currentState←to_visit.pop
    ∀ uc ∈useCases | currentState ⇒uc.pre do
      newState ← apply(currentState, uc)
      if newState ∉result then
        result.Q ←result.Q ∪ {newState}
        to_visit.push(newState) fi
      result.↪ ←result.↪ ∪ {(currentState,uc,newState)}
    done
  done
end
return result

function apply(currentS: STATE, uc: USECASE):STATE
-- returns the new current state obtained
-- when the instantiated use case uc is applied from state currentS
```

Listing 9.7 Algorithm producing the UCTS.

9.6.3.4 Generating Test Cases from Test Objectives and Sequence Diagrams

Once the main interfaces are designed, the analyst can detail the behavior of each use case using scenarios by giving examples of nominal and exceptional behaviors. These scenarios describe the exact messages that have to be exchanged between the system and the actors. The artifacts required to apply our approach are use cases enhanced with contracts and scenarios attached to these use cases. From these inputs, the generation of test scenarios is automatic: we just need to write a model-to-model transformation to replace the instantiated use cases with instantiated use case scenarios in the test objectives. Sequences of scenarios are thus obtained and are transformed into test scenarios using *weak sequential composition* (the weak sequential composition corresponds to a local merging of partial orders, and thus does not impose that every event of a use case scenario is executed before an event of the next scenario can be executed), once again implemented as a model-to-model transformation.

Of course, the quality of the test scenarios strongly depends on the use case contracts and on the scenarios, and the more those artifacts are relevant, the more the generated test scenarios can be relevant.

This two-phase method results in system test scenarios, that are valid and embed their oracle function. Several hard-points had to be taken into account:

- *Use case and contract validation*: the use cases have to be validated through simulation and model checking. The underlying model has to be compact enough to avoid combinatorial explosion of the internal states of the simulation model, called UCTS. This point is overcome by the two-step approach, which divides the complexity of high-level and detailed requirements into two levels (use cases and sequence diagrams), and by the introduction of use case parameters to deal with main systems concepts and actors.

- *Definition of system test criteria*: based on the UCTS model, test generation criteria have been proposed that automate the production of test objectives. The most efficient criteria have been identified through experimental comparisons.

9.7 EXERCISES

 Exercise 9.1 Improving VM Model Generation

Starting from the illustrative example of Section 9.5.1:

- In operation `generateInitialUniverseForAutomata`, replace the use of the **switch** by aspects on **Geometry** and its child classes.

- Evaluate the impact of dealing with extensions of the language (e.g., support for new geometries).

Variability Management

CONTENTS

T HIS chapter explores the usage of MDE for variability management. *Software Product Lines* (SPL) are now emerging as a paradigm shift toward modeling and developing software system families rather than individual systems. SPL engineering embraces the ideas of mass customization and software reuse and is strongly related to modeling.

After reading this chapter you will know:

– what software product lines are;

– how MDE assists in the definition and customization of SPLs;

– how to use MDE to model product line variability, and automatically derive products from product line models; and

– how to analyze SPLs and concrete configurations regarding consistency.

10.1 CONTEXT OF SOFTWARE PRODUCT LINES

Due to the increasing demand of highly customized products and services, software organizations now have to produce many complex variants accounting not only for differences in software functionalities but also for differences in hardware (e.g.; graphic cards, display capacities, input devices), operating systems, localization, user preferences, look and feel, etc. Of course, since they do not want to develop each variant from scratch and independently, they have a strong motivation to investigate new ways of reusing common parts to create new software systems from existing software assets.

Software Product Lines (SPL) [106], or *software product families* [141], are emerging as a paradigm shift toward modeling and developing software system families rather than individual systems. The basic vision underlying the SPL can probably be traced back to David Parnas seminal article [116] "On the Design and Development of Program Families." SPL engineering embraces the ideas of mass customization and software reuse. It focuses on the means of efficiently producing and maintaining multiple related software products (such as cellular phones), exploiting what they have in common and managing what varies among them [134].

SPL engineering is a process focusing on capturing the *commonalities* (assumptions true for each family member) and *variability* (assumptions about how individual family members differ) between several software products. Instead of describing a single software system, an SPL model describes a set of products in the same domain. This is accomplished by distinguishing between elements common to all SPL members and those that may vary from one product to another. Reuse of core assets, which form the basis of the product line, is a key to productivity and quality gains. These core assets extend beyond simple code reuse and may include the architecture, software components, domain models, requirements statements, documentation, test plans, or test cases.

The SPL engineering process consists of two major steps:

1. **Domain Engineering**, or *development for reuse*, focuses on core assets development.

2. **Application Engineering**, or *development with reuse*, addresses the development of the final products using core assets and following customer requirements.

Domain engineering consists of collecting, organizing, and storing past experiences in building systems in the form of reusable assets and providing an adequate means for reusing them for building new systems. It starts with a *domain analysis* phase to identify commonalities and variability among SPL members. During *domain design*, the product line architecture is defined in terms of software components and is implemented during the last phase.

Application engineering, also known as *product derivation*, consists of building the actual systems from the core assets.

10.2 MODELING VARIABILITY WITH FEATURE DIAGRAMS

Central to both processes is the management of **variability** across the product line. In common language use, the term *variability* refers to *the ability or the tendency to change*. Variability management is thus seen as the key feature that distinguishes SPL engineering from other software development approaches. Variability management is thus growingly seen as the cornerstone of SPL development, covering the entire development life cycle, from requirements elicitation [66] to product derivation [150] to product testing [103].

Software variation management is often split into two dimensions [120]:

Variability in time refers to the existence of different versions of an artifact that are valid at different times.

Variability in space refers to the existence of an artifact in different shapes at the same time.

Foundation 10.1 Modeling variability

Semantically, modeling of variability is rather equivalent to underspecification. The domain model $dm \in \mathbb{L}$ captures commonalities, while it leaves open variations.

The semantics $\mathbb{M}(dm)$ is therefore a large set of possible implementations reflecting underspecification.

In SPL, underspecification is operationalized by providing explicit alternatives, optional extensions, etc. The set of variants are defined in the *feature model* and a concrete selection given in the product configuration. Assuming $\mathbb{VL}$ is a language used to define a concrete variant, the variant $v \in \mathbb{VL}$ thus reduces underspecification by selecting a concrete implementation. The semantics definition is thus (roughly speaking) extended to:

$$\mathbb{M} : \mathbb{L} \times \mathbb{VL} \to \wp(\mathbb{S})$$

with $\mathbb{M}(dm, v) \subseteq \mathbb{M}(dm)$ enforcing that $\mathbb{M}(dm, v)$ is more specific.

The big difference between traditional forms of underspecification and variability modeling comes from the methodical use of variants and the explicit modeling of alternatives, which in practice is a much more usable approach, especially when a concrete family of applications needs to be maintained.

Variability in time is primarily concerned with managing program variation over time and includes a revision control system and the larger field of software configuration management. The goal of SPL engineering is mainly to deal with variability in space.

Weiss and Lai [146] defined variability in SPLs as *"an assumption about how members of a family may differ from each other."* From a software perspective, variability can be seen as *"the ability of a software system or artifact to be efficiently extended, changed, customized or configured for use in a particular context."*

Central to the modeling of variability is the notion of *feature*, defined as *"a system property relevant to some stakeholder used to capture commonalities or discriminate among systems in a family"* [27].

Based on this notion of *feature*, Kang et al. proposed to use a *feature model* [72] to model the variability in an SPL. A feature model consists of a *feature diagram* and other associated information: *constraints* and *dependency rules*. Feature diagrams provide a *graphical tree-like notation depicting the hierarchical organization of high-level product functionalities* represented as features. The root of the tree refers to the complete system and is progressively decomposed into more refined features (tree nodes). Relations between nodes (features) are materialized by *decomposition edges* and *textual constraints*. Variability can be expressed in several ways. Presence or absence of a feature from a product is modeled using *mandatory* or *optional features*. Features are graphically represented as rectangles while some graphical elements (e.g., unfilled circle) are used to describe the variability (e.g., a feature may be optional).

Features can be organized into *feature groups*. Boolean operators *exclusive alternative* (XOR), *inclusive alternative* (OR), or *inclusive* (AND) are used to select one, several, or all of the features from a feature group. Dependencies between features can be modeled using *textual constraints*: *requires* (presence of a feature imposes the presence of another) and *mutex* (presence of a feature automatically excludes another).

For the last 25 years, there have been a lot of contributions from research and industry in this area. Despite their popularity and widespread use, all these feature model variants only provide a hierarchical structuring of high level product functionalities, with very little connection to the actual software products. These limitations generated the need for other more expressive mechanisms for representing variability and linking it to the base assets.

10.3   ADVANCED VARIABILITY MODELING METHODS

Since SPLs revolve around the ideas of capturing commonalities and variations, an SPL can be fully modeled as

an assets model that models a set of core assets, i.e., reusable components used for the development of new products; and

a variability model that represents the commonality and variability between product line members.

Since standard languages are generally not developed to explicitly represent all types of variability, SPL models are frequently expressed by extending or annotating standard languages (models). The annotated models are unions of all specific models in a model family and contain all necessary variability concepts.

It is then clear that we need two different metamodels (i.e., two different sets of concepts) to handle both aspects of SPLs, but we also need to somehow *connect* these two sets of concepts to assess and manipulate models of SPLs. Consequently there are two categories of techniques to handle variability: *amalgamated* and *separated*. The amalgamated approach proposes to connect the asset model and the variability model at metamodel level, i.e., to augment the asset metamodel with variability concepts, while the separated approach proposes to connect them at the model level, i.e., the two modeling languages remain independent and the connection is made across model elements of either metamodels.

In turn, each of these two main styles of approaches decomposes into several threads that we are going to overview in the next subsections, taking into account issues such as addressing behavioral variability or handling variability at several stages in the software lifecycle (requirements time, design time, deployment time, runtime).

10.4   AMALGAMATED APPROACH

Techniques using an amalgamated approach extend a language or a general purpose metamodel with specific concepts that allow designers to describe variability. Their core characteristic is the mix of variability and product line asset concepts into a single model. Concepts regarding variability and those that describe the assets metamodel are combined into a new language, that may either have a new, mixed syntax, or one based on that of the base model extended by the syntax of the variability language. This applies at both metamodel and model level. We further distinguish three subcategories: ad hoc extensions to existing languages, generic extensions that can be woven into any language, and finally ad hoc languages.

10.4.1   Annotate a Base Model by Means of Ad hoc Extensions

One possible approach [23, 148] to introduce variability into a modeling language such as the UML is to leverage a UML extension mechanism such as *stereotypes*, *tagged values*, and *structural constraints* and gather them in a UML profile for product lines [150].

Class diagrams are extended with the concept of *optionality*. The

⟨⟨*optional*⟩⟩ stereotype marks model elements that can be omitted in some products. It is applied to the Classifier, Package and Feature meta-classes from UML. A *variation point* is modeled using UML inheritance and stereotypes: a variation point is defined by an abstract class and a set of subclasses which represent its variants. The abstract class is tagged with the ⟨⟨*variation*⟩⟩ stereotype while the sub-classes with ⟨⟨*variant*⟩⟩. The UML profile also contains *constraints* which specify structural rules applicable to all models tagged with a specific stereotype.

For sequence diagrams, variability is introduced through three concepts: *optionality*, *variation*, and *virtuality* (meaning, e.g., that parts of a sequence diagram can be redefined for individual products by another sequence diagram).

10.4.2 Combine a Reusable Variability Metamodel with Different Domain Metamodels

Instead of designing an ad hoc extension to a given modeling language, Morin et al. [96, 97] propose a generic solution that can be applied to any kind of metamodel. They propose a reusable variability metamodel describing variability concepts and their relations independent of any domain metamodel. Using aspect-oriented modeling (AOM) techniques, variability can be woven into a given base metamodel, allowing its integration into a wide variety of metamodels in a semi-automatic way. Harber et al. [55, 56] pushed this approach even further. For any given language $\mathbb{L}$, this approach generates a delta language $\mathbb{DL}$ that allows defining the changes necessary to evolve a model by adding or adapting features. The delta modeling approach starts with a small base model and allows configuring the product by applying a set of applicable deltas.

A key point of this method is the definition of a general variability metamodel, based on the work of Schobbens et al. [131] on feature modeling.

The process of creating the new metamodel that integrates concepts from both variability and base metamodels is easy: new meta-classes are created to connect the base metamodel with the variability aspect. The base metamodel is just extended; none of its elements are removed. This allows an easy translation of models encoded in the variability-woven metamodel into the original one and the reuse of already developed tools such as model editors or checkers. Once the weaving of variability is done to obtain an extended metamodel, product line models can be created. These are models with variability, conforming to the variability extended metamodel.

10.5 SEPARATING THE ASSETS AND THE VARIABILITY CONCERN

Techniques in this category have separate representations for the variability and for the assets model. Elements from the variability model relate to asset model elements by referencing them one way or another. The key characteristic of such methods is the clear separation of concerns they provide. This separation applies at both metamodel and model level, with the following advantages: each asset model may have more than one variability model; designers can focus on the product line itself and not on its variability, which is addressed separately. It also opens the way for a standardized *Common Variability Language* (CVL) as discussed below.

Another possibility is to combine a common variability language with different base languages. Regarding our classification, at the metamodel level there is a separate generic variability metamodel and an assets metamodel (AMM). The AMM is actually the metamodel of the base language on which the *common variability language* is applied. At the model level, variability model elements relate to asset model elements by referencing and using substitutions.

We discuss the CVL in more detail as proposed for standardization at the OMG.[1] It is based on several previous works, notably by Haugen et al. [61, 42]. CVL models specify both variabilities and their resolution. By executing a CVL model, a base SPL model is transformed into a specific product model as illustrated in Figure 10.1.

The variability model and the resolution models are defined in the CVL while the base model and resolved models can be defined in any MOF-defined language (see Figure 10.2).

The base model represents an instance of an arbitrary MOF metamodel, such as UML, on which variability is specified using CVL. From the standpoint of CVL, the base model is just a collection of objects and links between them.

---

[1]The CVL Revised Submission can be downloaded from: `http://variabilitymodeling.org`

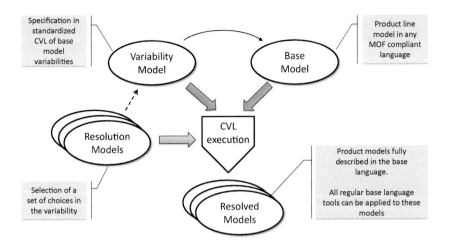

Figure 10.1 Example for using a CVL model.

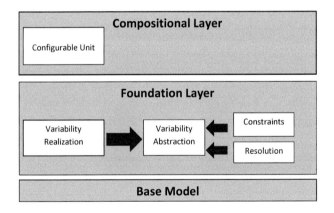

Figure 10.2 The structure of the CVL.

The foundation layer is a means to define abstract variability with proper constraints, how to resolve the variability to define products, and how to realize the products to produce products defined in the base language.

The compositional layer on top of the foundation layer includes ways to combine models in the foundation layer such that variability definitions can be reused, resolutions may have cascading effects, and several different base models (defined in different base languages) can be described. The *configurable unit module* provides the constructs that are needed for the modularization and encapsulation of variability as configurable units: i.e., component-like structures that may be configured through an exposed variability interface.

Let us now detail the foundation layer, which is made of the *variability realization model*, the *variability abstraction model*, as well as *constraints* and *resolutions*, as shown in Figure 10.2.

Variability Realization

The *variability realization model* provides constructs for specifying variation points on the base model. A variation point is an item that defines one step in the process of how the base model is modified to reach the specified product. This module is the part of the CVL that impacts the base model. The variation points refer to base model elements via base model handles.

The realization layer makes it possible to derive the products from the CVL description by transforming a base model in some MOF-defined language to another product model in the same language. Every construct of the realization layer defines a variation point of the base model representing a small modification of the base model into the product model. There are several kinds of variation points:

– *Existence* is an indication that the existence of a particular object or link in the base model is in question.

– *Substitution* is an indication that a single object, an entire model fragment, or the object at the end of a link, may be substituted for another. Object substitution involves two objects and means redirecting all links in which one is involved to the other and then deleting the former. Fragment substitution involves identifying a placement fragment in the base model via boundary element, thereby creating a conceptual "hole" to be filled by a replacement fragment of a compatible type.

– *Value assignment* is an indication that a value may be assigned to a particular slot of some base model object.

– *Opaque variation point* is an indication that a domain-specific (user-defined) variability is associated with the object(s) where the semantic of domain-specific variability is specified explicitly using a suitable transformation language.

Variability Abstraction

The variability abstraction module provides constructs for specifying and resolving variability in an abstract level, i.e., without specifying the exact nature of the variability w.r.t. the base model. It isolates the logical component of the CVL from the parts that manipulate the base model. The central concept in this module is that of a variability specification (abbreviated as VSpec), which is an indication of variability in the base model. VSpecs are similar to features in feature modeling, to the extent that the concrete syntax of the variability abstraction is similar to a feature diagram where the variability specifications are shown as trees.

The specifics of the variability, i.e., what base model elements are involved and how they are affected, is not specified, which is what makes VSpecs abstract. The effect on the base model may be indicated by binding VSpecs to variation points, which refer to the base model. VSpecs may be arranged as trees, where the parent–child relationship organizes the resolution space by imposing structure and logic on permissible resolutions.

There are three kinds of VSpecs provided in the base layer: choices, variables, and variability classifiers.

1. A choice is a VSpec whose resolution requires a yes/no decision. Nothing is known about the nature of the choice in the level of a VSpec tree, beyond what is suggested by its name. For example, the fact that there is a choice X in the tree indicates that in the resolution process there will be a need to decide *yes* or *no* about X, and that this decision may have some effect on the base model, the nature of which is unknown. It could decide for instance whether or not a given element will be deleted, a given substitution will be performed, a link will be redirected, etc.

2. A variable is a kind of VSpec whose resolution involves providing a value of a specified type. This value is meant to be used in the base model, but similar to choices, it is unknown in this level exactly where and how.

3. A variability classifier (abbreviated as VClassifier) is a kind of VSpec whose resolution means creating instances and then

providing per-instance resolutions for the VSpecs in its subtree. Like choices and variables, it is unknown at this level what the effect of each instance will be. Each VClassifier has an instance multiplicity which indicates how many instances of it may be created under its parent in permissible resolutions.

VSpecs are organized in a tree structure. The subtree under a node represents subordinate VSpecs in the sense that the resolution of a node imposes certain constraints on the resolutions of the nodes in its subtree:

- A negative resolution implies a negative resolution for its sub-choices and no resolutions for all other child VSpecs.

- Each choice has a field *isImpliedByParent* which, when true, indicates that if its parent is resolved positively then it must be decided positively. A resolution for a non-choice VSpec is always considered positive for this definition. The general rule is as follows: If a parent is resolved positively, i.e., it is either a positive choice decision or any variable resolution or any instance, then its sub-choices with *isImpliedByParent=True* must be resolved positively, its sub-variables must be resolved, i.e., given a value, and its subclassifiers must be instantiated according to their instance multiplicity.

Each VSpec may also have a group multiplicity indicating how many total positive resolutions there may be under it in case it is resolved positively, where positive resolution means the same as above, i.e., a positive choice decision or any variable value assignment or any instance of a VClassifier.

Constraints

Additional constraints can be used to express intricate relationships between VSpecs that cannot be directly captured by hierarchical relations in a VSpec tree. To this end, the CVL introduces a basic constraint language, a restricted subset of the OCL that is amenable to formal processing and practical constraint solving.

Resolutions

VSpecs are resolved by VSpec resolutions, and thus three kinds of VSpec resolutions mirror the three kinds of VSpecs. Choice resolutions resolve choices, variable value assignments resolve variables, and VInstances resolve VClassifiers. Each VSpec resolution resolves exactly one VSpec of the appropriate kind. In the absence of classifiers, each VSpec is resolved by at most one VSpec resolution.

10.6 EXPLOITATION OF VARIABILITY MODELS

Once variability is actually modeled, based on a well-defined metamodel, standard language engineering tools can be leveraged. These tools fall into two categories:

- endomorphic tools, processing variability models on their own, for either validation (self-consistency) or composition/decomposition; or

- exomorphic tools, generating other artifacts from variability models, such as concrete software products or test cases.

On the concrete side, one can rely once again on, e.g., well-tooled Eclipse standards such as E-MOF (cf. Chapter 3) to describe these metamodels, and then readily benefit from the set of tools we have described in the previous chapters. The use of such an MDE environment thus makes it quite straightforward to build a wide range of tools able to process variability models in several different ways.

10.6.1 Automated Analysis of Feature Models

Feature models may have interesting properties that can be automatically extracted by automated techniques and reported to an SPL engineer [3]. In particular, a feature model might represent no valid configuration, typically due to the presence of incompatible cross-tree constraints, or a feature model might have *dead* features, i.e., features not present in any valid configuration.

The automatic analysis of feature models is thus an active area of research that is concerned with extracting information from feature models using automated mechanisms. Since the introduction of feature models, the literature has contributed with a number of algorithms to support the analysis process, for example, the use of propositional logic techniques to reason about properties of a feature model [4].

The following steps are typically performed to encode a feature model as a propositional formula defined over a set of Boolean variables, where each variable corresponds to a feature:

1. Each feature of the feature model corresponds to a variable of the propositional formula.

2. Each relationship of the model is mapped into one or more formulas depending on the type of relationship (Xor- and Or-groups).

3. The resulting formula is the conjunction of all the resulting formulas of step 2.

4. Additional propositional constraints.

On the technical side, various kinds of automated support have been proposed:

- Propositional logic: SAT (for satisfiability) solvers or Binary Decision Diagram (BDD) take a propositional formula as input and allow reasoning about the formula (validity, models, etc.).

- Constraint programming: A constraint satisfaction problem (CSP) consists of a set of variables, a set of finite domains for those variables, and a set of constraints restricting the values of the variables. A CSP is solved by finding states (values for variables) in which all constraints are satisfied. In contrast to propositional formulas, CSP solvers can deal not only with binary values (true or false) but also with numerical values such as integers or intervals.

- Description logic (DL): DLs are a family of knowledge representation languages enabling the reasoning within knowledge domains by using specific logic reasoners. A problem described in terms of description logic is usually composed of a set of concepts (i.e., classes), a set of roles (e.g., properties or relationships), and set of individuals (i.e., instances). A description logic reasoner is a software package that takes as input a problem described in DL and provides facilities for consistency and correctness checking and other reasoning operations.

Benavides et al. [11] report that CSP solvers or DL solvers are mostly used for extensions of feature models (e.g., feature models with feature attributes), whereas propositional logic quite well fits basic feature models, as well as the core of the OMG's CVL proposal.

10.6.2   Multi-Views and Compositional Approaches

At the code level, when features are implemented separately in distinct modules (files, classes, packages, plug-ins, etc.), they can easily be composed in different combinations to generate variants. Voelter et al. [142] call this kind of variability *positive variability*, since variable elements are added together. Many techniques have been proposed to realize compositional approaches (frameworks, mixin layers [133], aspects [93], stepwise refinement [9], etc.). In model-based SPL engineering, the idea is that multiple models or fragments, each corresponding to a feature, are composed to obtain an integrated model from a feature model configuration. Aspect-oriented modeling techniques have been applied in the context of SPL engineering [82, 95, 97]. Apel et al. [5] propose to revisit a superimposition technique and analyze its feasibility as a model composition technique. Perrouin et al. propose a flexible, tool-supported derivation process in which a product model is generated by merging UML class diagram fragments [118].

Acher et al. [1] point out that quite often however, there is a need to compose and decompose variability models at the abstract modeling level, because variability exists across very different concerns of an SPL [50]: from functionality (e.g., particular function may only exist in some services or can be highly parameterized), deployment technology (e.g., operating system, hardware, libraries required, dependency on middleware), specificities of data format (e.g., image format), to non-functional property (like security, performance or adaptability), etc.

Acher et al. [2] coined the term *multiple feature models* to characterize a set of feature models, possibly inter-related, that are combined together to model the variability of a system. These multiple feature models can either come from the problem domain (e.g., variability of independent services that are by nature modular entities, when independent suppliers describe the variability of their different products, etc.) or as an engineering artifact to modularize the variability description of a large system into different criteria (or concerns). Acher et al. [2] thus proposed:

- A set of composition and decomposition operators to support Separation of Concerns in feature modeling. The operators are formally defined (using propositional logic), fully automated, guaranteeing properties in terms of sets of configurations and can be combined together or with other operators, for example, to realize complex reasoning tasks.

– A domain-specific, textual language, called FAMILIAR, that provides an operational solution for using the different operators and managing multiple feature models on a large scale.

10.6.3 Product Derivation

The product derivation process can be defined as a process of constructing products from software product lines, based on the modeling of variability and the choices made by the product configurator.

Feature diagrams are mostly used for *product configuration* during product derivation. A feature configuration corresponds to an individual product, but lacks details on how the selected features are combined into the actual software product. Many works thus started about 15 years ago to investigate the modeling and derivation of functional [12, 57, 143] and static [23, 151] aspects of SPL, with however much less emphasis on modeling and derivation of behavior [6, 49, 150], be it interaction-based (focusing on the global interactions between actors and components, e.g., UML sequence diagrams) or state-based (concentrating on the internal states of individual components, e.g., UML StateCharts).

Product derivation methods differ slightly depending on whether the variability modeling follows an amalgamated approach or a separated aspproach, as defined in Sections 10.6.3.1 and 10.6.3.2.

10.6.3.1 Derivation in Amalgamated Approaches

Jezequel et al. [150] propose an algebraic specification of UML sequence diagrams as reference expressions, extended with variability operators (optionality, choice, etc.). Generic and specific constraints then guide the derivation process. Behavioral product derivation is formalized using Reference Expressions for Sequence Diagrams (RESDs), which are expressions for basic Sequence Diagrams (bSDs) composed by interaction operators to provide the so-called Combined Sequence Diagrams introduced in UML2. These RESDs are extended with stereotypes as explained in Section 10.4.1 to give Product-Line RESDs, or PL-RESDs.

The first step toward product behavior derivation is to derive the corresponding product expressions from a PL-RESD. Derivation needs some decisions (or choices) associated with these variability expressions to be made to produce a product-specific RESD. A decision model is made of the following:

- The presence or absence of optional expressions.

- The choice of a variant expression for variation expressions.

- The refinement of virtual expressions.

An Instance of a Decision Model (noted hereafter IDM) for a product P is a set of pairs (name$_i$, Res), where name$_i$ designates a name of an optional, variation, or virtual part in the PL-RESD and Res is its decision resolution related to the product P. Decision resolutions are defined as follows:

- The resolution of an optional part is either TRUE or FALSE.

- For a variation part with E_1, E_2, E_3... as expression variants, the resolution is i if E_i is the selected expression.

- The resolution of a virtual part is a refinement expression E.

The derivation $[[PLE\ ]]_{DMi}$ can then be seen as a model specialization through the interpretation of a RESD-PL PLE in the DMi context, where DMi is the instance of the decision model related to a specific product. For each algebraic variability construction, the interpretation in a specific context is quite straightforward:

1. Interpreting an optional expression means deciding on its presence or not in the product expression. This is defined as:

$$[[\ \mathbf{optional}\ name\ [\ \mathtt{E}\ ]\ ]]_{DMi} = \begin{cases} \mathtt{E} & if\ (name, TRUE) \in DMi \\ \mathtt{E}_\emptyset & if\ (name, FALSE) \in DMi \end{cases}$$

2. Interpreting a variation expression means choosing one expression variant among its possible variants. This is defined as

$$[[\ \mathbf{variation}\ name\ [\ \mathtt{E}_1,\ \mathtt{E}_2,\ ..\ ]\ ]]_{DMi} = \mathtt{E}_j\ if\ (name, j) \in DMi$$

3. Interpreting virtual expressions means replacing the virtual expression by another expression:

$[\![$ **virtual** $name \; [\; E \;] \;]\!]_{DMi} = $ E' $if \; (name, E') \in DMi$, E $otherwise$

The derived product expressions are expressions without any variability left, i.e., expressions only involving basic SDs and interaction operators: alt, seq, and loop. Since the empty expression ($E_\emptyset$) is a neutral element for the sequential and the alternative composition, and idempotent for the loop, a derived RESD can be further simplified using algebraic rewriting rules:

- E seq $E_\emptyset$ = E ; $E_\emptyset$ seq E = E

- E alt $E_\emptyset$ = E ; $E_\emptyset$ alt E = E

- loop ($E_\emptyset$) =$E_\emptyset$.

The second part of the derivation process proposed in [150] is to leverage StateCharts synthesis from these scenarios [149], from which direct implementations can easily be obtained [21].

10.6.3.2 Product Derivation in Separated Approaches: The CVL Example

Beyond coming up with a metamodel and a set of well-formedness rules expressed in OCL, the proposed OMG standard for CVL also explicitly addresses the derivation process, which is seen as the dynamic semantics of CVL (i.e., deriving products is done by "executing" CVL on a given resolution model). Semantically, the aim of deriving a resolved model from a base model and a variability model (for a given resolution model) is to reduce the solution space cardinality (the set of all possible resolved models for a given base model and a given variability model). This derivation is thus obtained by considering a variability model as a *program* parameterized by the resolution model and operating on the base model, to provide a resolved model. Initially, the resolved model is equal to the base model. Then the execution of each *statement* of the variability model adds new constraints on the solution space, hence progressively reducing its cardinality, eventually down to 1 to get a fully resolved model, or to 0 if there are inconsistencies in the CVL model.

Since the CVL semantics is defined operationally for each statement as adding new constraints on the solution space, it boils down to giving the pre- and post-condition of the execution of each Variation Point meta-class of a CVL model. These constraints are defined using OCL pre- and post-conditions on an abstract *eval* operation, woven into each relevant class of the CVL metamodel. On the implementation side, Kermeta can readily be used to get an interpreter for deriving products from a product line, as implemented in [51].

10.6.4   Test Generation

Testing is an important mechanism both to identify defects and assure that completed products work as specified. This is a common practice in single-system development, and continues to hold in software product lines. However, in the early days of SPL research, very few SPL processes addressed the testing of the end product by taking advantage of the specific features of a product line (commonality and variabilities). It was indeed clear that classical testing approaches could not directly be applied on each product since, due to the potentially huge number of products, the testing task would be far too long and expensive [91]. Hence there was a need for testing methods, adapted to the product line context, that allow reducing the testing cost.

For example, the early approach presented in [101, 103] is based on the automation of the generation of application system tests, for any chosen product, from the system requirements of a product line [104]. These PL requirements are modeled using enhanced UML use cases which are the basis for the test generation. Product-specific test objectives, test scenarios, and test cases are successively generated through an automated process. The key idea of the approach is to describe functional variation points at the requirement level to automatically generate the behaviors specific to any chosen product. With such a strategy, the designer may apply any method to produce the domain models of the product line and then instantiate a given product: the test cases check that the expected functionalities have been correctly implemented. The approach is adaptive and provides automated test generation for a new product as well as guided test generation support to validate the evolution of a given product.

More recently the SPL testing field has attracted the attention of many more researchers, which results in a large number of publications regarding general and specific issues. Neto et al. [28] present a systematic mapping study, performed in order to map out the SPL testing field, through synthesizing evidence to suggest important implications for practice, as well as identifying research trends, open issues, and areas for improvement. Their goal was to identify, evaluate, and synthesize state-of-the-art testing practices in order to present what has been achieved so far in this discipline.

They identified four main test strategies that have been applied to software product lines:

- Incremental testing of product lines: The first product is tested individually and the following products are tested using regression testing techniques. Regression testing focuses on ensuring that everything that used to work still works, i.e., the product features previously tested are re-tested through a regression technique.

- Opportunistic reuse of test assets: This strategy is applied to reuse application test assets. Assets for one application are developed. Then, the application derived from the product line use the assets developed for the first application. This form of reuse is not performed systematically, which means that there is no method that supports the activity of selecting the test assets.

- Design test assets for reuse: Test assets are created as early as possible in domain engineering. Domain testing aims at testing common parts and preparing for testing variable parts. In application engineering, these test assets are reused, extended, and refined to test specific applications. General approaches to achieve core assets reuse are: repository, core assets certification, and partial integration. The SPL principle design for reuse is fully addressed by this strategy, which can enable the overall goals of reducing cost, shortening time-to-market, and increasing quality.

- Division of responsibilities: This strategy relates to select testing levels to be applied in both domain and application engineering, depending upon the objective of each phase, i.e., whether thinking about developing for or with reuse. This division can be clearly seen when the assets are unit tested in domain engineering and, when instantiated in application engineering, integration, system and acceptance testing are performed.

Specific testing activities are often split among the two types of activities: domain engineering and application engineering. Alternatively, the testing activities can be grouped into core asset and product development. From the set of studies they overview, around four adopt (or advocate the use of) the V-model as an approach to represent testing throughout the software development life cycle. However, there is no consensus on the correct set of testing levels for each SPL phase.

From the number of studies analyzed in [28], only a few addressed testing non-functional requirements. They point out that during architecture design, static analysis can be used to give an early indication of problems with non-functional requirements. One important point that should be considered when testing quality attributes is the presence of trade-offs among them, for example, the trade-off between modularity and testability. This leads to natural pairings of quality attributes and their associated tests. When a variation point represents a variation in a quality attribute, the static analysis should be sufficiently complete to investigate different outcomes. Neto et al. highlight that investigations toward making explicit which techniques currently applied for single-system development can be adopted in SPL are needed, since studies do not address this issue.

Their mapping study has also outlined a number of areas in which additional investigation would be useful, especially regarding evaluation and validation research. In general, SPL testing lacks evidence in many aspects. Regression test selection techniques, test automation, and architecture-based regression testing are points for future research as well as techniques that address the relationships between variability and testing and techniques to handle traceability among test and development artifacts.

10.7   MDE FOR SPL: WRAPUP

SPL engineering is a process focusing on capturing the *commonalities* (assumptions true for each family member) and *variability* (assumptions about how individual family members differ) between several software products. Models have long been used as *descriptive* artifacts, and proved themselves very helpful for formalizing, sharing, and communicating ideas. Modeling variability in SPL has thus already proven itself very useful, as highlighted by the popularity of feature modeling languages and their supporting tools.

In many cases we have shown that we could go beyond that, to be able to perform computations on variability models, for a variety of purposes, such as validation of the consistency of models, automatic composition or decomposition of variability models, production of new artifacts (e.g., tests), and of course concrete product derivation. These uses of variability models require that they are no longer informal, and that the language used to describe them has a well-defined abstract syntax (i.e., metamodel) and semantics. Model Driven Engineering (MDE) makes it possible to easily implement a set of tools to process variability models, either *endomorphic* tools, processing variability models on their own for validation (self-consistency) or composition/decomposition purposes, or *exomorphic* tools, i.e., generating other artifacts from variability models, such as concrete software products or test cases.

Scaling Up Modeling

CONTENTS

THIS chapter further explores advanced usages of MDE. Some of them are still at the forefront of research, but all have in common that they attempt to scale up MDE toward complex situations which go beyond the use of a single model and a single modeling language toward a potentially large set of small, dedicated models defined in a heterogeneous set of modeling languages.

This chapter completes the list of scaling techniques of which some have already been discussed in earlier chapters. In particular, we mention that variability management as discussed in Chapter 10 and in general, model transformations (Chapter 6) are a strong prerequisite for scaling up.

After reading this chapter you will

- understand the issues of heterogeneous modeling,

- be able to do aspect-oriented modeling and weave aspects at the modeling level, including behavioral aspects,

- be able to *model in the large* using the notions of model typing, polymorphism, and substitutability, and to reuse model transformations across different metamodels,

- be able to perform model slicing.

11.1 HETEROGENEOUS MODELING

One model is not enough to describe a complex system. In analogy, programs are typically written in many individual artifacts, namely files containing pieces of the code with crisp and clear boundaries, some internals that are encapsulated, and typically a meaningful function in terms of the system they implement. Programs consist of many of these artifacts. To scale up modeling, modeling languages must provide similar mechanisms. Model composition in its various forms is a core prerequisite to be able to manage many individual models, while describing an integrated system.

Furthermore, a modeling language typically concentrates on certain aspects of the system, e.g., interaction, structure, pre/post-conditions, but ignores others. As a consequence, one modeling language is not enough to describe the different aspects and viewpoints that are necessary to develop such a system. Therefore, we need to deal with heterogeneous languages that have an integrated semantics. The UML is such a language that is put together from currently 13 individual modeling languages. Also the cellular automaton example provides several languages, namely `CAIR` and `CAER`, for defining `Universe` layouts and their initialization respectively CA rules.

Even more languages need to be considered when systems instead of only software need to be developed. The software aspects are then accompanied by electrical, mechanical, safety, hydraulic, and potentially many more aspects. For example, the model of tracks in train stations is by law closely related to the software architecture of the controlling system and even the flow of crowds in crisis situations need to be modeled e.g., in large public buildings. Each of these aspects is denoted in its own models, using a different language.

Dealing with models from different languages at the same time means that we need an integrated semantics.

Foundation 11.1 Integrated Semantics for Heterogeneous Models

Assuming that there is an integrated semantics domain $\mathbb{S} = \mathbb{S}_1 = \mathbb{S}_2$ for languages $\mathbb{L}_1$ and $\mathbb{L}_2$, then heterogeneous models become an integrated mapping

$$\mathbb{M} : \mathbb{L}_1 \cup \mathbb{L}_2 \to \wp(\mathbb{S})$$

defined by $\mathbb{M}(l_i) = \mathbb{M}_i$ for $l_i \in \mathbb{L}_i$.

The meaning of a set of models is defined by

$$\mathbb{M} : \wp(\mathbb{L}) \to \wp(\mathbb{S})$$

which (for two models) is characterized by

$$\forall m_1, m_2 \in \mathbb{L} : \mathbb{M}\{m_1, m_2\} = \mathbb{M}(m_1) \cap \mathbb{M}(m_2)$$

Compatibility of models is semantically easy to define (the intersection needs to be nonempty), but in practice, developers need algorithmic checks that provide information about inconsistencies and their sources. Checks for existing names, for compatible signatures (e.g., for methods) and especially typing techniques are pivotal for understanding compatibility.

While understanding heterogeneity is conceptually relatively straightforward, to actually define an appropriate semantic domain [60] for a variety of heterogeneous languages is a tricky thing. For example, a combined semantics for UML's class diagrams and StateCharts needs obviously to reflect both structure and input/output behavior within the semantics domain. Klein et al. [74] provides a rather detailed system model that captures all the relevant aspects of an object-oriented system, but unfortunately does not abstract much from an actual implementation. To map into such a system model that is used as a semantic domain we may decompose the mapping by using an intermediate domain for each sublanguage. This for example works for StateCharts which are first mapped to input/output relations that are then embedded into the system model as relations between method calls and returns.

 Foundation 11.2 Semantics mapping and domains

If the semantics mapping $\mathbb{M}_i : \mathbb{L}_i \to \mathbb{S}_i$ is completely individual, then at first an integration of the semantic domains is necessary. Mapping

$$\mathbb{E}_i : \mathbb{S}_i \to \wp(\mathbb{S})$$

embeds the semantics into the composed domain. The overall mapping becomes

$$\forall m_i \in \mathbb{L}_i : \mathbb{M}(m_i) = \mathbb{E}_i(\mathbb{M}_i(m_i))$$

In the cellular automaton example, the CAIR and the CAER languages have their own semantics: CAIR gets its semantics in terms of a concrete cell universe and its structure. CAER is defined in terms of transformations on the values of such universes, while the structure of the universe remains unchanged. A suitable semantic domain for both would capture universe structure and rule execution behavior and therefore result in a trace of universes. These semantic considerations are a nice basis for the development of effective tooling on CAs because, e.g., tracing tools or analysis of temporal properties in fact need an efficient realization of this form of semantic domain.

It is noteworthy that the semantics of CAIR and CAER discussed here have a close relationship with the runtime data and their structure necessary for the interpretation of CAs in Chapter 7. The interpreter, however, doesn't need the history, so it only captures the current values in the universe. In contrast, using traces as the integrated semantic domain also allows understanding history. If for example detection of loops becomes interesting in CAs, then suddenly, at least an abstraction of the history would be necessary in the interpreter.

A similar decomposition of the mapping also applies, when the syntactic form of the models is too complex to deal with directly.

A mapping can safely abstract from the concrete syntax, let it be textual or graphical, by mapping it to abstract syntax first and starting the semantics considerations from there under the assumption that abstract syntax correctly reflects the concrete model.

While semantic considerations help to understand how heterogeneous models conform and can be used to describe different aspects of a system, operational tools that realize these semantics still need to be developed.

Today, developers often tend to come up with ad hoc integrations of their languages. This is quick and has some benefits in terms of agility, but may also exhibit problems in reliability, quality, or undetected errors in corner cases. However, using validation techniques for these ad hoc integrations helps to improve quality over time.

11.2 MODEL MERGING AND WEAVING

Given several models, it is important to know how they work together to describe a system. Several names, such as *model composition*, *merging* and *weaving* have been coined to describe techniques to relate models. While often used equivalently, we see slight differences in their meanings.

Definition 11.1 (Model Composition) *Given two independently defined models, model composition is the operator to combine both models into one, such that their individual semantics is retained and certain details of the models are encapsulated.*

Typically model composition works along the interfaces of models, which are the information a model exports and on which other models and code may rely. The composition results in a new model, with a composed interface that doesn't export anymore the elements that have been encapsulated in the composition. Examples of this are state machines or communication processes, which composition is based on exchange of shared messages. It is noteworthy to state that composition techniques very much rely on the semantics of a language and therefore need to be defined in a rather language-specific form.

One distinction between various existing approaches is whether the composition is fully automatic, assisted, or defined by hand. Furthermore, the point in time of the composition is relevant and whether it is expected by the developer to read or even manipulate the composed result. Three major variants exist:

- The composition is carried out as one shot only once: After the result is produced it is adapted by the developers. The original models are thrown away.

- The result can be read by developers for information, but should be adapted, because it is repeatedly generated: usually each time, when the sources change.

- The composition remains a conceptual construct and the result is never produced (or only very late) in the development or generation process.

While the first is obviously inefficient in the long run, the last one is the most helpful. Programming languages, such as Java, show that composition of sources is never carried out, but delayed through the compilation process to the loading and binding of class files when starting the program. That leads to agile and useful forms of composition that, e.g., libraries and frameworks heavily rely on.

It is also noteworthy that composition operations are in general able to compose independent models. So methodically, the models may have been developed independently and composed by a third developer, but may also have been developed in sequence, such that the second model could rely on the first.

Definition 11.2 (Model Weaving) *is a special form of model composition, where an aspect model is woven into a base model.*

Using this definition, it is allowed in model weaving that the aspect model can heavily rely on the elements provided by the base model. We will discuss this further in the rest of the section.

11.2.1 Models and Aspects

We have already seen that in engineering, one wants to break down a complex system into as many models as needed in order to address all the relevant concerns in such a way that they become understandable enough. These models may be expressed with a general purpose modeling language such as the UML, or with Domain Specific Languages when it is more appropriate (see Figure 11.1). Each of these models can be seen as the abstraction of an aspect of reality for handling a given concern. The provision of effective means for handling such concerns makes it possible to manage critical trade-offs early on in the software life cycle, and to effectively manage variation points in the case of product lines.

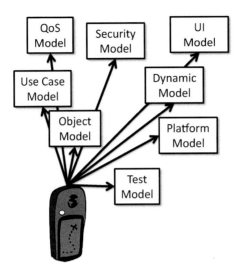

Figure 11.1 Representing several aspects in individual models.

Note that in the aspect-oriented programming community, the notion of aspect is defined in a slightly more restricted way as the modularization of a cross-cutting concern [41]. If we indeed have an already existing "main" decomposition paradigm (such as object orientation), there are many classes of concerns for which clear allocation into modules is not possible (hence the name "cross-cutting"). Examples include both allocating responsibility for providing certain kinds of functionality (such as logging) in a cohesive, loosely coupled fashion, as well as handling many non-functional requirements that are inherently cross-cutting, e.g., security, mobility, availability, distribution, resource management, and real-time constraints.

However, now that aspects also become popular outside of the programming world [123], there is a growing acceptance of a wider definition where an aspect is a concern that can be modularized. The motivation of these efforts is the systematic identification, modularization, representation, and composition of these concerns, with the ultimate goal of improving our ability to reason about the problem domain and the corresponding solution, reducing the size of the software model and application code, development costs, and maintenance time.

11.2.2 Design and Aspect Weaving

During the analysis activities, concerns in the problem domain are separated. If solutions to these concerns can be described as aspects, the design process can then be characterized as a weaving of these aspects into a detailed design model [70] (also called the solution space, see Figure 11.2). This is not new: this is actually what designers have been doing forever. Most often, however, the various aspects are not explicitly defined or given as informal descriptions. So the task of the designer is to do the weaving in her head more or less at once, and then produce the resulting detailed design as a big tangled program (even if one decomposition paradigm, such as functional or object-oriented, is used). While it works pretty well for small problems, it can become a major headache for bigger ones.

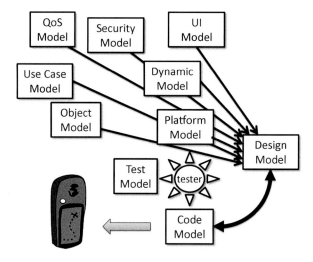

Figure 11.2 Design is weaving models.

Note that the real challenge here is not how to design the system to take a particular aspect into account: there is huge design know-how in industry for that, often captured in the form of design patterns. Taking into account more than one aspect at the same time is a little bit trickier. But many large-scale successful projects in industry demonstrate that engineers do ultimately manage to sort it out (most of the time).

The real challenge in a product-line context is that the engineer wants to easily decide on which version of which variant of an aspect she wants to build into the system. And she wants to conduct it cheaply, quickly and safely. For that, redoing by hand the tedious weaving of every aspect is not an option.

11.2.3 Weaving Aspects at Model Level

In practice, a base model is useful to provide a backbone on which other aspects are woven (see Figure 11.3).

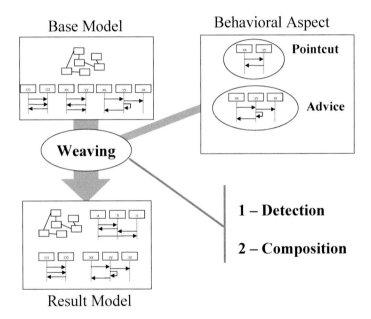

Figure 11.3 Principle of aspect weaving.

An aspect is then made of the following:

- **A pointcut,** which is a predicate over a model that is used to select relevant model elements called *join points*.

- **An advice,** which is a new behavior meant to replace (or complement) the matched ones.

Weaving an aspect consists of (1) identifying the join points matching the aspect pointcut and (2) replacing them (or composing them) with the aspect advice.

Both activities of join point identification and model composition can be more complex than it seems though.

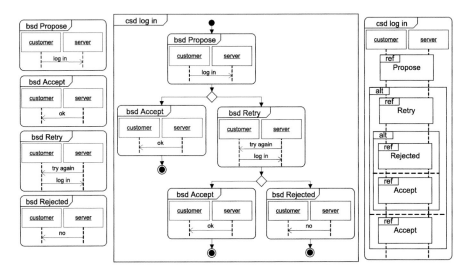

Figure 11.4 Examples of bSDs and cSDs.

First, many complex aspects involve dynamic behavior. This is usually a problem for AspectJ kinds of languages [90], which are limited by their join point models and pointcut expression mechanisms based on concrete syntax [20, 77]. With models, however, interrelations among model elements (not just classes and objects, but also method calls and other events) can be readily available and identifiable through e.g., dynamic diagrams. While class and object diagrams describe clientship and inheritance among the program elements, use cases, statecharts, activity, and sequence diagrams describe how and when the clientship takes place. Therefore, through a simple analysis of the models, we can get a much more direct outline of the system execution. In [122] we proposed a framework for expressing aspect pointcuts as model snippets. The idea is that model snippets are specified upon concepts in a given domain (metamodel), but that the pattern matching needed to find join points can be performed generically with respect to metamodels, using a Prolog-like unification. Still, as discussed in [20], it is in general difficult (or even undecidable) to identify join points when the patterns we are looking for are based on the properties of the computational flow. For instance, consider the following code snippet:

```
void f() {
  while(c()) {
    a(); b();
  }
}
```

Detecting a join point where a call to $a()$ is followed by a call to $b()$ depends on the analysis of $c()$. In that particular case, we can see that it would at least require some sort of loop unrolling.

The second dimension of complexity is related to model composition. While weaving a single aspect is pretty straightforward, weaving a second one at the same join point is not. When a second aspect indeed has to be woven, the join point may no longer exist, because it could have been modified by the first aspect advice. If we want to allow aspect weaving on a pair-wise basis, we must then define the join point matching mechanism in a way that takes into account these composability issues. However, with this new way of specifying join points, the composition of the advice with the detected part can no longer be just a replacement of the detected part by the advice: we also have to define more sophisticated composition operators.

The rest of this section investigates these issues taking the example of the simple modeling language of scenarios available in UML2 in the form of Sequence Diagrams. Note that even with such a model-level formalism that directly models possible execution flows, a restrictive hypothesis is needed on the input language to make it possible to statically identify the join points [78].

11.2.4 Weaving Aspects in Sequence Diagrams

Sequence diagrams are either basic sequence diagrams (bSDs), describing a finite number of interactions between objects of the system, or combined sequence diagrams (cSD), which are higher level specifications that allow the composition of bSDs with operators such as sequence, alternative, and loop. Formally, sequence diagrams in UML2 are partially ordered sets of event instances. Figure 11.4 (left) shows several bSDs which describe some interactions between the two objects *customer* and *server*. The vertical lines represent life lines for

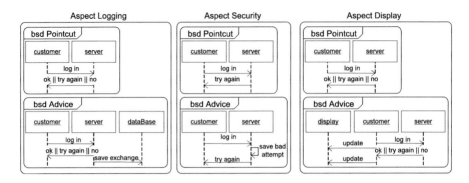

Figure 11.5 Three behavioral aspects.

the given objects. Interactions between objects are shown as arrows called messages, like *log in* and *try again*. Each message is defined by two events: message emission and message reception, which induce an ordering between emission and reception.

These bSDs can be composed with operators such as sequence, alternative and loop to produce a more complex sequence diagram (also called UML 2.0 Interaction Overview Diagram). In Figure 11.4 (center), the cSD *log in* represents a customer log in on a server. The customer tries to log in and either succeeds or fails. In this last case, the customer can try again to log in, and either succeeds, or the server answers with "no." Figure 11.4 (right) shows a more compact view of the same cSD, allowing an alternative between the bSDs Accept and Retry, and between the bSDs Accept and Rejected.

In this context, we define a *behavioral aspect* as a pair $A = (P, Ad)$ of bSDs. P is a pointcut, i.e., a bSD interpreted as a predicate over the semantics of a base model satisfied by all join points. Ad is an advice, i.e., the new behavior that should replace the base behavior when it is matched by P.

When we define aspects with sequence diagrams, we keep some advantages related to sequence diagrams. In particular, it is easy to express a pointcut as a sequence of messages. Figure 11.5 shows three behavioral aspects. The first one allows the persistence of exchanges between the customer and the server. In the definition of the pointcut, we use regular expressions to easily express three kinds of exchanges that we want to save (the message *log in* followed by either the message *ok*, the message *try again*, or the message *no*). The second aspect allows the identification of a login that fails. The third aspect allows

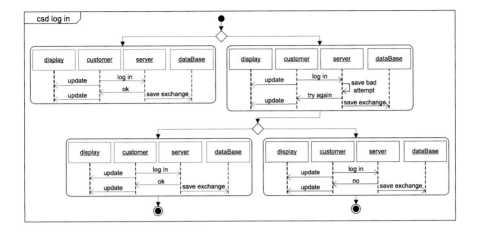

Figure 11.6 Result of the weaving.

the addition of a display and its update.

The expected weaving of the three aspects depicted in Figure 11.5 into the cSD *log in* is represented by the cSD in Figure 11.6.

11.2.5 Weaving More than One Aspect: The Detection Problem

Weaving several aspects at the same join point can be difficult if a join point is simply defined as a strict sequence of messages, because aspects previously woven might have inserted messages in between. In this case, the only way to support multiple static weaving is to define each aspect in function of the other aspects, which is clearly not acceptable.

The weaving of the three aspects depicted in Figure 11.5 allows to better explain the problem. If the join points are defined as the strict sequence of messages corresponding to those specified in the pointcut, the weaving of these three aspects is impossible. Indeed, when the aspect *security* is woven, a message *save bad attempt* is added between the two messages *log in* and *try again*. Since the pointcut only detects a strict sequence of messages, after the weaving of the aspect *security*, the aspect *display* cannot be woven anymore. We obtain the same problem if we weave the aspect *display* first and the aspect *security* afterward.

To solve this problem of multiple weaving, we need definitions of join points which allow the detection of join points where some events can occur between the events specified in the pointcut. In this way, when the aspect *security* is woven, the pointcut of the aspect *display* will allow the detection of the join point formed by the messages *log in* and *try again*, even if the message *save bad attempt* has been added.

In our approach, the definition of join point will rely on a notion of *part of a bSD*, which is a subset of a bSD where any kind of messages can occur between the messages of the pointcut. A join point will then be defined as a part of the base bSD such that this part corresponds to the pointcut.

The notion of correspondence between a part and a pointcut is defined as an isomorphism between bSD, made of a set of 3 isomorphisms between the base SD and the pointcut SD:

f_0 is an isomorphism for matching objects,

f_1 is an isomorphism for matching events, and

f_2 is an isomorphism for matching message names (taking into account wildcards).

As an example, Figure 11.7 shows a bSD morphism $f =< f_0, f_1, f_2 >: pointcut \rightarrow M2$ where only the morphism f_1 associating the events is represented (for instance, the event ep_1, which represents the sending of the message $m1$, is associated with the event em_2).

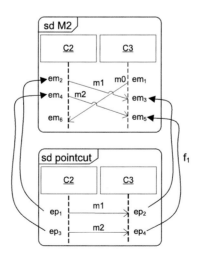

Figure 11.7 Example of a morphism between bSD.

11.2.6   Weaving More than One Aspect: The Composition Problem

Detecting a join point in a bSD then boils down to constructing such an isomorphism between a pointcut and a base bSD. Once such a join point has been detected, it remains to compose the bSD Advice with the join points. Since some messages can be present between the messages forming the join point, it is not possible to simply replace a join point by an advice because we would lose the "in-between" messages. Therefore, we have to define a new operator of composition which takes into account the common parts between a join point and an advice to produce a new bSD, which does not contain copies of similar elements of the two operands [76]. We use an operator of composition for bSDs called the *left amalgamated sum*, inspired by the amalgamated sum proposed in [75]. We add the term *left* because our operator is not commutative, as it imposes a different role on each operand.

Figure 11.8 shows an example of a left amalgamated sum where the two bSDs *base* and *advice* are amalgamated. For that, we use a third bSD, which is the *pointcut* and two bSD morphisms, $f : pointcut \rightarrow base$ and $g : pointcut \rightarrow advice$, which allow the specification of the common parts of the two bSDs *base* and *advice*.

f is the isomorphism from the *pointcut* to M' that has automatically been obtained with the process of detection described in the previous section.

The morphism g, which indicates the elements shared by the advice and the pointcut, has to be specified when the aspect is defined. In this way, g allows the specification of abstract or generic advices which are "instantiated" by the morphism. For instance, it is not mandatory that the advice contains objects having the same names as those present in the pointcut. In the three aspects in Figure 11.5, the morphism g is not specified but it is trivial: for each aspect, we associate the objects and the actions having the same names, and the events corresponding to the same-named actions. The advice of the aspect Display in Figure 11.5 could be replaced by the "generic" Advice in Figure 11.8. It is the morphism g which indicates that the object *customer* plays the role of the object *subject* and that the object *server* plays the role of the object A.

In Figure 11.8, the elements of the bSDs *base* and *advice* having the same antecedent by f and g will be considered as identical in the bSD *result*, but they will keep the names specified in the bSD *base*. For instance, the objects *subject* and A in the bSD *advice* are replaced by the objects *customer* and *server*. All the elements of the bSD *base* having an antecedent γ by f such that γ has no image by g in the bSD *advice* are deleted. This case does not appear in the example proposed, but in this way we can delete messages of the bSD *base*. For instance, in an amalgamated sum, if the right operand (the bSD advice in the example) is an empty bSD, then the part of the left operand, which is isomorphic to the *pointcut* (that is to say the join point), is deleted. Finally, all the elements of the bSDs *base* and *advice* having no antecedent by f and g are kept in the bSD *result*, but the events of the bSD *advice* will always form a "block" around which the events of the bSD *base* will be added. For instance, in Figure 11.8, in the bSD *base*, if there were an event e on the object *customer* just after the message *try again*, then this event e would be localized just after the sending of the message *update* (event ea_7) in the woven SD.

Note that if we are interested in carrying on an implementation based on these woven SDs, we could easily synthesize state charts from them [149], and then either derive test cases [119] or an implementation [22].

11.2.7   Discussion

This example with sequence diagrams illustrates several difficult issues of weaving aspects at the model level, involving both semantic based pattern matching and semantic-based composition. While our solutions are very specific to the semantics of sequence diagrams, we can find related problems and solutions in other modeling languages, for instance Statecharts or Activity Diagrams.

It probably means that there is no hope for a fully general-purpose, metamodel-independent, model-level aspect weaver. Still, it should be possible to develop aspect weaving software components handling several parts of aspect weaving, from general purpose model-level pattern matching [122] to automated support for composing models written in a particular language (through a definition of model composition behavior in the metamodel defining the language [45]), to specializable model composers [65]. These aspect weaving components could then be customized and combined to build domain-specific or even project-specific aspect weavers.

From a higher viewpoint, what we are trying to achieve is to reify the design process into a weaver program that makes it possible to re-build the target software from its models as often as needed. The goal is

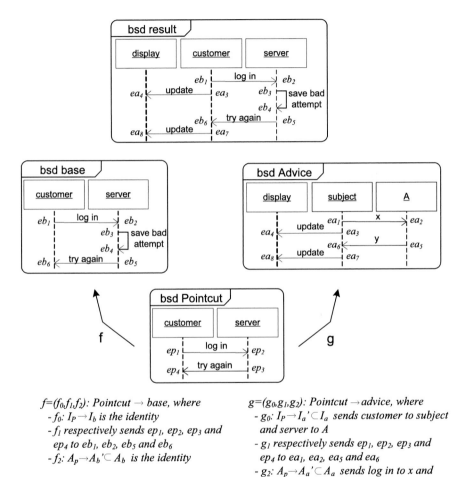

Figure 11.8 An example of left amalgamated sum.

to have only small modifications to make when requirements do change. Actually we need a family of weavers that for a given product-line are just variants of one another [83].

11.2.8 Building Project-Specific Aspect Weavers with Kermeta

As illustrated in Listing 11.1, the weaving implemented with Kermeta consists of two steps. First, the detection step uses the pointcut model and the base model to compute a set of join points. Each join point is characterized by a morphism from the pointcut to a corresponding element in the base model. Secondly, using these morphisms, the advice is composed with each join point in the base model.

Kermeta

```
package bsd.weaver;

import bsd.BSD
import bsd.morphism.BSDMorphism
import bsd.impl.BsdFactoryImpl
import detection.algorithm.Detection
import amalgamatedsum.LeftSum
import java.util.HashSet
import java.util.Set

class Weaver{
  public def BSD weave(BSD base, BSD pointcut, BSD advice, BSDMorphism g){
    var BSD result = BsdFactoryImpl.eINSTANCE.createBSD()        Initialization
    // declaration of the various components we need
    val Detection detection = new Detection
    val LeftSum sum = new LeftSum
    var BSDMorphism f
    val Set<BSDMorphism> setOfMorphisms = new HashSet<BSDMorphism>

    //Detection Step                                              Detection Step
    f = detection.detect(pointcut, base)
    while(f != null){
      setOfMorphisms.add(f)
      f = detection.detect(pointcut, minus(base, f))
    }

    //Composition Step                                           Composition Step
    for(BSDMorphism f1 : setOfMorphisms){
      result = sum.merge(result, pointcut, advice, f1, g)
    }

    return result
  }
}
```

Listing 11.1 Weaving aspects in Kermeta.

The first step processes models to extract join points and the second is a model transformation. Figure 11.9 gives another view of the overall process, concentrating on the input and output models of these two steps (each ellipse is a model and the black rectangle on the top left-hand corner indicates its metamodel). Except for morphisms (which are defined with their own metamodels), all models are SDs.

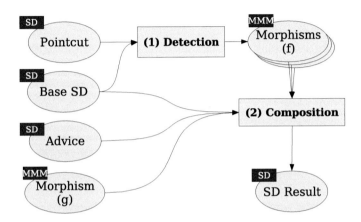

Figure 11.9 Example for a process for a transformation of models.

11.2.9   Merging and Weaving: Wrapup

From an engineering point of view, modeling and weaving aspects are complementary activities: weaving aspects is the process by which analysis models are decomposed into a modular design model. Model Driven Engineering makes it possible to automate this process: i.e., to have software built automatically instead of building it by hand. In this section we have described the overall vision of a design process based on these ideas.

We have highlighted, however, that both activities of join point identification and model composition can be more complex than it looks at first. Beyond the well-known fact that it is in general difficult (or even undecidable) to identify join points when the patterns we are looking for are based on the properties of the computational flow, additional difficult join point detection and composition problems may arise if more than one aspect has to be woven. In case a second aspect has to be woven, the join point might no longer exist because it could have been modified by the first aspect advice. As already said if aspect weaving is defined on a pair-wise basis, the join point matching mechanism must take into account these composability issues.

We have illustrated these issues on a smaller example where simple aspects, described as sequence diagram pairs (representing the aspect pointcut and advice), had to be woven into a base sequence diagram.

While it probably means that there is no hope for a fully general purpose model-level aspect weaver, we have shown that it is possible to develop aspect weaving software components handling several aspects of aspect weaving, from general purpose model-level pattern matching to ad hoc and specializable model composers. These aspect weaving components could then be customized and combined to build domain-specific or even project-specific aspect weavers using for instance an executable metamodeling environment as available in Kermeta.

11.3 LANGUAGE REUSE WITH MODEL TYPING

As we use models for more and more applications, creating more and more modeling languages, and writing more and more model transformations and syntaxes, the likelihood increases that we will perform repeating tasks. Different modeling languages will share similar characteristics. Perhaps a metamodel for modeling automobiles and a metamodel for modeling airplanes will share a set of constructs for representing 3D geometries, or perhaps a metamodel for hospitals and another for occupational health and safety monitoring will share classes for modeling organizational structures. Perhaps there will be a transformation of optimizing 3D structures for occlusion, or for determining supervision relationships, which will need to work against multiple metamodels.

Semantics definitions for modeling languages show that a model may belong to several languages. For example a state machine is always a Mealy machine (that has no output) and also always a Statechart (that is by coincidence flat). While a model may semantically be an element of many languages, we have to ensure that neither complete models nor parts thereof are reused with different semantics. A (piece of) model should always have the same semantic essence.

How can we construct our metamodels and transformations in a modular way, so that when we build a new modeling language, we can reuse or share parts of languages that have been built previously? And more importantly, how can we do this in a way that is semantically consistent and that protects us against certain kinds of errors?

11.3.1 Limits of the Conformance Relations

To determine whether a model is a valid statement of a DSL, MDE relies on the conformance relation that stands between a model and a metamodel (i.e., the DSL implementation). While no standard definition of the conformance relation exists, a recurring definition has emerged from the literature: a model conforms to a metamodel if every element of the model is an instance of (has been created from) one of the elements of the metamodel [7, 48, 34, 125].

Examples of de facto technological metamodeling standards in the MDE community are the Meta-Object Facility (MOF) [112] from the Object Management Group (OMG), and the Eclipse Modeling Framework (EMF) [140] used by multiple metamodeling tools and frameworks. The way these standards define the relation between models and metamodels is thus central to how tools currently manipulate models with regard to metamodels. In particular, MOF, a language for defining the abstract syntax of DSLs in the form of an object-oriented metamodel, does not explicitly provide a conformance relation between a model and a metamodel. Ecore, a meta-language within EMF and aligned with MOF, relies on Java classes for language element instantiation and XML Schema for model serialization.

From the above analysis, three important properties of currently used conformance relations can be inferred:

- *The conformance relation is a construction-based relation.* Since the conformance relation relies heavily on the instantiation relation, the relation between a model and a metamodel is set up at the time the model is constructed.

- *The conformance relation is hardcoded.* The conformance relation is set up once and for all at the creation of the model. Moreover, the relation is kept throughout the lifetime of a model, even through serialization. Indeed, during the serialization of a model, the URI of its metamodel is one type of meta-information that is serialized with the description of the model elements and their relations.

- *A model conforms to one and only one metamodel.* This property is a consequence of the two previous ones. Because the conformance relation is construction based, hardcoded, and only one metamodel is used to create a model, a model conforms to this metamodel only. Indeed, an object (a model element) is an instance of (i.e., is built from) only one class (a meta-class in the metamodel), which defines the fields and operations of the object. A given class only belongs to one package, belonging itself to one metamodel. Thus, one and only one metamodel exists to which a given model conforms: the metamodel defining all the classes from which the elements of the model are instances.

In practice, a model is often stored in an XML file (XMI format), with an explicit URI that identifies the metamodel used to create it. The URI makes explicit the language and tools that must be used to manipulate a model.

11.3.2 Model Typing

Model typing [139] proposes to abstract the overly restrictive conformance relation with a typing relation which stands between a model and a language to provide a sound and uniform approach for:

- model reuse through model polymorphism (the ability to assess and manipulate a model as belonging to different but closely related languages),

- model transformation reuse through language substitutability (the ability to substitute a language to another one for reusing existing model transformations), and

- language reuse through language inheritance (the ability to inherit a language implementation into another one).

In order to abstract from the instantiation relation, on which the conformance relation relies, model typing proposes to separate the concepts of interface and of implementation of the models, as is done for interface and implementation of objects. Types (either object types or model types) thus exhibit an interface through which it is possible to manipulate (or check the validity) the entities they type (objects or models). Classes and metamodels provide the implementation of objects and models, and allow creating them. Similar to an object that has only one class, but can have a set of types, a model has only one metamodel (the one from which the model was created), but can have a set of model types (see Figure 11.10).

Among the different types of an object or of a model, if it exists, the exact type is the most precise type of the object or the model. To build the model typing relation between a model and its set of model types, a model-type system would rely on these exact types of models and model elements, and on model subtyping relations [54].

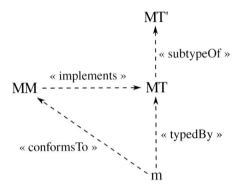

Figure 11.10 Relationship between Models, Model Types, and Meta-models.

Figure 11.11 details the concepts and relations reified in a modeling framework supported by a dedicated model-oriented type system.

A model type exhibits the interface through which it is possible to manipulate the models typed by the model type. A model type consists of object types, themselves exhibiting the interface of model elements. Model transformations are defined with respect to model types, i.e., the interface of models. Model transformations manipulate models typed by given model types, and not models created from given metamodels. A subtyping relation relates model types. A subtyping relation states the substitutability of metamodels implementing a model type to metamodels typed by the supertypes, and allows reusing all the model transformations defined on the model type and super model types. Similarly, a subtyping relation states the polymorphism of models typed by the subtype to models typed by the supertype, and allows us to manipulate a model as belonging to different languages (all metamodels that implement a model type and super model types). Variants of subtyping relations can be considered to increase reusability through model polymorphism and language substitutability [54].

A metamodel implements one or more model types by providing the implementation corresponding to the interface these model types exhibit. The implementation relationship can be explicitly defined or

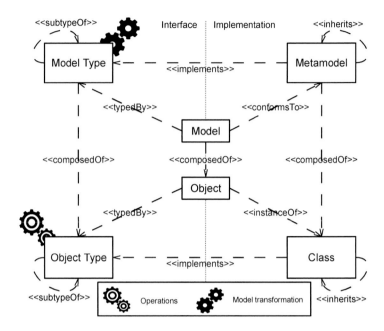

Figure 11.11 Model, model transformation, and language reuse with model typing.

automatically inferred (i.e., structural typing).

Metamodels are related through the inheritance relation: the super-metamodel and the sub-metamodel. The inheritance relation allows us to reuse the structure (classes) and the behavior (operations) from one metamodel to another.

All these principles are currently supported by the Melange workbench[1] to provide modeltypes, model transformation, and language reuse. The listing shown in Figure 11.12 gives an example of such a reuse in the family of Finite State Machines, reusing FSM and common model transformation (here *execute()*) in the definition of TFSM, a timed extension of FSM.

11.4 MODEL SLICING

Model slicing is a model comprehension technique inspired by program slicing [145]. The process of model slicing involves extracting a subset of model elements which represent a *model slice*. The model slice may

---

[1] Cf. http://melange-lang.org

```
1   metamodel Fsm {
2     ecore   "FSM.ecore"
3     exactType FsmMT
4     aspect fsm.ExecutableFSM
5     aspect fsm.ExecutableState
6     aspect fsm.ExecutableTransition
7   }
8   metamodel TimedFsm inherits Fsm {
9     exactType TimedFsmMT
10    // Redefinition of the fire() method
11    // in Transition to take time into account
12    aspect timedfsm.ExecutableTimedTransition
13  }
14  transformation execute(FsmMT fsm) {
15    val root = fsm.contents.head as fsmmt.FSM
16    root.execute("some_word")
17  }
18  @Main transformation main() {
19    val m1 = Fsm.load("ExFsm.xmi", FsmMT)
20    val m2 = TimedFsm.load("ExTFsm.xmi", FsmMT)
21    execute.call(m1)
22    execute.call(m2)
23  }
```

Figure 11.12 Model typing with melange.

vary depending on the intended purpose. For example, when seeking to understand a large class diagram, it may help to extract the sub-part of the diagram that includes only the dependencies of a particular class. For other comprehension purposes, one might want to know the footprint of model operations [67] or extracting information from several interdependent models [84].

Program slicing transposed to models can be divided into static and dynamic slicing as well. Static model slicing consists of slicing models according to structural criteria. For instance, slicers relying on the MOF or UML will slice the structure of models (classes, properties, etc.). Dynamic model slicing considers the behavioral semantics of the input metamodel and requires the execution of the sliced model. For example, slicing an automaton with respect to a specific event as a slicing criterion consists of extracting a sub-automaton, which reacts to the selected event.

11.5 SOFTWARE LANGUAGE ENGINEERING

Incorporating domain-specific concepts, best practices, and development experience into modeling languages can significantly improve software and systems engineer's productivity and systems quality. To address this challenge, the modeling community is starting a technology revolution in software development, and the shape of this revolution is becoming more and more clear. Little, *domain-specific modeling languages* (DSMLs) are increasingly being developed to continuously leverage business or technical domain expertise of various stakeholders, and are then used as formalizations of the domains to define relationships among them and to support the required integration activities. A DSML provides a bridge between the (problem) space in which domain experts work and the implementation (solution) space. DSMLs are usually small and simple languages, focused on a particular problem or aspect of a (software) system. Domains in which DSMLs have been developed and used include those for automotive, avionics, and cyber-physical systems. Hutchinson et al. recently provided some indications that DSMLs can pave the way for wider industrial adoption of MDE [147]. This leads to a *language-oriented modeling*[2] that emerges in various guises (e.g., metamodeling, model transformation, generative programming, compilers, etc.), and in various shapes (from API or fluent API, to internal or external DSMLs).

Although there are many examples of the use of DSMLs to overcome the semantic gap between problem space and solution space, it has only been recently recognized that the development of a DSML is itself a significant software engineering task. Indeed, many DSMLs were designed in an ad hoc way and without proper language engineering principles with clearly identified phases (e.g., decision, analysis, design, implementation, deployment, maintenance, evolution, and adaptation) and artifacts. The development of DSMLs conceptually follows a unified partially ordered process (see the previous chapters of this book): identification of the abstract syntax (i.e., the concepts and structures that constitute a DSML of interest); specification of the concrete syntax (i.e., the symbols and notations to be used by stakeholders); mappings from abstract to concrete syntax; specification of the semantics (which captures the

---

[2]By analogy with language-oriented programming [144].

meaning of the concepts and structures in the DSML, e.g., using mathematics, simulation, transformation); and elaboration of an integrated development environment that allows stakeholders to write models in the DSML, check that models are well formed, and support simulation, code generation, etc. While conceptually all approaches to DSML development generally follow this process, in practice they all use different techniques and technologies, all resulting from specific foundations. In the modeling community, *metamodeling* foundations have been defined in the last two decades. The core idea is that the very same notion of model is used to formalize models (see Chapter 3). We call such a special kind of model a metamodel. This vision has led to work, starting in the late 1990s, on language workbenches that support the development of DSMLs and associated tools (e.g., model editors and code generators) [37].

Research on systematic development of DSMLs has produced a technology base that is robust enough to support the integration of DSML development processes into large-scale industrial system development environments. Current DSML workbenches support the development of DSMLs to create models that play pivotal roles in different development phases. Workbenches such as Microsoft's DSL tools,[3] MetaCase's MetaEdit+,[4] JetBrains's MPS,[5] Eclipse Modeling Framework (EMF),[6] MontiCore,[7] and the Generic Modeling Environment (GME)[8] support the specification of the abstract syntax, concrete syntax, and the static and dynamic semantics of a DSML. These workbenches address the needs of DSML developers in a variety of application domains.

While DSMLs have been found useful for structuring development processes and providing abstractions to stakeholders [64], their ultimate value has been severely limited by their user-understanding ambiguity, the cost of tooling, and the tendency to create rigidity, immobility, and paralysis (the evolution of such languages is costly and error-prone). The development of DSMLs is a challenging task also due to the specialized knowledge it requires. A language engineer must own not only quite solid modeling skills but also the technical expertise

---

[3]Cf. http://www.microsoft.com/en-us/download/details.aspx?id=2379
[4]Cf. http://www.metacase.com/fr/mwb/
[5]Cf. https://www.jetbrains.com/mps
[6]Cf. http://www.eclipse.org/modeling/emf
[7]Cf. http://www.monticore.de
[8]Cf. http://www.isis.vanderbilt.edu/projects/gme/

for conducting the definition of specific artifacts such as grammars, metamodels, compilers, and interpreters. *"Software languages are software too"* [40] and, consequently, language development inherits all the complexity of general software development; concerns such as maintainability, re-usability, evolution, and user experience are recurring requirements in the daily work of language engineers. As a result, there is room for application of software engineering techniques that facilitate the DSML construction process. This results in the emergence of what we know as *Software Language Engineering* (SLE), which is defined as the application of systematic, disciplined, and measurable approaches to the development, use, deployment, and maintenance of software languages [79].

11.6 EXERCISES

Exercise 11.1 Code the Weaver Using Lambda

In Section 11.2.8, in order to ease understanding of the algorithm, Listing 11.1 uses a classic programming style. With some adaptations, refactor the algorithm in order to use Lambdas such as `map` and `reduce`.

Wrapup: Metamodeling Process

CONTENTS

THIS chapter describes how the techniques shown in previous chapters can be organized into an engineering process for tooling a DSML. After reading this chapter you will be able to:

- identify the development activities for building typical tooling for a new DSML, and the dependencies that exist between them;

- organize these activities along best practices; and

- reuse DSML libraries or DSML components in order to minimize development efforts.

The previous chapters have shown how to build various tools, each supporting a particular aspect of a DSML. Used together, these tools constitute a modeling environment for a given domain. We are now going to present a general process to orchestrate the creation of such an environment.

12.1 ACTORS

Developing an application that leverages metamodeling tools involves several roles for the stakeholders. Figure 12.1 shows the roles of the users implied in a typical process.

- *The metamodeling (M2) team* develops modeling tools (for example, it will develop a model editor or a code generator).

- *The modeling (M1) team* uses the modeling tools to develop the final system (for example, a web application). The M1 team then iteratively shares its experience and its needs with the M2 team, which upgrades the modeling tools accordingly. For example, the M2 team could enhance a code generator to support a new pattern for supporting the functionality of the web application.

- *The final user* is the client who is going to use the system. He expresses his needs to the M1 team, for example, by describing the features and functions of the expected web application.

Depending on the size of the project, some of these roles (M2, M1 or final user) can be fulfilled by the same persons, who would then interleave their activities. For example, people in a small modeling team who are building a system may have to change their hats to improve their modeling tools. The new version of the tool will then allow the team to be more productive. Conversely, in larger companies, the roles will typically be assigned to different specialized people.

12.2 TOOLS TO BUILD

To build a dedicated environment around a business domain, we typically find a common set of recurring tools (see Figure 12.2). Depending on the area and intended applications, these tools include editors, model checkers, documentation generators, simulators,

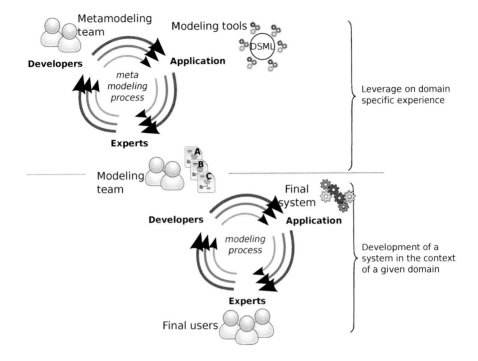

Figure 12.1   Roles in a modeling and metamodeling process.

compilers, translators (or converters) to other areas, refactoring tools, test suite generators, etc. All these tools rely on model manipulation techniques.   In most cases, it will of course not be necessary to create all of these tools: for example, sometimes we might prefer an interpreter/simulator, and sometimes a compiler is better. Also, some of these tools can be automatically generated thanks to model transformation. In other situations, general purpose tools can be reused with only a slight customization.

12.3   METAMODELING PROCESS

In most cases, the domain for which we are developing a modeling infrastructure, platform, or application will not be a green field. There will exist standards, tools, frameworks or languages which need to be integrated into the final tool suite, either for building upon them or for using them as targets for import/export/transformation. Identifying these is an important early step in planning the processes for developing

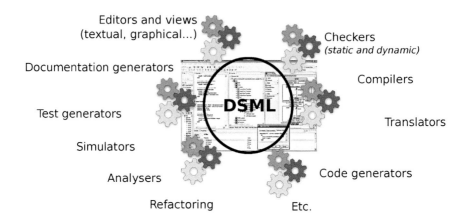

Editors and views
(textual, graphical...)

Checkers
(static and dynamic)

Documentation generators

Compilers

DSML

Test generators

Translators

Simulators

Analysers

Code generators

Refactoring

Etc.

Figure 12.2 Example of tools for a modeling workbench.

a modeling suite, and can be a very strong determinant of the order in which you attack the other activities (this case is going to be discussed in Section 12.4 below).

Still, the design, development and tooling of a metamodel generally follows an iterative process that is summarized in Figure 12.3. The advantage of the iterative aspect of this process is to quickly assess whether the metamodel fulfills the requirements of the domain. In addition, this process can be freely adapted to the needs of the domain that is to be tooled. Except for the initial phase of creating the metamodel, all other steps may be omitted or delayed. For example, a DSML used as intermediate representations in a toolchain may not have an immediate need for a concrete syntax.

The metamodel really plays the role of a pivot for the M2 team. Once agreed upon, all the other tools can be designed separately, and live their own life cycle. Their designs can then be assigned to different teams, for example to be developed in parallel. Each one can be developed incrementally. For example, we can build an editor and simulator in the first iterations to quickly prototype the behavior of the business domain. In subsequent iterations, we can develop a compiler and more sophisticated editors in order to obtain better performance and increased usability.

The process of metamodeling then typically follows these steps:

1. Definition of a business domain. To build tools around a business domain, it is first necessary to define the abstract syntax that

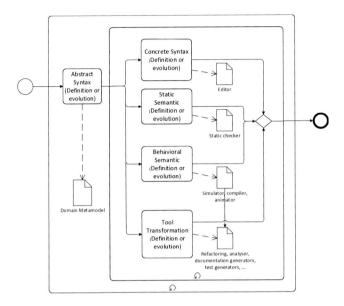

Figure 12.3   Workflow for building a modeling environment.

allows the expression of the concepts that are of importance for
the domain. This is typically done through the creation of a
metamodel. This step was described in detail in Chapter 3. It
consists of identifying the key concepts that need to be modeled,
considering the level of abstraction that is needed relative to the
purpose (inasmuch as it is known; purpose can change over time)
for which you are modeling the domain. For instance, if you're
only interested in high-level details, there is no need to build
fine-grained concepts into the metamodel.

This step frequently involves sample modeling/sketching, discussion of what other tools you eventually want to build, what the
competition is, etc.

2. Definition of the static semantics using so-called well-formedness
constraints. When using only abstract and concrete syntax, it is
often possible to create models that are incorrect with respect
to the domain (e.g., violating business rules). Well-formedness
constraints restrict the set of models that are valid to only those
respecting these constraints. Pragmatically, we most often add
constraints in an ad hoc fashion, i.e., when we encounter models

that should not be allowed, rather than seeking completeness from the start. This step was illustrated in Chapter 4.

Tip 12.1 Start by Creating Sample Models

It is of help to create sample models on which to validate constraints and to search for counter-examples (models that satisfy the well-formedness constraints but shouldn't, or models that don't satisfy the well-formedness constraints but should)

---

3. Definition of concrete syntaxes. This step is to ensure the expressiveness of the metamodel in terms of its goal. For an assisted creation of the first models, we can automatically generate editors. We can initially focus on fully generic editors such as the EMF tree editor, or text editor based on a generic concrete syntax such as HUTN. Thereafter, as the business domain metamodel stabilizes, we build other editors to provide more user-friendly ways of creating models, either with graphic editors or a dedicated textual editor featuring highlighting, completion, etc. This step has been presented in Chapter 5.

4. Definition of behavioral semantics. This task (which may not be necessary for all languages) is intended to express the expected behavior of models. As seen in Chapter 6, several techniques are possible, either by interpretation or by compilation to another domain. The choice of one or the other of these techniques depends on the goals but also on the needs in terms of performance and development time. The existence of a target domain already equipped with a semantics that is sufficiently close to the semantics we want for our model could also be of importance. This step is illustrated in Chapter 7 for the definition of a simulator and in Chapter 9 for the definition of a compiler.

5. Definition of transformations. As discussed in Chapter 6, the alternative to making a model to do something (by defining a behavioral semantics), is to apply appropriate model transformations. There are many uses that in practice will require model transformations. Common uses include, for example:

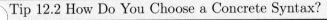

Tip 12.2 How Do You Choose a Concrete Syntax?

There are no hard and fast rules, but some of the steps which are very useful include:

- Characterizing the intended users in terms of their expertise and experience.

- Consideration of users' expectations; what syntaxes/interfaces are they used to, for example? Are there any de facto standard interfaces in the domain? These may affect or even determine users' expectations.

- Consideration of the processes they will use (is speed of editing important, for example?), and the environments in which they will be working (mobile vs. desktop, offline vs. online, etc.).

Even more than in the previous step, this step depends on having some sample models, which can be used to assess first whether the chosen concrete syntax is appropriate for the models that will be represented, and secondly for evaluating its effectiveness and relevance.

Tip 12.3 Sample Model when Defining Behavioral Semantics

This step, again, benefits a lot from having some sample models that are going to play the role of input test data.

– Refactoring, e.g., for optimization, design pattern injection, or model refinements.

– Analysis of models in order to to understand models, to reason about models, or to extract metrics. These metrics are particularly interesting to automate the phases of testing and validation.

– Weaving and/or composition of models, which is used to assemble models with a homogeneous or heterogeneous nature.

– Conversion to other areas, which allows for analysis or treatment by exploiting the characteristics of the target domain. This is particularly useful when you want to take advantage of tools from related fields.

– Documentation generation, for example in the style of Javadoc, but also as design documentation.

– Test generation (known as model-based testing), allowing us to validate the system design and construction.

Chapters 6 and 8 show the techniques to implement such transformations, both generally and in the specific contexts of refactoring and refinement.

Note 12.4 Classical Development Processes Applied to MDE

This overall process is only about orchestrating the development of all the tools of a DSML. Each tool development by itself can of course follow classical software development processes such as waterfall or agile methodologies.

12.4 METAMODELING PROCESS VARIANTS

The process proposed in Section 12.3 is applicable in many cases and is particularly efficient for domains with few background constraints. However, depending on the tools used and the DSML requirements, this process can be adapted.

One of the main alternatives is the creation order between the concrete syntax and the abstract syntax. It is indeed possible to begin the overall process with concrete syntax and only then to have the metamodel be produced (to some extent at least). For example, if there is a dominant standard concrete representation in the domain, then it can make sense to take that as a starting point for your development. Alternatively, if your target users have very strong views on how they would interact with their system, then the strength of this driver can lead to the early design of a concrete syntax (or even of editors) as one of the first steps in the process.

Thus, the choice between starting from the concrete syntax or the abstract syntax is mostly driven by the need of reusing existing documents or tools and start with the most stable of them.

Here is a list of questions that could guide you to an alternative process:

- Do some normative documents or habits in the domain exist that need to be taken into account?

- Do models need to be printable or are electronic versions always good enough?

- Does the metamodeling team have some preferences regarding modeling tools, development environment, etc.?

- Is the concrete syntax more important than the abstract syntax? (i.e., some intermediate models might accept a non-optimal concrete syntax)

- Do the DSMLs need to simultaneously support several concrete syntaxes? Are these concrete syntaxes close enough so that their parsers would be able to share their tree structure?

- Are the algorithms of the model manipulation complex enough so that we need to optimize the structure for it? Is a central representation valid for several different algorithms?

12.5 METAMODELING GUIDELINES

As for code where best practices are captured through guidelines and coding conventions and design patterns, modeling and DSML design also have best practices and modeling conventions and patterns. Some have already been outlined in dedicated sections of this book.

12.5.1 Decompose Large Transformations into Smaller Ones

In many situations, transformations can be large or complex. As for any kind of software that has to be developed, tested, and maintained, building new transformations by reusing existing ones helps in reducing their cost and increasing their quality. It also greatly increases the confidence on the common parts since they are tested more extensively in wider situation ranges.

The transformation languages may internally support modularization or extension mechanisms such as inheritance, modularity or aspect weaving. A good practice for complex transformations is to consider splitting them into smaller ones to decrease the overall complexity.

As seen in Chapter 6, transformations may use several metamodels (one or many metamodels for both inputs and outputs). Adding an extra step in a transformation can also introduce new metamodels dedicated to this intermediate step.

Typical cases where splitting a transformation is useful are:

– reuse of an existing small transformation that is shared by several other transformations,

– reuse of a transformation generator that will generate a part of a complex transformation at the cost of a small manual adaptation, and

– decrease the complexity of a large transformation.

12.5.2 Illustrative Example: Reusing Existing Smaller Transformations

A typical use of transformation splitting is when a DSL must support several import/export transformations from/to other similar languages. If the imported/exported languages are similar enough, it is interesting to use an intermediate metamodel allowing capture of their similarity. This intermediate model acts as a pivot reducing the development cost for all the required importers.

Conversely, it also works for export.

12.5.3 Illustrative Example: Using a Transformation Generator

The parser generators used while creating textual concrete syntaxes seen in Section 5.6 are an example of use of transformation generators.

They generate a tool able to parse the textual representation and create the model from it. They optionally generate a second transformation that is able to pretty print the model into a text conforming to the grammar.

They automate quite an error-prone task and are very useful in practice. Note that Chapter 5 simplified the problem by considering that the generator is able to map the domain model to the representation. In more complex cases, both the grammar and the metamodel of the domain may be constrained by other requirements such as normalization, usage, or the need to also support a rather different graphical syntax. In these cases, the tool might not be able to handle the mapping. It is then a good practice to use an intermediate tree that allows us to still use the editor generator and then complement it with an additional transformations to define the missing mapping.

12.5.4 Illustrative Example: Reducing Transformation Complexity

If the algorithm is very complex, it can often be split into smaller parts. This ensures that the complete transformation is easier to write, understand, and maintain. This principle is commonly applied in compilers that need several steps and intermediate representations before being able to get to the final binary.

For example, in a C-like language the `for` loop can be reduced to the use of only the `while` loop. This decreases the number of concepts and then reduces the development costs for an interpreter or a compiler.

Another usual case in code generation is the combination of model-to-model transformations with model-to-text ones. We have seen that model-to-text transformations, especially using a template-based approach, are very easy to use and customize. However, they work optimally only when a mere traversal of the model is needed to generate the code (i.e., there is a one-to-one mapping between the source concepts and the target concepts). If intermediate computations are needed, such as navigating the model to accumulate information that is needed for the generation, or even restructuring the model, then it might be very difficult to implement it into the template-based transformation. A model-to-model transformation is then very helpful to cleanly separate the concerns, i.e., to first put the model into the form that is optimal for the model-to-text transformation.

12.6 ILLUSTRATIVE EXAMPLE: PROCESS FOLLOWED TO BUILD CELLULAR AUTOMATON TOOLING

As seen in previous chapters, the cellular automata example combines several collaborating DSMLs. Each of these DSMLs followed the proposed process. The development of the cellular automata example proceeds as follows:

Part 1, CAIR

- Definition of cellular automata topology.

- Definition of cellular automata reusable rules.

- Definition of cellular automata initialization rules based on the assembly of CA Topology and CA reusable rules.

- Tree editor for cellular automata initialization rules.

- Textual editor for cellular automata initialization rules.

- OCL constraints for cellular automata initialization rules.

- Definition of VM (target of initialization rules).

- Tree editor for VM.

- Transformation of cellular automata initialization rules to VM; modularizes the part that applies to the reusable rules.

Part 2, CAER

- Definition of cellular automata evolution rules based on CA reusable rules.

- Tree editor for cellular automata evolution rules.

- OCL constraints for cellular automata evolution rules.

- Textual editor for cellular automata evolution rules.

- Simulator for cellular automata evolution rules.

CHAPTER 13

Language Engineering: The Logo Example

CONTENTS

13.1 INTRODUCTION

One of the most straightforward application domains for the ideas and technologies presented in this book is the *Software Language Engineering* domain.

The term "software language" refers to artificial languages used in software development. These include general-purpose programming languages, domain-specific languages, modeling and metamodeling languages, data models, and ontologies.

Software Language Engineering is the application of systematic, disciplined, and measurable approaches to the development (design, implementation, testing), use, deployment, and maintenance (evolution, recovery, and retirement) of these languages.

In this chapter, we are going to develop the example of the Logo language. This example was chosen because Logo is a simple yet real (i.e., Turing-complete) programming language, originally created for educational purposes. Its most popular application is *turtle graphics*: the program is used to direct a virtual turtle on a board and make it draw geometric figures when its pen is down.[1] Listing 13.1 presents a sample Logo program that draws a square.

In the following, we propose to build a complete Logo environment using Model Driven Engineering techniques.

Logo

```
# definition of the square procedure
TO square :size
  REPEAT 4 [
    FORWARD :size
    RIGHT 90
  ]
END

# clear screen
CLEAR
# draw a square
PENDOWN
square(50)
PENUP
```

Listing 13.1 Logo square program.

13.2 METAMODELING LOGO

The first task in the model-driven construction of a language is the definition of its abstract syntax. The abstract syntax captures the concepts of the language (these are primitive instructions, expressions, control structures, procedure definitions, etc.) and the relations among them (e.g., an expression is either a constant or a binary expression, that itself contains two expressions). In our approach the abstract syntax is defined using a metamodel.

Figure 13.1 presents the metamodel for the abstract syntax of the Logo language. The Logo metamodel includes:

---

[1] A complete history of the Logo language and many code samples can be found on Wikipedia. (`http://en.wikipedia.org/wiki/Logo\_(programming\_language)`).

- Primitive instructions (`Forward`, `Back`, `Left`, `Right`, `PenUp` and `PenDown`). These instructions allow moving and turning the Logo turtle and controlling its pen.

- Arithmetic expressions (`Constant`, `BinaryExp` and its subclasses). In our version of Logo, constants are integers and all operators only deal with integers.

- Procedures (`ProcDeclaration`, `ProcCall`, `Parameter` and `ParameterCall`) allow defining and calling functions with parameters (note that recursion is supported in Logo).

- Control structures (`Block`, `If`, `Repeat` and `While`). Classical sequence, conditional and loops for an imperative language.

In practice, the Logo metamodel can be defined within the Eclipse Modeling Framework (EMF). EMF is a metamodeling environment built on top of the Eclipse platform and based on the Essential-MOF/ Ecore standard. Within Eclipse several graphical editors can be used to define such metamodels. Once the metamodel is defined, the EMF automatically provides editors and serialization capabilities for the metamodel. The editor allows creating instances of the classes of the metamodel and saving these instance models in the XMI standard format.

As soon as the metamodel of Figure 13.1 has been defined, it is possible to instantiate it using the generated editor in order to write Logo programs. Figure 13.2 presents a screen-shot of the generated editor with the square program presented previously. The program was defined in the tree editor and the right part of the figure shows how the Logo program was serialized.

13.3 WEAVING STATIC SEMANTICS

13.3.1 The Object Constraint Language

A metamodel can be seen as the definition of the set of allowed configurations for a set of objects representing a domain. All structures are represented as classes, relations, and structural properties. In MDLE, a metamodel defines a set of valid programs. However, some constraints (*formulas* to the logician, *Boolean expressions* to the programmer) cannot be directly expressed using EMOF. For example there is no easy way to express that formal parameter names should

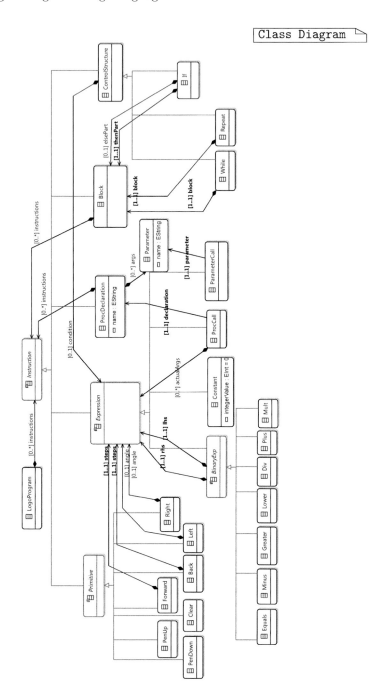

Figure 13.1   Logo abstract syntax.

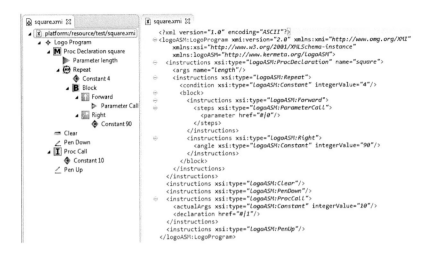

```
square.xmi ⊠
▲ X platform:/resource/test/square.xmi
   ▲ ◆ Logo Program
      ▲ M Proc Declaration square
         ▷ Parameter length
         ▲ ● Repeat
            ◆ Constant 4
            ▲ B Block
               ▲ Forward
                  ▷ Parameter Call
               ▲ Right
                  ◆ Constant 90
      ⌐ Clear
      ∠ Pen Down
      ▲ I Proc Call
         ◆ Constant 10
      ∠ Pen Up
```

```
square.xmi ⊠
<?xml version="1.0" encoding="ASCII"?>
<logoASM:LogoProgram xmi:version="2.0" xmlns:xmi="http://www.omg.org/XMI"
    xmlns:xsi="http://www.w3.org/2001/XMLSchema-instance"
    xmlns:logoASM="http://www.kermeta.org/LogoASM">
  <instructions xsi:type="LogoASM:ProcDeclaration" name="square">
    <args name="length"/>
    <instructions xsi:type="LogoASM:Repeat">
      <condition xsi:type="LogoASM:Constant" integerValue="4"/>
      <block>
        <instructions xsi:type="LogoASM:Forward">
          <steps xsi:type="LogoASM:ParameterCall">
            <parameter href="#/0"/>
          </steps>
        </instructions>
        <instructions xsi:type="LogoASM:Right">
          <angle xsi:type="LogoASM:Constant" integerValue="90"/>
        </instructions>
      </block>
    </instructions>
  </instructions>
  <instructions xsi:type="LogoASM:Clear"/>
  <instructions xsi:type="LogoASM:PenDown"/>
  <instructions xsi:type="LogoASM:ProcCall">
    <actualArgs xsi:type="LogoASM:Constant" integerValue="10"/>
    <declaration href="#/1"/>
  </instructions>
  <instructions xsi:type="LogoASM:PenUp"/>
</logoASM:LogoProgram>
```

Figure 13.2 Logo square program in the generated editor and serialized in XMI.

be unique in a given procedure declaration, or that in a valid Logo program the number of actual arguments in a procedure call should be the same as the number of formal arguments in the declaration. This kind of constraint forms part of what is often called the static semantics of the language.

In Model Driven Engineering, the Object Constraint Language (OCL) [124] is often used to provide a simple first-order logic for the expression of the static semantics of a metamodel. OCL is a declarative language initially developed at IBM for describing constraints on UML models. It is a simple textual language that provides constraints and object query expressions on any Meta-Object Facility model or metamodel that cannot easily be expressed by diagrammatic notation. OCL language statements are constructed using the following elements:

1. a context that defines the limited situation in which the statement is valid,

2. a property that represents some characteristics of the context (e.g., if the context is a class, a property might be an attribute),

3. an operation (e.g., arithmetic, set-oriented) that manipulates or qualifies a property, and

4. keywords (e.g., if, then, else, and, or, not, implies) that are used to specify conditional expressions.

13.3.2 Expressing the Logo Static Semantics in OCL

The Logo metamodel defined on Figure 13.1 only defines the structure of a Logo program. To define the subset of programs which are valid with respect to Logo semantics, a set of constraints has to be attached to the abstract syntax. Figure 13.2 presents the OCL listing of two constraints attached to the Logo metamodel. The first one is an invariant for class `ProcCall` that ensures that any call to a procedure has the same number of actual arguments as the number of formal arguments in the procedure declaration. The second invariant is attached to class `ProcDeclaration` and ensures that the names of the formal parameters of the procedure are unique.

OCL ⌐

```
context logoASM::ProcCall
  inv same_number_of_formals_and_actuals :
    actualArgs->size() = declaration.args->size()

context logoASM::ProcDeclaration
  inv unique_names_for_formal_arguments :
    args->forAll( a1, a2 | a1.name = a2.name implies a1 = a2 )
```

Listing 13.2 OCL constraints on the Logo metamodel.

13.3.3 Adding the Logo Static Semantics to Its Metamodel

One of the easiest ways to add OCL constraints on an Ecore model is to use the `oclinecore` editor that is present in the *EMF Validation framework*. This editor allows opening the core model using a textual representation and adding annotations that will contain the OCL expressions.

Once the Logo metamodel has been annotated with these constraints (see Figure 13.3.3), a right-click in the Logo editor allows us to validate the model. As shown in Figure 13.4, the validation framework will highlight the invalid elements in the editor. In case of a high number of violated constraints, the *Validity view* sorts them according the constraint or the violating element.

```
 0 ASMLogo.ecore 🖾
33      \
34          attribute integerValue : ecore::EInt[?];
35      }
36⊖   class ProcCall extends Expression
37    {
38          property actualArgs : Expression[*] { ordered composes };
39          property declaration : ProcDeclaration;
40          invariant same_number_of_formals_and_actuals: actualArgs->size() = declaration.args->size();
41    }
42⊖   class ProcDeclaration extends Instruction
43    {
44          attribute name : String[?];
45          property args : Parameter[*] { ordered composes };
46          property instructions : Instruction[*] { ordered composes };
47⊖        invariant unique_names_for_formal_arguments:
48          args->forAll( a1 , a2 | a1.name = a2.name implies a1 = a2);
49    }
50⊖   class Block extends Instruction
51    {
52          property instructions : Instruction[*] { ordered composes };
53    }
54⊖   class If extends ControlStructure
55    {
56          property thenPart : Block { composes };
57          property elsePart : Block[?] { composes };
58    }
59⊖   class ControlStructure extends Instruction
```

Figure 13.3   Defining constraints on Logo program using oclinecore.

Tip 13.1 Textual Editor for Ecore Files

The **oclinecore** is a convenient editor for those who are more efficient in writing their Ecore metamodels with a textual syntax than using the default tree editor or a graphical editor. A similar textual editor for the Ecore files is **emfatic**.

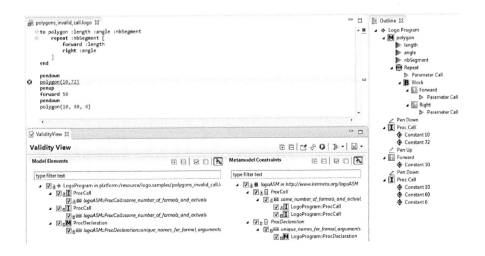

Figure 13.4   Checking OCL constraints on Logo programs.

> **Note 13.2 Weaving OCL Using EMF Validation Framework**
>
> Using `oclinecore` allows adding the OCL constraint in the Ecore metamodel. This is fine for general constraints that must apply on all models conforming to this metamodel. A more flexible approach would be to weave these constraints while keeping them in a separate file. Thanks to plugin extension declarations, the EMF validation framework allows us to declare `Validators` that uses separate OCL files. In addition, when validating a model the user is able to enable or disable these `Validators` according to his needs.

13.4 WEAVING DYNAMIC SEMANTICS TO GET AN INTERPRETER

The next step in the construction of a Logo environment is to define Logo operational semantics and to build an interpreter. In our approach this is done in two steps. The first one is to define the runtime model to support the execution of Logo programs, i.e., the Logo *virtual machine*. The second one is to define a mapping between the abstract syntax of Logo and this virtual machine. This is going to be implemented as a set of *eval* functions woven into the relevant constructs of the Logo metamodel.

13.4.1 Logo Runtime Model

As discussed earlier, the most popular runtime model for Logo is a turtle that can draw segments with a pen. As for the language abstract syntax, the structure of the runtime model can be defined by a metamodel. The advantage of this approach is that the state of the running program is then also a model. Like for any model, all the tools available in a framework like EMF can then readily be used in order to observe, serialize, load, or edit the state of the runtime.

Figure 13.5 presents a diagram of the Logo virtual machine metamodel. The metamodel only defines three classes: `Turtle`, `Point` and `Segment`. The state of the running program is modeled as a single instance of class `Turtle` which has a position (which is a `Point`), a heading (which is given in degrees), and a Boolean to represent whether the pen is up or down. The Turtle stores the segments which were drawn during the execution of the program. In practice the metamodel

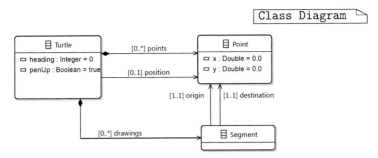

Figure 13.5 Logo runtime metamodel.

was defined without operations using EMF tools. The operations, implemented in Kermeta, are later woven into the metamodel to provide an object-oriented definition of the Logo virtual machine. Listing 13.3 presents an excerpt of the Kermeta listing. It adds three operations to the class **Turtle** of the metamodel.

Kermeta

```
package example.logo.interpreter
import fr.inria.diverse.k3.al.annotationprocessor.Aspect
import fr.inria.diverse.k3.al.annotationprocessor.OverrideAspectMethod
import vmLogo.Point
import vmLogo.Segment
import vmLogo.Turtle
import static extension example.logo.interpreter.PointAspect.*
import static extension example.logo.interpreter.SegmentAspect.*
import static extension example.logo.interpreter.TurtleAspect.*
...
@Aspect(className=typeof(Turtle))
class TurtleAspect {
  def Turtle initialize(){
    _self.reset()
    return _self
  }
  def void reset() {
    _self.position = vmLogo.VmLogoFactory.eINSTANCE.createPoint().
        initialize(0,0)
    _self.heading = 0
    _self.penUp = true
    _self.drawings.clear
  }
  def void setPenUp(boolean b) {
    _self.penUp = b
  }
  def void rotate(int angle) {
```

```
    _self.heading = (_self.heading + angle) % 360
  }
  def void move(double dx, double dy) {
    var Point newPos = _self.position.getDelta(dx,dy)
    if(_self.penUp) {
      println("Turtle move to "+ newPos.asString)
    }
    else {
      println("Turtle trace to "+ newPos.asString)
      _self.drawings.add(vmLogo.VmLogoFactory.eINSTANCE.createSegment.
          initialize(_self.position,newPos))
    }
    _self.position = newPos
  }
  def void forward(int steps) {
    var double radian = Math.toRadians(_self.heading)
    _self.move(_self.scale(steps,Math.sin(radian)), _self.scale(steps
        ,Math.cos(radian)))
  }
  /**
   * scale the "steps" by factor
   */
  def double scale(int steps, double factor) {
    return steps * factor
  }
}
```

Listing 13.3 Runtime model operations in Kermeta.

13.4.2 Operational Semantics

We are now going to define the operational semantics for each
construct of the abstract syntax. The idea is again to weave operations
implemented in Kermeta directly into the metamodel in such a
way that each type of statement would contain an `eval` operation
performing the appropriate actions on the underlying runtime model.
To do that, a context is provided as a parameter of the `eval` operation.
This context contains an instance of the Turtle class of the runtime
metamodel and a stack to handle procedure calls. Listing 13.4 presents
how the `eval` operations are woven into the abstract syntax of
Logo. An abstract operation `eval` is defined on class **Instruction**
and implemented in every subclass to handle the execution of all
constructions.

```
package example.logo.interpreter

import fr.inria.diverse.k3.al.annotationprocessor.Aspect
import fr.inria.diverse.k3.al.annotationprocessor.OverrideAspectMethod
...
import static extension example.logo.interpreter.InstructionAspect.*
import static extension example.logo.interpreter.ForwardAspect.*
import static extension example.logo.interpreter.GreaterAspect.*
import static extension example.logo.interpreter.PenUpAspect.*
import static extension example.logo.interpreter.PlusAspect.*
...
@Aspect(className=typeof(Instruction))
abstract class InstructionAspect {
   public def abstract int eval (Context context )
}
...
@Aspect(className=typeof(Forward))
public class ForwardAspect extends PrimitiveAspect{
  @OverrideAspectMethod
  def int eval (Context context) {
    var int param = _self.steps.eval(context)
    context.turtle.forward(param)
    return 0
  }
}
@Aspect(className=typeof(PenUp))
public class PenUpAspect extends PrimitiveAspect{
  @OverrideAspectMethod
  def int eval (Context context) {
    context.turtle.setPenUp(true)
    return 0
  }
}
@Aspect(className=typeof(If))
public class IfAspect extends ControlStructureAspect{
  @OverrideAspectMethod
  def int eval (Context context) {
    if ( _self.condition.eval(context) != 0) {
      return _self.thenPart.eval(context)
    }
    else{
      return _self.elsePart.eval(context)
    }
  }
}
@Aspect(className=typeof(Plus))
public class PlusAspect extends BinaryExpAspect{
```

```
@OverrideAspectMethod
def int eval (Context context) {
  return _self.lhs.eval(context) + _self.rhs.eval(context)
}
}
@Aspect(className=typeof(Greater))
public class GreaterAspect extends BinaryExpAspect{
  @OverrideAspectMethod
  def int eval (Context context) {
    if(_self.lhs.eval(context) > _self.rhs.eval(context)) {
      return 1
    }
    else{
      return 0
    }
  }
}
```

Listing 13.4 Logo operational semantics.

For simple cases such as the `PenDown` instruction, the mapping to the virtual machine is straightforward: it only boils down to calling the relevant VM instruction, i.e., `context.turtle.setPenUp(false)` (see `PenUpAspect` in Listing 13.4).

For more complex cases such as the `Plus` instruction, there are two possible choices. The first one, illustrated in `PlusAspect` of Listing 13.4, makes the assumption that the semantics of the Logo `Plus` can be directly mapped to the semantics of "+" in Kermeta. The interest of this first solution is that it provides a quick and straightforward way of defining the semantics of that kind of operators. If however the semantics we want for the Logo `Plus` is not the one that is built into Kermeta for whatever reason (e.g., we want it to handle 8-bit integers only), we can define the desired `Plus` operation semantics in the Logo Virtual Machine (still using Kermeta of course) and change the `eval` method so that it first calls `eval` on the left-hand side, pushes the result on the VM stack, then calls `eval` on the right-hand side, again pushing the result on the VM stack, and finally calls the `Plus` operation on the VM.

13.4.3 Getting an Interpreter

Once the operational semantics for Logo has been defined as described above, getting an interpreter is pretty straightforward: we first have to import each relevant aspect to be woven into the Logo metamodel (using `import static extension` instructions, see the import statements at the beginning of Listing 13.3, Listing 13.4, and Listing 13.5). We then need to load the Logo program into Kermeta (see `load` in Listing 13.5), instantiate a `Context` (that contains the Logo VM), and then call `eval(Context)` on the root element of the Logo program.

Kermeta

```
package example.logo.interpreter
...
import static extension example.logo.interpreter.LogoProgramAspect.*
class LogoInterpreter{
  public def run(String fileName) {
    var LogoProgram prog
    if(fileName.endsWith(".logo")){
      prog = load(fileName)
    }
    else{
      prog = loadXMI(fileName)
    }
    var Context context = new Context()
    prog.eval(context)
    new Window(context.turtle)
  }
  ...
  public def LogoProgram load(String fileName){
    var Injector injector = new LogoTextualSyntaxStandaloneSetup().
        createInjectorAndDoEMFRegistration()

    var XtextResourceSet resourceSet = injector.getInstance(
        XtextResourceSet);
    resourceSet.addLoadOption(XtextResource.OPTION_RESOLVE_ALL, Boolean
        .TRUE);
    val Resource res = resourceSet.getResource(URI.createURI(fileName),
        true);

    return res.contents.get(0) as LogoProgram
  }
```

Listing 13.5 Getting an Interpreter.

Loading the *Square* program of Figure 13.1 and executing it this way will change the state of the model of the Logo VM: during the execution, four new `Segments` will be added to the `Turtle`, and its position and heading will change. Obviously, we would like to see this execution graphically on the screen. The solution is quite easy: we just need to put an Observer on the Logo VM to graphically display the resulting figure in a Java widget. The Observer is implemented in Kermeta and calls relevant Java methods to notify the screen that something has changed as shown in Figure 13.6.

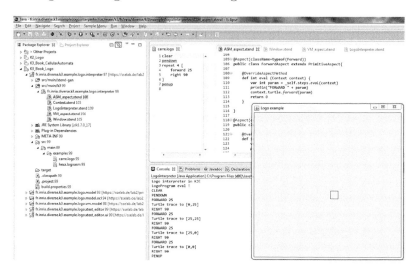

Figure 13.6 Simulation of Logo.

13.5 COMPILATION AS A KIND OF MODEL TRANSFORMATION

In this section we are going to outline how to build a compiler for our Logo language. The idea is to map a Logo program to the API offered by Lego Mindstorm so that our Logo programs can actually be used to drive small robots mimicking Logo turtles. These *Robot-Turtles* are built with Lego Mindstorms and feature two motors for controlling wheels and a third one for controlling a pen (see Figure 13.7).

A simple programming language for Lego Mindstorms is NXC (standing for Not eXactly C). So building a Logo compiler for Lego Mindstorms boils down to writing a translator from Logo to NXC. The problem is thus much related to the Model Driven Architecture (MDA) context as promoted by the OMG, where a Logo program would play the role of a Platform Independent Model (PIM) while the NXC program would play the role of a Platform Specific Model (PSM). With this interpretation, the compilation we need is simply a kind of model transformation.

Figure 13.7   A Lego mindstorm robot-turtles.

We can implement this model transformation either using model-to-model transformations or model-to-text transformations:

Model-to-text transformations are very useful for generating code, XML, HTML, or other documentation in a straightforward way, when the only thing that is needed is actually a syntactic-level transcoding (e.g., pretty-printing). Then we can resort on either:

– Visitor-based approaches, where some visitor mechanisms are used to traverse the internal representation of a model and directly write code to a text stream.

– Template-based approaches, based on the target text containing slices of meta-code to access information from the source and to perform text selection and iterative expansion. The structure of a template resembles closely the text to be generated. Textual templates are independent of the target language and simplify the generation of any textual artifacts.

Model-to-model transformations would be used to handle more complex, semantic-driven transformations.

For example, if complex, multi-pass transformations had been needed to translate Logo to NXC, it could have been interesting to have an explicit metamodel of NXC, properly implement the transformation between the Logo metamodel and the NXC one, and finally call a pretty-printer to output the NXC source code.

In our case, however, the translation is quite simple, so we can for example directly implement a visitor-based approach. In practice, we are once again going to use the aspect weaving mechanism of Kermeta to simplify the introduction of the Visitor pattern. Instead of using the pair of methods `accept` and `visit`, where each `accept` method located in classes of the Logo metamodel would call back the relevant `visit` method of the visitor, we can directly weave a `compile()` method into each of these Logo metamodel classes (see Listing 13.6).

Kermeta

```
package logo.compiler
import logo.model.*
import static extension logo.compiler.PenUpAspect.*
import static extension logo.compiler.ClearAspect.*
...

@Aspect(className=PenUp)
class PenUpAspect extends PrimitiveAspect{
   def void compile (Context ctx) {
    ...
   }
  }
@Aspect(className=Clear)
class ClearAspect extends PrimitiveAspect{
   def void compile (Context ctx) {
    ...
   }
}
...
```

Listing 13.6 The Logo compilation aspect in Kermeta.

Integrating this compilation aspect into our development environment for Logo is done as usual, i.e., by using **import static extension** in the main Kermeta program.

13.6 MODEL-TO-MODEL TRANSFORMATION

For the Logo compiler described above to work properly, we have to assume that all Logo function declarations are performed at the outermost block level, because NXC does not support nested function declarations. Since nothing in our Logo metamodel prevents the Logo user from declaring nested functions, we need to either add an OCL constraint to the well-formedness rules of the language, or we need to do some pre-processing before the actual compilation step. For the sake of illustrating Kermeta capabilities with respect to model-to-model transformations, we are going to choose the latter solution.

We thus need a new aspect in our development environment, that we call the *local-to-global* aspect (See Listing 13.7). We are using a very simple OO design that declares an empty method local2global (taking as a parameter the root block of a given Logo program) in the topmost class of the Logo metamodel hierarchy, Instruction. We are then going to redefine it in relevant metamodel classes, such as ProcDeclaration, where we have to move the current declaration to the root block and recursively call local2global on its block (containing the function body). Then in the class *Block*, the local2global method only has to iterate through each instruction and recursively call itself.

Kermeta

```
package kmLogo
import logo.model.logoASM.*
...

@Aspect(className=Instruction)
class InstructionAspect{
  def void local2global(Block : rootBlock) {}
}
@Aspect(className=ProcDeclaration)
class ProcDeclarationAspect
  def void local2global(Block : rootBlock) {
  rootBlock.add(_self)
  block.local2global(rootBlock)
  }
}
@Aspect(className=Block)
class BlockAspect
  def void local2global(Block : rootBlock) {
    instructions.forEach[i| i.local2global(rootBlock)]
  }
}
```

Listing 13.7 The Logo *local-to-global* aspect in Kermeta.

Note that if we also allowed ProcDeclaration inside control structures such as Repeat or If, we would also need to add a local2global method in these classes to visit their block (thenPart and elsePart in the case of the If statement).

Once again this *local-to-global* concern is implemented in a modular way in Kermeta, and can easily be added or removed from the Logo programming environment without any impact on the rest of the software. Further, new instructions could be added to Logo (i.e., by extending its metamodel with new classes) without much impact on the *local-to-global* concern as long as these instructions do not contain any block structure. This loose coupling is a good illustration of Kermeta advanced modularity features, allowing both easier parallel development and maintenance of a DSML environment.

13.7 CONCRETE SYNTAX

Metamodeling is a natural approach in the field of language engineering for defining abstract syntaxes. Defining concrete and graphical syntaxes with metamodels is still a challenge. Concrete syntaxes are traditionally expressed with rules, conforming to EBNF-like grammars, which can be processed by compilers such as ANTLR [117] to generate parsers. Unfortunately, these generated parsers produce concrete syntax trees, leaving a gap with the abstract syntax defined by metamodels, and further ad hoc hand-coding is required to produce the complete editor.

Fortunately, the MDE community has contributed tools for concrete syntaxes, which take advantage of metamodels to generate fully operational tools (such as parsers or text generators). The principle is to map abstract syntaxes to concrete syntaxes via bidirectional mapping-models with support for both model-to-text and text-to-model transformations.

Similarly, to get usable graphical editors for your domain-specific language (DSL), several projects provide the tooling to create component and runtime infrastructure for building graphical editors.

We have used Xtext [33] and Sirius to respectively build the Logo textual syntax, the Logo graphical syntax, and their associated editors. Listing 13.8 presents the Xtext grammar for Logo.

xtext 🗋

```
grammar example.logo.xtext_editor.LogoTextualSyntax with org.eclipse
    .xtext.common.Terminals
import "platform:/resource/example.logo.model/model/ASMLogo.ecore"
import "http://www.eclipse.org/emf/2002/Ecore" as ecore
...
LogoProgram returns LogoProgram:
  {LogoProgram}
  instructions+=Instruction ( instructions+=Instruction)*
```

```
  ;
Instruction returns Instruction:
  Back | Forward | Left | Right | PenDown | PenUp | Clear | ProcCall |
      ProcDeclaration | Block | If | Repeat | While ;
...
Forward returns Forward:
  'forward' steps=LiteralsExpression;
Left returns Left:
  {Left}
  'left' angle=LiteralsExpression;
...
PenUp returns PenUp:
  {PenUp}
  'penup' ;
...
Constant returns Constant:
  {Constant}
   integerValue=EInt ;
ProcCall returns ProcCall:
  declaration=[ProcDeclaration|EString]
  '(' (actualArgs+=LiteralsExpression)?
      ( "," actualArgs+=LiteralsExpression)* ')' ;
ProcDeclaration returns ProcDeclaration:
  {ProcDeclaration}
  'to' name=EString
    ( args+=Parameter)*
    instructions+=Instruction ( instructions+=Instruction)*
  'end' ;
Block returns Block:
  {Block}
  '[' ( instructions+=BInstruction)* ']';
If returns If:
  ('ifelse' condition=LiteralsExpression
     thenPart=Block
     elsePart=Block) |
  ('if' condition=LiteralsExpression
     thenPart=Block) ;
...
AddExpression returns Expression:
  MultExpression ((({Plus.lhs=current} '+')|({Minus.lhs=current} '-') )
      rhs=MultExpression)* ;
MultExpression returns Expression:
  LiteralsExpression ((({Mult.lhs=current} '*')|({Div.lhs=current} '/')
      ) rhs=LiteralsExpression)* ;
LiteralsExpression returns Expression:
  ParameterCall | Constant | '(' EqualExpression ')' ;
```

Listing 13.8 Xtext grammar definition for Logo.

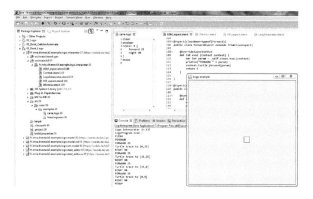

Figure 13.8   Simulation of a Logo model.

13.8   EXERCISES

Exercise 13.1 Logo with Multiple Pens

Extend Logo with the possibility to have multiple pens of different colors.

Exercise 13.2 Logo with Variables

Extend Logo with variables and variable assignments.

Exercise 13.3 Logo with Multiple Turtles

Extend Logo with multiple turtles.

Exercise 13.4 Logo for Your Own Robot

If you own a robot (rover, humanoid...), write a compiler (or extend the existing one) that targets this platform.

CHAPTER 14

Model-Driven Engineering of a Role-Playing Game

CONTENTS

14.1 INTRODUCTION

One common characteristic of all games is that they are defined with *rules*. These rules can of course be coded into some programming language to allow either the automatic computation of complex data (such as scoring) or even playing with (or against) the computer. Then the usual trade-off applies: if the rules are stable for centuries, as in chess, there is probably no better way than hard coding the rules using the abstractions provided by the chosen programming language (or for a minimum of flexibility use a design pattern such as the type-object pattern [71]). However when the rules are unstable, or evolve often, or have many variants, having these rules as data that is interpreted by a rule engine can be a better choice.

A typical example of this is all the video games (such as *Angry Birds*) having the notion of *level*, or role-playing games, in which players assume the roles of characters in a fictional setting, such as *Dungeons and Dragons* featuring complex rules described with hundreds of pages. In this latter case, the rules are interpreted to allow a Playing Character (PC) to convert the experience it gained in adventures into the acquisition of new powers and competencies. Thus beyond being mere "dead" data, these rules can be seen as programs that are interpreted to make the PC evolve over time. Recast in terms of MDE, these rules are expressed in a language, whose operational semantics is the mapping of the rules into the semantic domain made of the PC's powers and competencies.

In this chapter, we are going to develop the example of building a game support system for a real-sized role-playing game: The System Reference Document (SRD). The SRD is a comprehensive toolbox consisting of *rules*, *races*, *classes*, *feats*, *skills*, *various systems*, *spells*, *magic items*, and *monsters* compatible with the d20 System version of *Dungeons and Dragons* and various other role-playing games from the company Wizards of the Coast.[1]

---

[1]System Reference Document ("SRD") is Open Game Content as described by the Open Gaming License, Version 1.0a. *Dungeons & Dragons*® and the d20 system are registered trademarks of Wizards of the Coast, Inc. in the United States and other countries. All images and text associated therewith are the copyrighted property of Wizards of the Coast, Inc. All rights reserved. "d20 System" and the "d20 System" logo are trademarks of Wizards of the Coast, Inc. and are used according to the terms of the d20 System License version 5.0. More information about the licenses cited above can be found at `www.opengamingfoundation.org`, `www.wizards.com/d20` and on this book companion website at `mdebook.irisa.fr`.

In the SRD, players take responsibility for acting out their roles within a narrative (provided by a Game Master), through a process of structured decision making or character development: Actions taken within the game succeed or fail according to a formal system of rules and guidelines, whose description makes up the bulk of the SRD. The core mechanics are simple however: Whenever a player attempts an action that has some chance of failure (as trying to hit a dragon with a sword), she rolls a twenty-sided die (d20), adds any relevant modifiers, and compares the result to a target number. If the result equals or exceeds the target number, the character succeeds. If the result is lower than the target number, it fails.

The rich game mechanism then comes from the set of rules that describe how a character can turn its powers into numerical bonuses on its actions. The more actions the character does, the more *experience* it gains to gain *levels*, which provide it with new powers. One of the key success factors of these types of games is that the Game Masters are encouraged to extend the base system with so-called *house rules*, for instance new *races*, new *classes*, or new *magic items*.

Since the actual rules of the SRD are rather long and complex, they cannot be fully described within this book. Even the SRD metamodel has to care for many aspects of the rules, and cannot be fully described here. For the sake of clarity, we are thus going to work with a slightly simplified metamodel, which is going to be instantiated in a tiny set of rules for an SRD-like game. However the full SRD has been programmed using this very same approach: the interested reader can get the result at `opendd.free.fr`.

14.2 METAMODELING THE SRD 3.5

The first task in the model-driven construction of a language is the definition of its abstract syntax, which is in practice the domain model of the SRD: the notions of ability scores, alignment, races, classes, skills, feats, equipment, spells, etc.

14.2.1 Main Concepts of the SRD 3.5

Ability scores Each Stat, such as Strength, Constitution, Intelligence, or Charisma partially describes a character and affects some of his or her actions. It is modeled as a positive integer.

Alignment A character's general moral and personal attitudes are represented by its alignment: lawful good, neutral good, chaotic good, lawful neutral, neutral, chaotic neutral, lawful evil, neutral evil, or chaotic evil. Beyond character development, the impact of alignment on the game is that it might restrict some choices. For instance a Paladin can only be lawful good. In MDE terms, that means that the Alignment can be used as a *precondition* in the choice of a new level for a character.

Race The race of a character, such as Human, Dwarf or Elf, has an impact on many other things, for example language command. All characters know how to speak Common. A dwarf, elf, gnome, half-elf, half-orc, or halfling also speaks a racial language, as appropriate. A character who has an Intelligence bonus at 1st level speaks other languages as well, one extra language per point of Intelligence bonus as a starting character. Also, races have different sizes, ranging from tiny (for e.g., a bee) to gigantic (for an ancient dragon). Medium characters such as humans have no bonus. A Small character (halfling, gnome, etc.) gets a $+1$ size bonus to Armor Class, a $+1$ size bonus on attack rolls, and a $+4$ size bonus on Hide checks. A small character's carrying capacity is three-quarters that of a Medium character. A Small character generally moves about two-thirds as fast as a Medium character. A Small character must use smaller weapons than a Medium character. Finally, some races have specific advantages: Humans have 1 extra feat at 1st level, 4 extra skill points at 1st level and 1 extra skill point at each additional level, while Dwarves have a bonus of $+2$ in Constitution, and -2 in Charisma.

Classes A character may add new classes as he or she progresses in level, thus becoming a multiclass character. The class abilities from a character's different classes combine to determine a multiclass character's overall abilities. Multiclassing improves a character's versatility at the expense of focus. There are 11 standard character classes defined in the SRD. They are Barbarian, Bard, Cleric, Druid, Fighter, Monk, Paladin, Ranger, Rogue, Sorcerer, and Wizard. For instance, a Wizard can be of any alignment, has a Hit Die of 4, Skill Points at 1st Level is defined as $(2 + IntModifier) * 4$, and Skill Points at Each Additional Level are defined as $2 + IntModifier$, while a Paladin must be Lawful Good, has a Hit Die of 10, etc. On top of that, a Wizard can cast a choice of Spells depending on its intelligence and level, while the Paladin gets special powers at some specific levels (e.g., at level 2 *Divine grace* and *Lay on hands*) and typically more attack and damage bonuses than the Wizard. Each class also defines a number of skills that are called *class skills* (see below).

Skills such as Bluff, Climb, Hide, Jump, Swim, etc. are used to make skill checks, i.e., roll a d20 and add a skill modifier that is defined as skill rank + ability modifier + miscellaneous modifiers.

> **Skill ranks:** A character's number of ranks in a skill is based on how many skill points a character has invested in a skill. Many skills can be used even if the character has no ranks in them; doing this is called making an untrained skill check.

> **Ability modifier:** The ability modifier used in a skill check is the modifier for the skill's key ability (the ability associated with the skill's use). The key ability of each skill is noted in its description.

> **Miscellaneous modifiers:** Miscellaneous modifiers include racial bonuses, armor check penalties, and bonuses provided by feats, among others.

> Each skill point spent on a class skill gets the character 1 rank in that skill. Class skills are the skills found on the character's class skill list. Each skill point spent on a cross-class skill gets the character 1/2 rank in that skill. Cross-class skills are skills not found on the character's class skill list. The maximum rank in a class skill is the character's level + 3. If it's a cross-class skill, the maximum rank is half of that number (do not round up or down).

> Regardless of whether a skill is purchased as a class skill or a cross-class skill, if it is a class skill for any of your classes, the maximum rank equals the total character level + 3.

Feats Some feats are general, meaning that no special rules govern them as a group. Examples of these Feats are: Acrobatic (character gets a +2 bonus on all Jump checks and Tumble checks), or Endurance (character gets a +4 bonus on Swim checks made to resist nonlethal damage, Constitution checks made to continue running, etc.). Others are item creation feats, which allow spellcasters to create magic items of all sorts. A metamagic feat lets a spellcaster prepare and cast a spell with greater effect, albeit as if the spell was a higher spell level than it actually is.

Some feats have prerequisites: Diehard requires that the character already has Endurance, or Dodge requires the character to have a Dexterity of at least 13. More generally the character must have the indicated ability score, class feature, feat, skill, base attack bonus, or other quality designated in order to select or use that feat. In MDE terms, all these aspects must thus be seen as preconditions for obtaining a feat. A character can gain a feat at the same level at which he or she gains the prerequisite. A character cannot use a feat if he or she has lost a prerequisite.

Equipment includes weapons, armor, goods, and services. Each piece of equipment has a price, a weight, and can give defense and/or attack bonuses to characters using them. For instance, a Longsword is a slashing weapon that weights 4 lb., is worth 15 gold pieces, makes 1d6 damage[2] in its small version and 1d8 in its medium version, etc. A magical longsword would add several bonuses to this basic longsword, such as +1 to hit and to the damage rolls, and even special powers such as being intelligent, cursed, or a life-drinker.

Spells A spell is a one-time magical effect. Spells come in two types: arcane (cast by bards, sorcerers, and wizards) and divine (cast by clerics, druids, and experienced paladins and rangers). Some spellcasters select their spells from a limited list of spells known, while others have access to a wide variety of options. Most spellcasters prepare their spells in advance (whether from a spellbook or through devout prayers and meditation) while some cast spells spontaneously without preparation. Hundreds of spells are described in the SRD, with many different effects.

From this short description of the SRD rule system, we can see that the game rules are quite complex and intricate. At the dawn of role-playing games, players used to spend hours browsing the books

---

[2]Dice rolls are described with expressions such as $3d4 + 3$, which means *roll three four-sided dice and add 3* (resulting in a number between 6 and 15). The first number tells you how many dice to roll (adding the results together). The number immediately after the d tells you the type of die to use. Any number after that indicates a quantity that is added or subtracted from the result.

containing the rules to decide what to do with their characters. With the advent of computers, this tedious task can now be supported by software implementing these rules and guiding the players in choosing legal options for their characters.

14.2.2 Metamodeling the SRD Rules

One obvious solution to implement the SRD rules would be to directly encode them in Java. For instance you would have an abstract class Race with as many subclasses as they are actual races: Human, Dwarf, etc. and another abstract class called ClassLevel with subclasses such as Wizard1, Paladin1, Wizard2, Paladin2 etc. Each of these subclasses would encode the complex SRD rules using Java. An obvious drawback of this approach is that you need a Java programmer to extend or maintain the rules, somehow ruling out the idea of house rules. Also in the end you get a very big and very rigid program.

So the alternative is to define a language for letting game designers *encode* their own rules using a dedicated editor: the actual SRD rules would then become data. By the way, looking more closely at the SRD, one would realize that Human or Dwarf is not really a subclass of Race but an instance of it, as Wizard1 or Paladin1, are not subclasses but instances of ClassLevel. Indeed the SRD notions of races, classes, feats, skills, etc. are meta-level concepts that can be instantiated in actual races, classes, feats, skills, etc.

These concepts are linked together: a ClassLevel has a set of class skills, and gives the character a set of benefits that can be attack or defense bonuses, feats, spell access, etc.

We already have seen that we also need the notions of preconditions: a Paladin can only be lawful good means that the levels of Paladin are only available to lawful good characters. The feat Diehard requires that the character already has Endurance, or Dodge requires the character to have a Dexterity of at least 13. That means that we need a language for letting the game designers express those kinds of preconditions.

Similarly, we are going to need an expression language, working at least on the domain of integer, for caring about all the bonuses that can be added to dice rolls.

14.2.3 Implementing the SRD Metamodel

The various parts of the SRD metamodels are implemented as packages: actions, core, expressions, precondition, spellcasting.

> **Tip 14.1 Getting a Metamodel from POJO**
>
> Even if the book is mainly illustrated using EMF, modeling techniques can also be achieved directly on the class structure. The metamodel diagrams of the SRD have been generated thanks to a generator that uses the POJO[a] structure of the the Java implementation. It produces an yUML[b] file which takes care to create diagrams with an automatic layout.
>
> ---
> [a]Plain Old Java Object
> [b]plantuml is an opensource alternative to yUML

14.2.3.1 The Core Package

The core package is presented in Figure 14.1. Probably the most important class there is ClassType, which models the type of a ClassLevel. It features a *hitDice* that tells which dice must be rolled to get the hit points gained by a Character gaining a level in that ClassType (e.g., D4 for a wizard, D10 for a Fighter), the *maxClassLevel* offered in that ClassType, the type of spell offered (e.g., arcane, divine, psionic or none), and the *spellCastingTable* associated with this ClassType if any. There might be preconditions to acquire this ClassType (e.g., a Paladin must be Lawful Good), which is inherited through AbstractClassType and AbstractPrecondType.

Upon a Character acquiring a ClassType (through Abstract-ClassType), a Character gets a set of bonuses that are modeled as an ActionList, which is going to be described below in the Actions package.

Another interesting class in the core package is the RaceType class, modeling the race of the Character. Through AbstractTraitType, a raceType is an AbstractContributorType, meaning it also gives a Character a set of bonuses, modeled as an ActionList. AbstractContributorType also handles vision features such as night vision or blind vision. AbstractTraitType defines the number of hands and legs the Character gets (allowing for non-humanoid characters such as animals

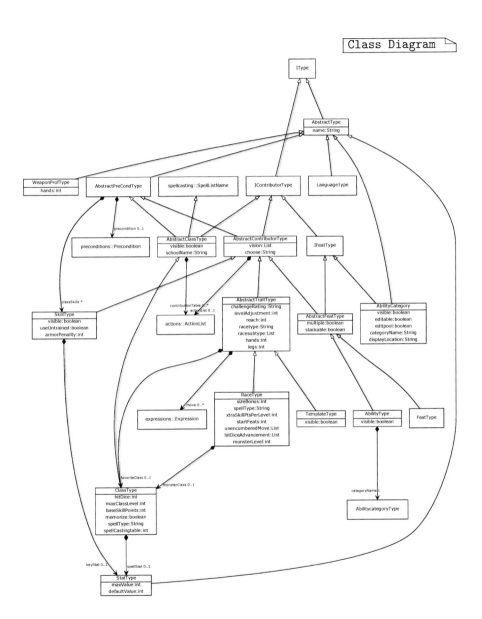

Figure 14.1   The core package.

or other monsters), and has a number of move modes (such as walk, swim, fly, etc. called *move*), each associated with a speed that is modeled as an Expression (from the Expression package). A RaceType handles the bonus (resp. malus) brought by small sizes (resp. large or even huge sizes), as well as possible extra skill points or extra feats given by a specific race (e.g., humans gets extra skill points). Some monster races also have built-in levels in some ClassType (e.g., some Dragons have built-in Wizards like abilities).

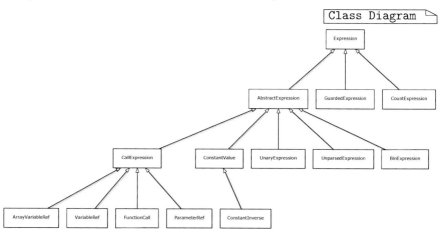

Figure 14.2   The expressions package.

14.2.3.2   The Expression Package

Once again in this book, we need an expression language to create and evaluate integer expressions. In this case it is quite simple, as illustrated in Figure 14.2. It supports both scalar and array variables, and simple functions, as well as the usual ConstantValue and BinExpression. ConstantInverse makes it possible to easily model values such as $1/2$ or $1/3$ that sometimes appear in some rules, without the need to extend the domain of the expressions from integers to rational numbers. Also available is GuardedExpression, which is an expression guarded by a Condition (from the package Preconditions): if the condition is false then the value of the Expression is 0.

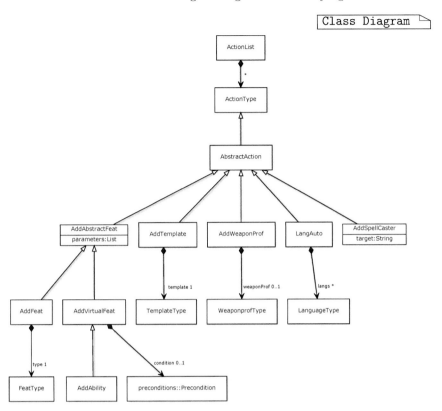

Figure 14.3   The action package.

14.2.3.3   The Action Package

The action package, presented in Figure 14.3, contains the possible upgrades a Character gets when acquiring a new level in some class, or a new race (as well as in some other occasions). They are seen as actions (class AbstractAction) performed on the Character data sheet, for example adding a new Feat (class AddFeat), a new Weapon Proficiency (class AddWeaponProf), a new spoken Language, or a new Spell Caster Ability.

14.2.3.4   The Bonus Package

Another important subtype of AbstractAction is AbstractBonus, presented in Figure 14.4. An AbstractBonus has a value, which is a GuardedExpression from the Expression package. Examples of

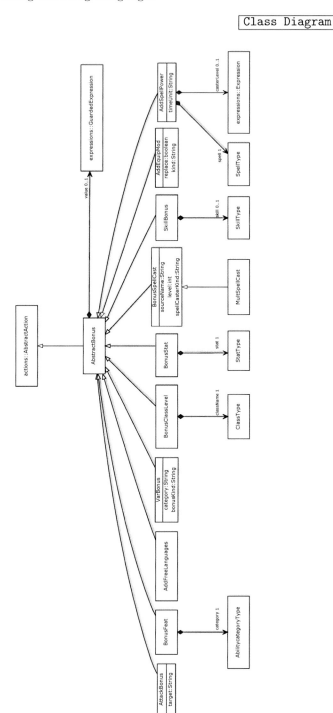

Figure 14.4 The bonus package.

AbstractBonus subtypes are AttackBonus (that grants a specific attack such as melee attack a bonus), AddFreeLanguages (the number of extra languages that can be learned by the Character), BonusClassLevel (the number of extra levels in a given ClassType given to the Character, themselves bringing their own bonuses), or SkillBonus (that add bonus points in a specific skill).

14.2.4 Example: Creating a Tiny Rule Set

The SRD metamodel described above can be instantiated into a set of rules for a specific version of the SRD game. Making house rules boils down to editing the rule set: adding, modifying or removing classes, races, feats, etc. While that can readily be done using the native EMF reflective editor, this is of course not a user-friendly approach. So in Section 14.4 we describe how to generate a web-based editor for the game designer.

For now, Figure 14.5 shows a tiny example of a rule set as an instance diagram of the SRD metamodel described above. This Tiny Rule Set only contains two possible races, Elf and Human (instances of RaceType). Each one has a favorite class, either Wizard of Fighter, each instance of ClassType.

Wizard has an associated ActionList that contains an instance of AddSpellPower, for adding the Sleep spell to a Wizard.

Fighter also has an associated ActionList that contains:

- an instance of BonusStat that gives a bonus of +2 to the Character StatType called Str (for Strength); and

- an instance of AddFeat that adds the Acrobatic FeatType to the Character, itself adding a SkillBonus of +2 to the Jump SkillType.

Creating and modifying game rules is of course nice, but in the end the goal is to *play* them, that is, to apply the rules to a specific adventure where a party of characters is created and evolved according to these rules. In MDE terms we say that the rules must be *interpreted*. This is described next.

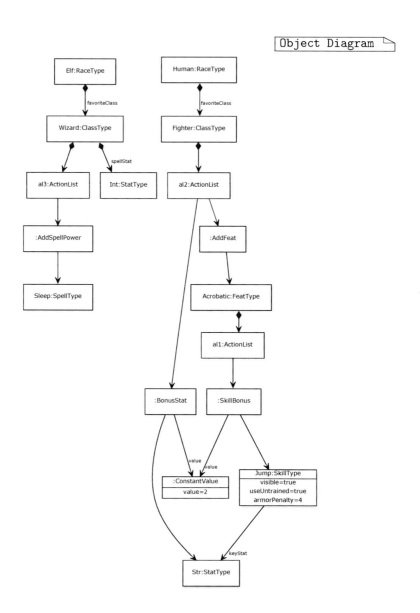

Figure 14.5 Object diagram for a tiny rule set.

14.3 WEAVING DYNAMIC SEMANTICS TO GET AN INTERPRETER

The next step in the construction of an SRD environment is to define SRD operational semantics and to build an interpreter. As usual, this is done in two steps. The first one is to define the runtime model to support the execution of SRD rules, i.e., the notion of Character that can be considered as the *virtual machine* on which the rules apply. The second one is to define a mapping between the abstract syntax of the SRD and this virtual machine. As in the Logo chapter, this is going to be implemented as a set of *eval* functions woven into the relevant constructs of the SRD metamodel.

14.3.1 SRD Runtime Model

The runtime model of the SRD is a *party* consisting of a set of *characters* (cf. Figure 14.6). All the rules are applied to the party, and thus to the characters. For instance if the party successfully defeats some monsters, it may win a number of experience points (XPs) depending on the difficulty of the encounter. These XPs are then divided among the characters of the party. Once a given character has enough XPs, it can get a new level that brings it new abilities and bonuses. The basic operations of a Character are thus:

Create a new character with a default race, typically human.

Modify its attributes such as name, sex, alignment.

Change race: remove previous race and add new one.

Gain XPs

Add class level, which is allowed only if the Character has enough XPs.

Remove class level, because some rules allow some monsters (such as Vampires) or weapons (cursed sword) to steal vital energy from their targets, which in game terms corresponds to loosing levels.

Change feat, remove a feat and add the newly chosen one.

Add points to skill, to add (or remove) points to (from) a skill.

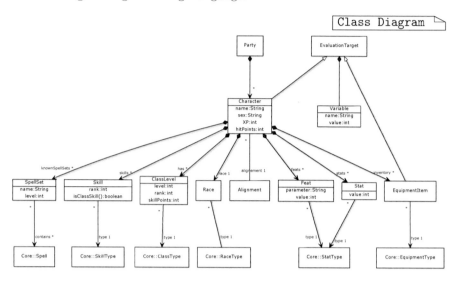

Figure 14.6   A simplified model of the SRD runtime.

14.3.2   Mapping the Abstract Syntax to the Runtime Model

Adding a Class level to a Character boils down to *executing* the actions (such as gain bonus, gain skill points, add feat...) listed for this class level with the Character as a target. In programmatic terms, that means that the *eval()* method of the Add class level action is going to call the *eval()* method of each of the listed actions.

If we get back to the Tiny Rule Set presented in Figure 14.5 to illustrate the algorithm, then adding a class level of Fighter will call the *eval()* method on each action of its action list, that is,

– *eval()* on an instance of BonusStat, that looks into the set of Stats of the Character for the one with the relevant StatType, and add 2 to it;

– *eval()* on an instance of AddFeat, that adds a new Feat (typed with the Acrobatic FeatType) to the set of feats of Character. Then *eval()* is called on the Acrobatic FeatType own action list to add a SkillBonus of +2 to the Character's Skill typed by the Jump SkillType.

Remove class level plays a symmetrical role, and can be seen as a kind of *undo()* action of Add Class level. Adding or removing a race works in the same way.

14.4 COMPILATION OF A WEB-BASED EDITOR

14.4.1 Requirements

Creating (or modifying) a game based on the SRD metamodel boils down to editing the rule set: adding, modifying or removing classes, races, feats, etc. A popular way to edit such objects nowadays is to use a web browser, because it can be deployed everywhere and it allows cooperative editing.

It is however not so easy to build such a web application from scratch if we want all the bells and whistles that are expected from a professional-grade web application: responsive web design, connection to a database (either classical or NoSQL) located somewhere in the cloud, security, administration support (logs, performance monitoring, etc.), internationalization support, and Maven configuration for building, testing and running the application.

Fortunately enough, there are a bunch of well-designed frameworks that considerably help developers in their endeavors. One of these frameworks that recently became quite popular on Github is JHipster.

14.4.2 Overview of JHipster

JHipster, or "Java Hipster," is an application generator that will create a Spring Boot (that's the Java part) and AngularJS (that's the hipster part) application for you.

JHipster focuses on generating a high-quality application with a Java back-end using an extensive set of Spring technologies; Spring Boot, Spring Security, Spring Data, Spring MVC (providing a framework for websockets, REST and MVC), etc., an Angular.js front-end, and a suite of pre-configured development tools like Yeoman, Maven, Gradle, Grunt, Gulp.js and Bower. JHipster creates a fully configured Spring Boot application with a set of pre-defined screens for user management, monitoring, and logging. The generated Spring Boot application is specifically tailored to make working with Angular.js a smoother experience.

JHipster gives you the tools to update, manage and package the resulting application. A Maven build uses the Spring Boot Maven plugin to create a single executable .war file, and Grunt or Gulp.js tasks to test, minify, and optimize JavaScript, HTML and CSS code.

On the client side the technology stack is based on the single web page application paradigm:

- Responsive Web Design

- HTML5 Boilerplate

- Twitter Bootstrap

- AngularJS

- Compatible with IE9+ and modern browsers

- Full internationalization support with Angular Translate

- Optional Sass support for CSS design

- Optional WebSocket support with Spring WebSocket

The Yeoman development workflow allows an easy installation of new JavaScript libraries with Bower, building, optimization and live reload with Grunt or Gulp.js, and testing with Karma and PhantomJS.

Conversely on the server side the technology stack is made of a complete Spring application:

- Spring Boot for easy application configuration

- Maven or Gradle configuration for building, testing and running the application

- "development" and "production" profiles (both for Maven and Gradle)

- Spring Security

- Spring MVC REST + Jackson

- Optional WebSocket support with Spring Websocket

- Spring Data JPA + Bean Validation

- Database updates with Liquibase

- Elasticsearch support if you want to have search capabilities on top of your database

- MongoDB support if you prefer a document-oriented NoSQL database instead of JPA

– Cassandra support if you prefer a column-oriented NoSQL database instead of JPA

It provides professional-grade server-side software, ready to go into production with:

– Monitoring with metrics

– Caching with ehcache (local cache) or hazelcast (distributed cache)

– Optional HTTP session clustering with hazelcast

– Optimized static resources (gzip filter, HTTP cache headers)

– Log management with Logback, configurable at runtime

– Connection pooling with HikariCP for optimum performance

– Builds a standard WAR file or an executable JAR file

14.4.3 Targeting JHipster

What JHipster expects as input is a set of Entity classes, representing the data to be edited and stored in the web application. That is exactly the level of abstraction provided by our SRD metamodel: each concrete class in the SRD metamodel is going to be a JHipster Entity.

So the only thing we have to do is to write a model transformation taking as input the SRD metamodel and producing the set of Entity classes in the format expected by JHipster, which append to be a set of JSON files, one for each class of the SRD metamodel.

For instance the JSON that is expected for a StatType class is the following:

JSON

```
{
  "inheritanceFromClass": "AbstractType",
  "relationships": [

  ],
  "fields": [
    {
      "fieldId": 1,
      "fieldName": "maxValue",
      "fieldType": "Integer",
```

```
    "fieldNameCapitalized": "MaxValue",
    "fieldNameUnderscored": "maxValue"
  },
  {
    "fieldId": 2,
    "fieldName": "defaultValue",
    "fieldType": "Integer",
    "fieldNameCapitalized": "DefaultValue",
    "fieldNameUnderscored": "defaultValue"
  }
],
"changelogDate": "1441004153446"
}
```

Another example is BonusStat, which shows how the relationship between BonusStat and StatType is encoded:

JSON

```
{
  "inheritanceFromClass": "AbstractBonus",
  "relationships": [
    {
      "relationshipId": 1,
      "otherEntityName": "stat",
      "relationshipType": "one-to-one",
      "otherEntityNameCapitalized": "StatType",
      "fieldNameUnderscored": "stat"
    }
  ],
  "fields": [

  ],
  "changelogDate": "1441004153479"
}
```

Generating the relevant JSON files for each class in the SRD metamodel is pretty straightforward with a template-based approach such as Acceleo, as explained in Section 9.2. Once that is finished and a basic JHipster environment is deployed in your computer (see https://jhipster.github.io/installation.html), you can simply call:

```
yo jhipster:entity StatType
yo jhipster:entity BonusStat
...
```

to generate all the relevant files, both for the server and client side. Of course our generator actually generates a script to call these commands at once. Finally, you just need to deploy and run everything with

```
mvn spring-boot:run
```

Et voila: The application is available on `http://localhost:8080`. Figure 14.7 gives a screenshot of the resulting web-based editor, ready to be used.

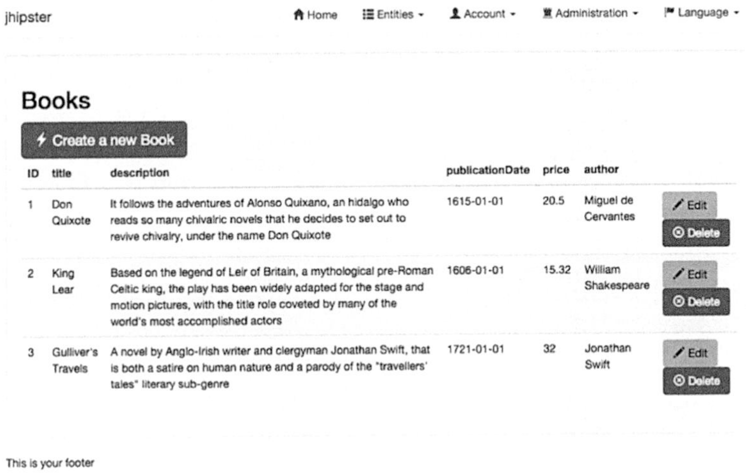

Figure 14.7   Web-based editor for games based on the SRD metamodel.

Clicking on Edit on the presented objects will show the editor screen.

On top of the user-oriented views, JHipster also provides administration screens visible from the browser (see Figure 14.8).

Several thousand lines of code have been generated to obtain this state-of-the-art piece of web-based software. However most of the technical complexity of it stays cleanly separated from the domain know-how: MDE and generative techniques clearly demonstrate here their ability to empower domain experts.

14.5   TESTING A RULE SET

When rule sets are as complex as the *Dungeons and Dragons* one, including user extensions and home rules, there is a chance that there might be inconsistencies or dead ends. Of course we can test the rules by hand: we create a new Character, have it gain some experience points, and choose some new classes, feats, skills, etc. But this way

Figure 14.8   JHipster monitoring screen.

we can only try a very small fraction of the several billion possible Characters.

We thus need to provide a better way to validate the rule sets.

14.5.1   Random Intensive Testing

Among the various V&V techniques that have been outlined in Section 9.6, we can start with random intensive testing because it provides a good trade-off between fault-revealing power and ease of implementation.

The principle of the random testing algorithm is:

```
loop (for a fix amount of time)
   initialize a new character
   randomly choose its race
   foreach level in 1..maxlevel
```

```
      randomly choose an allowed classlevel
      randomly choose feats
      randomly choose spells
      ...
      check character consistency
    endforeach
  endloop
```

Checking character consistency can be done in several ways. Once again an easy test is to try to save the character, then load it again, and check that it is the same. If at some point an invariant is violated, or it is impossible to perform an action (such as randomly choosing an allowed class level because no class is allowed for the character at some point), then an exception is raised, and the current character printed out for further inspection of the problem.

This random testing algorithm is surprisingly efficient at detecting big problems after only a few seconds, so it can be run as often as needed during the development of the game rules.

14.5.2 Exhaustive Testing

Random intensive testing is good at efficiently finding big problems with the rule set, but what if the problem only has a very low probability to manifest itself? The only way to get a better confidence level on a rule set is then to try all the possibilities, which of course is going to take quite some computing power and time. But the principle of the algorithm is once again very simple:

```
foreach possible race
  initialize a new character with that race
  foreach level in 1..maxlevel
    foreach allowed classlevel
      add that classlevel to the character
      foreach allowed feats
        add all the possible combinations of feats
        in each of them check character consistency
      ...
    endforeach
  endforeach
endforeach
```

Running this algorithm however takes ages. Actually, for the d20 rule set, after running it for one week on a decent modern computer, it did not finish. Still it allowed us to detect quite a number of errors, but not to make sure that everything was correct.

14.5.3 Pairwise Testing

A good trade-off to that kind of validation is known as pairwise testing [105]. The basic idea is that instead of testing all the possible combinations, we only test all the possible interactions between any two elements. Of course we can combine that to exhaustive testing to somehow degrade exhaustive only where there are too many combinations, e.g., for choosing feats in the d20 system.

The algorithm then becomes something like this:

```
foreach possible race
  initialize a new character with that race
  foreach level in 1..maxlevel
    foreach allowed classlevel
      add that classlevel to the character
      foreach allowed feats f1
      add f1
      foreach still allowed feats f2
        add f2
        check character consistency
        remove f2
        ...
      endforeach
    endforeach
  endforeach
endforeach
```

With this approach, we got down to less than 30 minutes execution time for the d20 rule set, and were able to catch some tricky bugs involving improbable combinations of magical weapon properties.

14.6 EXERCISES

Exercise 14.1 Extending Game Rule Set

Extend the tiny rule set as you see fit: Introduce a new class, race, etc.

Exercise 14.2 Possible Options for Saving Character Runtime Data

What are the possible options for saving Character runtime data? Which of them could be resilient to a change in the game rules, and to what extent?

Exercise 14.3 Editor Generator for Another Technology

Propose an editor generator for another technology, such as C# or Android.

Exercise 14.4 Extending Game Support System to Combats

Until now the game support system is only for managing the evolution of characters. It does not handle combats. Extend the metamodel to deal with a party fighting against another one. First, only consider physical combat (with an effect on Characters' hit points only), and then introduce special effects brought by magical spells.

Exercise 14.5 Type-Object Pattern versus MDE Approach

Discuss the pros and cons of using the type-object pattern [71] instead of an MDE approach in the case of the *Dungeon and Dragons* example.

CHAPTER 15

Civil/Construction Engineering: The BIM Example

CONTENTS

In this chapter we discuss the use of models in software targeted at the building and construction sector. In doing so we demonstrate how problems in the domain can be addressed by techniques presented earlier: the creation of a metamodel from an existing standard, the storage of large models using database mapping, the use of model merging to detect simple design problems, and the use of model transformations to aid in the estimation of project cost.

15.1 INTRODUCTION

The design and construction of a building is a complex endeavor. Even for small buildings, it brings into play dozens of different expert skills, and will involve dozens of stakeholders: architects, structural engineers, electrical engineers, mechanical engineers, quantity surveyors, project managers, subcontractors, plus building owners and users. There are hundreds of things that can go wrong during the process, which can result in problems with the building, blow-outs in costs, or even danger to the people who construct or use the building.

To anticipate these problems before commencing construction, and to facilitate communication between the various stakeholders in the process, the building and construction industry has long made use of models. Most traditionally this has been in the form of drawings and other documents describing either the building or the construction process. On many projects, this has also involved the use of physical small-scale models. In recent decades, however, the industry has come to rely heavily on the use of digital models.

In the early years of digital design, these models, often dubbed CAD (Computer-Aided Design) models, were 2-dimensional, showing the building or part of the building as seen from a specific perspective (such as plan, elevation or section). Over time, tools evolved to incorporate 3-dimensional representations. In recent years, models have increasingly come to incorporate other information about the building: the materials of each element, performance (structural, thermal, or operational) characteristics, cost information, etc. These models are commonly referred to as Building Information Models.

Having captured this information in models, there is a huge range of analyzes that can be done. Later in this chapter we will explore two of these—clash detection and quantity take-off—in greater depth. Other analyses that can be performed, depending on the nature of the project, include:

- Some of the most important analyzes that need to be performed are *structural analyzes*. These consider the different loads on the building and its constituent elements based on different usage patterns and environmental conditions, by considering the different structural characteristics of the beams, columns, slabs and other structural elements of the building.

- All building projects are subject to codes which must be satisfied depending on the nature of the building and in which jurisdiction it is being built. These codes can cover the safety of construction processes, the quality of workmanship, accessibility, fire safety, and others. *Code-checking* tools can often be used to check whether or not a building model satisfies the rules in these codes (or whether more information needs to be included in the model).

– Not all designs that can be represented as a model can actually be built. *Constructability* analysis considers whether it is possible, and how long it will take, to construct a building design given specific resources (e.g., labor, cranes and other machinery) and using specified construction techniques. This includes consideration of the structural dependencies between different elements, the necessity to protect a partially completed building against the elements, and often attempts to try and minimize the cost of construction by optimizing the use of different resources (labor, rental equipment, etc.).

– One of the biggest determinants of the cost of operating a building is its energy efficiency, which is highly dependent on usage patterns, heating/cooling equipment, exterior finishes, and local/geographic conditions such as seasonal temperate ranges, wind directions, etc. There are a variety of tools available which can estimate the building's energy usage based on this kind of information.

– The use of *natural light* can often greatly improve the experience of building users, and can help to optimize the building's use of artificial light. There are a number of tools which can analyze a building model, in combination with information about the surrounding environment and local conditions, to show the levels of natural light which can be expected in different parts of the building at different times of the day and at different times of the year.

– In many buildings, it is important to consider the level of noise which will be present in the different spaces of the building. By specifying the kinds of activities (either human or otherwise) which must be supported in different spaces, in terms of the levels they generate and the levels they can tolerate, and considering factors such as the transmission of sound through walls, floors, etc., *acoustic analyses* can provide information about the acoustic consequences for the different users of a building.

- In large cities, there are complex relationships between different buildings in terms of *wind flow*, and *heat effects*, based on the shape of the buildings, their finishes and the local wind, temperate and light conditions. An number of tools can perform these analyses to ensure that new buildings do not significantly detract from the operation of existing buildings.

- The paths that people take through buildings can be of great importance. For example, hospitals need to have efficient paths for transporting patients and medical professionals between different parts of the building. There are also important rules which must be satisfied about evacuation routes from a building in the event of fire or other emergencies. Analyses are often performed for checking these based on navigable paths through the building and including width and inclines of corridors, the types of doors which are present, and other movement mechanisms such as elevators, escalators, or stairs.

- *Lifecycle analysis* considers the energy and materials being used in the building and their environmental emissions. For example, different finishes, or the use of certain equipment, can result in chemical emissions either during the construction process, during the early occupancy of the building, or as the building ages. Using automated tools to evaluate the impact of design details can aid in decision making to reduce cost or environmental impact, or increase user satisfaction.

As well as being used for analyses during the design process of a building, building information models can also be used throughout the rest of the lifecycle of the building. For example, models used in the design of the building can often be used to aid in the development of visualizations of the building for use in sales. Models can also be used to manage building operations, such as tracking maintenance or repair activities. The models can also aid in planning or carrying out renovations, or in the decommissioning/destruction of buildings.

The following sections discuss how the modeling techniques presented in earlier chapters can be brought to bear upon the domain of building and construction to build software solutions that address real problems of the domain.

15.2 ABSTRACT SYNTAX OF BUILDINGS

There are a variety of different ways to represent building designs. In some cases, analysis tools propose a relatively concise language which represents only those aspects of the building which are relevant. For example, a language such as gbXML, used for performing energy analyzes, includes constructs for modeling basic geometries, and information about adjacent spaces and the thermal absorption or transmittance between them, but will not have information about, e.g., structural characteristics, or the richness of geometry that is required for modeling objects such as fittings or furnishings. Other languages, such as those used in the major CAD tools, are more general, and include constructs that cover a large range of the disciplines involved in the design process.

One of the most significant of the general languages used is the Industry Foundation Classes (IFC)[18]. In the next section we discuss the structure of the IFC, and how it can be used as a modeling language for capturing and analyzing building models.

15.2.1 Industry Foundation Classes

The Industry Foundation Classes (IFC), defined by the building-SMART alliance®, represent the accepted industry standard for design models. IFC models are semantically rich in that they capture not only the 3-dimensional geometry of the objects, but metadata related to many other aspects of the building. For example, if we consider an instance of a door object, this door will be situated in a wall, on a defined building story, within the building. It will have attributes associated with it that describe its thermal performance, costing, fire safety performance, etc. Which building components need to be accessed to resolve an issue can be determined by tracing system descriptions within the model, for example, the thermal zones system, cost breakdown structure, and the fire safety system. The necessary attribute definitions and the system descriptions are derived from legislative requirements and analysis software input requirements.

IFC data model is defined using a metamodeling system known as STEP (Standard for the Exchange of Product model data), standardized by the ISO. STEP has a similar architecture to that presented here, with a language for metamodeling, called EXPRESS (analogous to Ecore), a mapping to a concrete interchange format, known as Part 21 (analogous to XMI), and mappings to various programming language interfaces.

Many of the significant BIM tools currently used by industry support import and export of IFC files.

Although the metamodels (STEP/EXPRESS as opposed to Ecore) and syntaxes (Part 21 as opposed to XMI) are different, the essential structure of the STEP modeling environment is broadly similar to that described in this book (for example, in Chapter 3). Nonetheless, there are elements such as model transformations that are less well supported, which can make it appealing to bring the IFC models into a MOF/Ecore world. Techniques such as technical space bridging [13] can be used to do this in the case of building information models [138].

Perhaps the most prominent example of integrating the technical spaces of building information modeling and the model-driven technologies used in this book is the Open BIM Server [10][1].

15.3 MODEL STORAGE: LARGE MODELS

One of the challenges faced when dealing with models of buildings is that of size. IFC is a very large language, and takes the approach of providing modeling constructs for an overwhelming range of concerns. The Ecore translation of the original IFC schema checks in at around 700 classes and more than 1600 attributes and references.

More importantly, individual building models can also be extremely large. As an example, a mechanical service (incorporating the heating, ventilation and air-conditioning systems) model for a 19-story office building shown in [137] contained 7.3 million computational objects; comparable sizes could reasonably be expected for other architectural, structural, electrical, and interior models of the building[2]. This kind of scale of model is well beyond the capacity of file-based storage mechanisms such as XMI.

As was introduced briefly in Section 3.5, dealing with models of this size very quickly renders file-based serializations such as XMI unworkable, so for BIM applications it is generally necessary to look into tools such as CDO for managing the models.

---

[1]Cf. http://bimserver.org

[2]This is by no means a large building. The *BIM Handbook* [32] includes a number of large projects incorporating building modeling. Parametric models tend to be bigger still. The parametric model used in the design of the One Island East was 5 Gb in size.

Note 15.1 Parametric Modeling

One of the recent developments in building modeling has been the increasing prevalence of *parametric modeling*. This is supported by software such as Grasshopper (based on the Rhino 3D tool) from McNeel & Associates, and Generative Components from Bentley Systems.

When creating a building model, we frequently find a high degree of interdependency between the things being modeled. Imagine we are modeling a simple room with 2 slabs (floor and ceiling) and four walls. Each of these 6 objects have 6 properties—a placement expressed as x,y and z coordinate values, as well as length, width, and depth—giving us 36 property values. However, in the case of a typical room, we are only interested in varying a handful of these values—the placement of the room itself, the length and width and height of the room, and the thickness of the walls and slabs. All other values in the model are some function of these. Including all of the 36 values is redundant, and introduces the possibility of error, e.g., changing the length of the walls but not of the slabs.

Parametric modeling allows us to model values as being a function of some other value in the model. In the example, we could create a placeholder for the values we care about—room position, room length, room width, room height—then define the other values as functions of these placeholders. This simplifies our design (by reducing the number of parameters' it has), and more importantly simplifies the process of modifying our design. It also means that the design better captures the design intent, since it more explicitly captures the metaphors the designer has used in creating the design.

The real contribution of parametric modeling is that it allows the individual modeler (and not only the modeling language designer) to create and use higher, or different, abstractions, than those offered by the modeling language. In effect, it allows them to embed their own modeling language within the host language, and to define the mapping from this ad hoc language to the host. When used judiciously, this can greatly increase the effectiveness of modeling. For example, if the building design is based on a helical shape (for example, the Gherkin office tower building in London), then the Cartesian, element-by-element abstractions offered by a traditional geometric modeling system can be replaced by variables for the curvature of the shell, the floor-to-ceiling height of the stories, and the rotation rate of the exterior panels.

15.4 CONCRETE SYNTAX

The most obvious concrete representation of a building is how it looks. Since building models including information about 3-dimensional geometry, as well as potentially information about color and even texture of building elements, the obvious way to represent the model is using a 3D rendering.

However, there is also a lot of information in the building model that is not as easy to represent in 3D. Material choices, structural properties, heating/cooling capacities of HVAC systems, and other metadata are all present in the model and have no logical representation in 3 dimensions.

Most tools used in building information modeling incorporate two distinct representations of building models: the first, a customized tree representation of the building model, and the second, a 3-dimensional representation (using technologies such as OpenGL). It is important to note that these representations are best used in parallel. For example, if we are interested in the structural properties of a certain beam, then we can find and select the beam using the 3D model, then inspect its properties in the tree viewer. Or, we can restrict the 3D view to a single story of the building by selecting the story using the tree viewer.

The tree representation, which can be built in the style described in Section 5.4, is useful because large buildings frequently have their many components organized into clear hierarchies. For example, a site will contain a building, a building will contain stories, and elements such as doors and windows will be contained within a story. However, there are typically multiple hierarchies available. For example, an electrical wire might be considered to reside with a certain story, but it might equally be considered to reside within the building's electrical system, or the lighting subsystem.

A three-dimensional view is clearly more difficult to construct, since it requires rendering a wide range of possible 3D constructs, including colors and textures. Like the tree view, it is often useful to have multiple 3D renderings. A representation which closely resembles the building's visual form is obviously desirable, for communicating the design to clients, but it is also useful to have more symbolic representations, for example, in which colors might represent material choices or expected space usage.

Having multiple representations like this can represent a challenge in interface design. This often necessitates the use of techniques such as selection sharing, whereby a user can select an element or elements in one view, and see the selection in another view. This can even be extended to query interfaces that highlight sets of elements to certain selection criteria, very useful in facilitating inspection of designs by stakeholders and engineers during the design process.

15.5   CASE STUDY: CLASH DETECTION

When we are implementing a software system and we discover that something in our design is incorrect, it becomes very expensive to correct the design, then follow this through to correct the implementation.

Design problems encountered during the construction of a building are even worse. Material costs are significant, and the structural and other dependencies between different elements in the design can be extremely complex. On-site corrections of design problems represent a significant part of the cost of constructing a building, and detecting these problems before commencing construction is of the utmost value.

To do this, the building and construction industry has long made use of models to perform analyses to detect any problems before construction begins. One of the most common analyzes is finding cases where two building elements in the design occupy the same physical space. The process of finding these situations is called *clash detection.*

Clashes might seem like an easy thing to avoid. Certainly, in a single model, it is a relatively simple thing to ensure that this does not occur. However, even in moderately sized projects, it is typical to have 3 or 4 models for different aspects of the building. On a large project this could include multiple architectural models, structural models, electrical models, models of heating/ventilation/air-conditioning (HVAC) models, civil engineering models, landscaping models, and interiors models. These models are built by different engineers, who are generally only concerned with their own discipline, and who each interact with only some of the other designers. With all of these models existing in parallel, it is not uncommon to have, for example, an electrical duct running through a heating duct.

The first step, then, in performing clash detection, is to create a merged model incorporating all of the different discipline models. We can do this using the model-merging techniques presented in Section 11.2.

Having done this, and keeping in mind that our building models include all the information about the geometry of its individual elements, the process of detecting clashes can be reduced to a search problem, using OCL or the models' programmatic APIs.

15.6 CASE STUDY: QUANTITY TAKE-OFF

Another interesting problem in the building and construction industry is that of managing the cost of a building project as it progresses from initial concept through design, construction, and delivery. In this section we describe a project that uses the model-driven techniques described in earlier chapters in order to help automate the process of managing estimates and costs [136].

15.6.1 Background: Description of the Domain

Two roles have emerged within the building industry to assist in controlling project costs. The quantity surveyor (in UK/Australian practice) works for the project client and provides advice to the building design team on the expected cost to complete the project as the building is being designed. This is an iterative process where cost plans (predictions) are developed several times through the design/documentation process to minimize the risk of cost overruns. On completion of the design, the contract documents will be handed over to an estimator within a building contracting company. The estimator needs to prepare an accurate estimate of the cost of the building within a short period (normally 4–6 weeks).

The fundamental operation underlying cost planning and estimation is the preparation of a Bill of Quantities (BoQ). This consists of an itemized list of the components required to construct a building, prepared at a level of detail enabled by the state of project documentation at the time the BoQ is prepared (top right panel in Figure 15.1). Once the BoQ is prepared the quantity surveyor/estimator will examine the building components referenced by each item in the BoQ and will apply a "unit rate" from the company or personal database to calculate the estimated cost of the item. A weighting factor may be applied if there are unusual circumstances regarding the buildings element(s). The unit rates are built up statistically over a long period of time and are the major intellectual property of the quantity surveyor/estimator.

Traditionally, the quantity surveyor/estimator reads the plans, sections, elevations, details, and specifications of the building project to identify all of the building elements, infer information that was not explicit and then select the items needed for the project from a standard BoQ. The type, structure and units of measurement used are defined in industry standards (i.e., [8]) or in company standards. One organization does not always use the same measurement rules.

Measurement against the unit rates is not trivial. For some trades, such as masonry wall construction, openings in walls less than $1m^2$ are ignored since the extra work of forming the opening makes up for the reduction in wall material. Other items, such as areas of formwork underneath or around concrete need to be inferred as these are not explicitly represented. Of the two distinct stages within the quantity surveyor's/estimator's work processes, the extraction of building elements does not require significant levels of intelligence if the source information contains appropriate semantic content. This is also the most time-consuming stage, requiring several man-months for a complex building. The addition and modification of unit rates does require a considerable amount of background knowledge and intelligence. Consequently, the extraction stage is the most promising for automation.

15.6.2 Automated Estimator: Buildings and Bills

The Automated Estimator (Estimator) is a program developed by the Cooperative Research Centre (CRC) for Construction Innovation which aims to automate much of the quantity take-off process by

1. reading an IFC file;

2. identifying the building elements in the model against a predefined method of measurement;

3. matching the elements against item descriptions in the generic BoQ;

4. adding information that can be inferred from the model (e.g., areas of formwork);

5. extracting the relevant quantities and adding them to the BoQ items; and

6. presenting the BoQ and model information in a variety of "views" that support the estimating process (Figure 15.1).

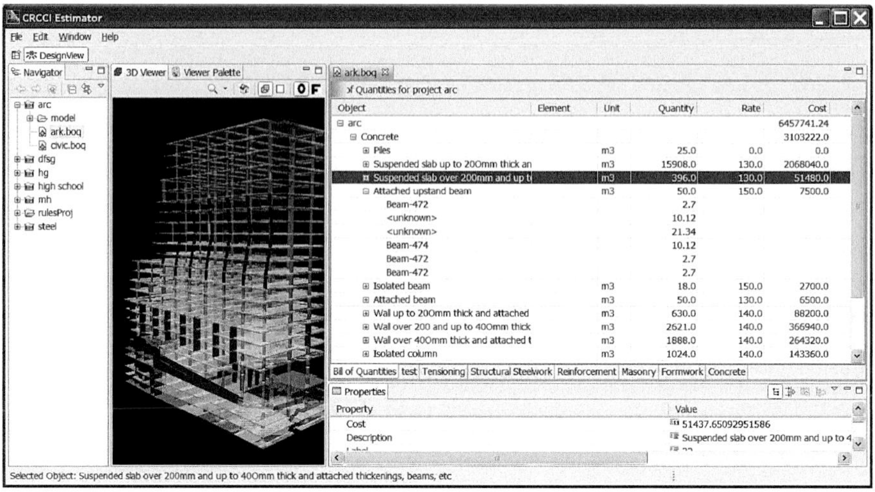

Figure 15.1 The Bill of Quantities editor.

Estimator is built on a generalized framework for BIM-based analysis of design models called DesignView. DesignView provides features for the import of IFC files, and for querying, inspecting, and visualizing the imported models in hierarchical and 3-dimensional views (these views are described in more detail in Section 15.6.2.1).

Estimator is able to handle most quantity take-off tasks. A range of take-off rules can be used depending on need and level of detail of information in the BIM. Implicit information, such as formwork and surface finishes, can be automated through defining rules that add such items to the BoQ together with the geometric queries necessary to calculate the results. Errors in the original BIM can be identified through built-in queries that select "all objects measured" within a trade package and also "all items not measured." Building designers will always come up with new building components that do not fit established types. Additional rules can be added to Estimator to support the gradual evolution of the standard item set. Since BoQs are often prepared by a team, additional rules should be added by a single expert so that the implications can be supported across all trade packages within the project. The major constraint on improved functionality and performance of Estimator is the level of detail and consistency of models currently provided by BIM generating software. These are being addressed both through research projects (by the authors and others) and also developments by the commercial software vendors.

One important aspect of traditional practice that is perhaps threatened by automating quantity take-off in Estimator and similar software is the identification of errors by the quantity surveyor/estimator. The ability to browse the model through the geometric and textual panels provides an alternative method for identifying errors. Additionally, this supports filtering of outputs by element, by material, by type, and by story.

15.6.2.1 The Intelligent Building Model Language

Because of the imposing size of the IFC language, the DesignView platform (and, by implication, Automated Estimator) uses a simplified language for representing design models, called the Intelligent Building Model (IntBM). IFC models are converted into the IntBM language through an import wizard. An extract of the IntBM metamodel is shown in Figure 15.2. As can be seen, this language includes only about 30 classes, as opposed to more than 600 in IFC—a reduction aimed at simplifying the development of design analysis tools, and achieved through a few significant language design decisions.

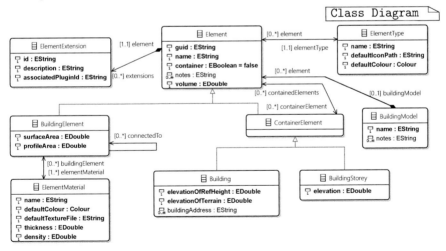

Figure 15.2 The intelligent building model metamodel.

The first economy is that a lot of elements are not considered during import. Discipline-specific information such as structural moment models, property sets containing metadata for lifecycle or performance data, or information about organizational responsibility for building elements, are not interesting for many design analyses, so these are stripped out during import.

Rather than including classes for all the possible building element types, the IntBM language uses a flattened type hierarchy in which elements and element types are included within the same model. This is facilitated by a standard library of common building element types which are populated during import, and a standardized mapping for IFC building element types outside this set.

Because the focus of DesignView is on analysis and visualization of models rather than creation or modification, it uses triangles for the surface geometry rather than IFC's wide variety of 3D geometry modeling constructs. Conversion from the richer IFC geometry constructs to triangles is done during import. Triangularization can lead to variation in calculation of geometrical properties, particularly volumes, so some of this calculation is also performed during import and stored in the model.

The IntBM language also includes a facility for extension of model elements with extra information. This is used for two purposes within Automated Estimator. Quantity take-off sometimes requires elements to be classified at a finer grain than normal. For example, most building models will use the Slab element type, but for quantity take-off it is important to distinguish between ground slabs, suspended slabs, or thickening slabs. These extra classifications are included as tags through the `ElementExtension` mechanism. The other use of extensions is for the area-height information for suspended slabs, which are taken off differently based on their height above the slab immediately below them. For this purpose, each suspended slab is annotated with a set of values to show what proportions of its under-surface areas are at what heights. These Estimator-specific extensions are populated using registered processes that run at the end of IFC model import.

Within the DesignView platform, the user can inspect the model using a number of different views. The model browser provides a tree-view of the model elements in the style common to the EMF framework, with separate tabs to see elements arranged according to the physical object hierarchy (element within space within story within building within site), by material, or by element type. The 3D view uses the triangle representations of the building elements to present a graphical presentation of the design. Since the chief purpose is typically per-element analysis of the model, coloring of the 3D model is typically done by element-type in order to distinguish, e.g., walls from beams from columns from slabs, etc. The hierarchy and 3D viewers use two levels of selection sharing in order to facilitate inspection of the models. Clicking on an element or a set of elements in either view will highlight these elements in the other view. Dragging a container element or a set of elements from the hierarchy view to the 3D view will restrict the 3D visualization to just those elements that are dragged. This is particularly useful for inspecting a single floor.

15.6.2.2   The Bill of Quantities Language

The language used for describing bills of quantities is based on an analysis of the existing documents used by quantity surveyors. The result is the metamodel shown in Figure 15.3.

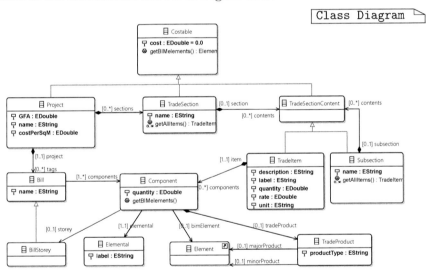

Figure 15.3 The Bill of Quantities metamodel.

The BoQ is broken down into a series of trade sections, each of which can in turn have a hierarchical structure within them. At the bottom of these hierarchies are `TradeItems`, each of which has a description, a quantity, a unit of measurement for the quantity, and a cost per unit. These trade sections and the trade items within them are not hard-coded in the metamodel; they are created by the take-off rules that populate the model, in order to provide flexibility in the structure of the bills being generated. The default rules shipped with Automated Estimator correspond to the trade sections and items from the Australian Standard Method of Measurement [8].

In some cases, elements are considered as aggregated units called `TradeProducts`. For example, in situ (as opposed to precast) concrete elements such as slabs with attached thickenings or support beams, are constructed in a single pour, and calculations for their surface areas or volumes must be done as an aggregate, not separately for each element. Within the quantities model defined in Automated Estimator, we further allow `TradeItems` to be broken down into `Components`, to show the contribution made to the item's quantity by each building element or trade product. In addition to being defined within a certain `TradeItem`, `Components` can also be tagged, for example by story, which allows for breakdowns of the BoQ by characteristics other than the dominant hierarchy of `TradeSections`.

BoQ models are accessed using the table-based Bill of Quantities Editor, shown in Figure 15.1. This editor supports selection sharing in a similar way to that used between DesignView's 3D and Hierarchy views. Selecting building elements in the 3D or Hierarchy views will highlight the BoQ items that are contributed to by the selected elements. Similarly, selecting a `TradeSection`, `Subsection` or `Item` in the Bill of Quantities Editor will highlight the building elements that contribute to the selection. Furthermore, if the user drags a selection of elements into the 3D view, the BoQ will be narrowed to show only the totals for the selected elements.

15.6.3 The Take-Off Rules Language and Tool Support

The rules that govern the generation of a bill of quantities from an IntBM model are expressed using the Take-Off Rules language. The design of this domain-specific transformation language and its implementation in the take-off rules engine were based on consultation with quantity surveyors and cost engineers, in an effort to ensure that the resultant language would be usable by its target users. These users are already familiar with the idea of using rules in order to populate a bill of quantities, and the Take-Off Rules language within Automated Estimator has been designed to reflect this and provide a familiar formalism.

The next sections describe the Take-Off Rules language and the implementation of its engine within Automated Estimator. We also discuss the mechanism for storing the trace information between the building model and the generated BoQ, and the facilities for inspecting/debugging the generated bill.

15.6.3.1 Take-Off Rules

Figure 15.4 shows the metamodel of the rule-based Take-Off Rules language used within Automated Estimator. There are two parts to this language—the structural part and the expression part. The high-level structures in the take-off language are based on those from the Bill of Quantities metamodel. The `RuleModule`, `Subsection` and `TakeoffRule` concepts correspond to, and result in the instantiation/population of the `TradeSection`, `Subsection`, and `TradeItem/Component` concepts, respectively, from the Bill of Quantities metamodel. Unlike bills of quantity, however, Take-Off Rule modules are stored with one `RuleModule` per file—the collection of rule modules is not modeled.

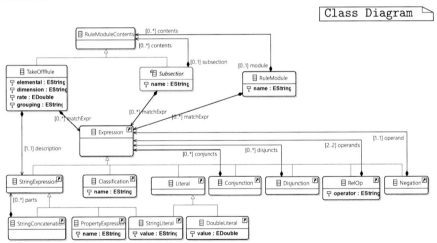

Figure 15.4 The Take-Off Rules metamodel.

The expression language used in the Take-Off Rules language is a simplified variant of the expression language from the Tefkat model transformation language [86]. It includes negation, conjunction, and disjunction, literals for strings and numbers, and binary relation operators for value comparison ($=$, $<$, $>$, etc). There are also unary operators for checking a building element's type or classification; these include IFC-style element types such as wall, beam or column, as well as Estimator-specific classifications, as outlined in Section 15.6.2.1, such as *plinth*, *pile_cap* or *upstand_beam*. Lastly, the expression language also includes *PropertyExpressions*, which allow the retrieval of 16 different string-, number- or Boolean-valued properties of elements—either simple properties such as `length`, `height`, or `material`, or take-off-specific "view" properties such as `height_from_floor` or `isCambered`.

The description for each `RuleModule`, `Subsection` and `TakeoffRule` element in the hierarchical structure of a Take-Off Rules model is expressed using a `StringExpression`. In the majority of cases this is a `StringLiteral`, but some rules include variable elements, which result in the generation of multiple `TradeItems` for a single `TakeoffRule`, each with a different description. One of the motivating cases for this was structural steel members, which must be grouped based on their lengths. The structural elements also include a match expression— a Boolean-valued expression which determines whether the section or rule matches in the context of a given element or, if specified in the rule, a certain `TradeProduct` grouping. For `RuleModules` and `Subsections`, this narrows the range of objects that can be matched by the contained `TakeoffRules`. For example, the concrete `RuleModule` might have a match expression such as `material = "concrete"`, which ensures that all the `TakeoffRules` in that `RuleModule` will only match concrete elements.

Most of the work in the take-off process is, unsurprisingly, involved in the evaluation of `TakeoffRule` objects. When the rules engine finds a `BuildingElement` which satisfies the rule's *matchExpr*, it will create a `TradeItem` (if it doesn't already exist), then populate (if it already exists) it with a `Component`, as the element's contribution to the quantity. The main link between the a `TakeoffRule` and the `TradeItem` that is either created or modified is the *description*, which uniquely identifies the trade item within its `TradeSection`. The rule also contains information for the population of a `TradeItem`, including a reference number, default rate, and elemental classification, and these are copied across into the new or modified `TradeItem`. It also includes the dimension to be taken off, a string value taken from a list of twelve dimensions understood by the engine: `No` (a count of matching elements), `Item` (for bill items that appear only once, regardless of how many elements they match, such as requirement

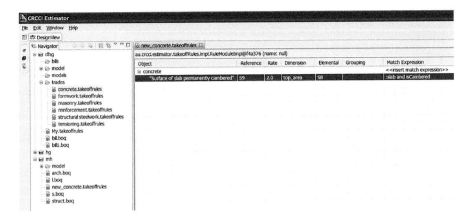

Figure 15.5 The Take-Off Rules editor.

for a crane), `volume`, `height`, `tonnes` (for structural steel elements), and various area measures for total, top, bottom, side or specific face areas. These dictate how the engine calculates a quantity from the `BuildingElement` for inclusion in the `TradeItem`.

15.6.3.2 Tool Support for Quantity Take-Off

Take-Off Rules models are created and modified in a tabular editor, shown in Figure 15.5. This shows the structure of the rules (corresponding to the structure of the bill to be generated) in the left-most column, with further columns for the reference number of the target `TradeItem`, the rate, the dimension, elemental classification, the `TradeProduct` grouping, and the match expression. Of these, only the first and last columns are required.

Both the description of the `TradeItem`, and the match expression, in the left-most and right-most columns respectively, are handled using an expression parser implemented using the Emfatic[29] framework. Using a tabular view emphasizes the relationship between the structure of the take-off rules and the bills that they will generate. Mixing tabular and textual representations is also done to seek a trade-off between the accessibility of tabular presentation and the expressive power of a textual syntax. The example match expression in Figure 15.5, : *slab and isCambered*, will match elements classified as *slab* and which satisfy the *isCambered* test (defined as a Boolean-valued `PropertyExpression`).

The take-off process is initiated using a contextual command on a building model, which prompts the user to nominate a target bill of quantities, and invokes the engine. The engine then evaluates a registered set of take-off rule modules, managed by the user in a preferences dialog, and populates the new bill. The matching phase of the engine is largely based on the EMF Query[3] framework, and the target model population is done in Java/EMF.

15.6.3.3 Traceability and Debugging

The issue of traceability is very important within Automated Estimator. Much of the time spent by a quantity surveyor within the tool will be spent inspecting an automatically generated bill to check whether the correct quantities have been taken off the building model. Of course, this does not negate the benefit of automating the bill's generation, reproducing several man-weeks of manual effort in less than an hour—much repetitive work is alleviated, and over time, a user will gain a deeper understanding of how a rule works, and gain more confidence in its operation. There are a number of typical questions that the QS will ask:

- What building elements have contributed to this cost item?

- To which cost items have this/these element/s contributed?

- Are there building elements that are not represented in this bill, or within this part of a bill?

The first two questions are primarily answered using the selection sharing mechanism between the bill of quantities editor, and the 3D and Hierarchy views on the building model. Selecting a cost item (including sections or subsections) will highlight all building elements that contribute to it, i.e., that are referenced by a `Component` object within the bill. Similarly, selecting a building element or set of building elements will highlight the cost items to which the element/s contribute, i.e., those `TradeItems` containing a `Component` which refers to one of the selected elements, or to a `TradeProduct` that contains them. These `Component` objects effectively function as in situ traceability relations within the bill of quantities model.

To address the third question, the Bill of Quantities Editor provides a command for detecting unmatched elements, which can be run either

---

[3]Cf. `http://www.eclipse.org/modeling/emf/?project=query`

relative to the whole bill, or to some subsection of the bill. This command will highlight any elements in the currently visible selection that are not matched by the bill or part-of-bill. Once again, this is done by consulting the Component objects within TradeItems.

The currently visible selection is an important factor in the task of inspecting and debugging a bill generated from a building model. The building model will frequently be very large, containing many thousand building elements. Particularly using a 3D view, it is frequently the case that highlighted building elements will be partially or totally hidden from view behind other elements. This is partly addressed using transparency, but a more powerful technique is by reducing the set of objects shown in the view. A popular use observed has been to inspect the bill story-by-story, which allows for a "roof-off" view of a more manageable subset of the building, and a more manageable size of bill. Another approach is to inspect one trade at a time, e.g., considering only concrete or only structural steelwork.

At present, the selection-sharing approach to debugging the quantity take-off process has not been extended to take-off rules. That is, it is not currently possible to select a take-off rule and show the building elements and cost items that the rule has matched and generated, respectively. Doing so would not be complicated, but at this point it is felt that because there is such a strong correlation between the rules and the bills that they generate, it is not necessary to provide selection sharing for rules, since selecting the cost item that the rule generates has a similar result.

References

[1] Mathieu Acher, Philippe Collet, Philippe Lahire, and Robert B. France. Decomposing feature models: language, environment, and applications. In *26th IEEE/ACM International Conference on Automated Software Engineering (ASE 2011), Lawrence, KS, USA, November 6-10, 2011*, pages 600–603. IEEE Computer Society, 2011.

[2] Mathieu Acher, Philippe Collet, Philippe Lahire, and Robert B. France. A domain-specific language for managing feature models. In *Proceedings of the 2011 ACM Symposium on Applied Computing*, pages 1333–1340. ACM, 2011.

[3] Mathieu Acher, Philippe Collet, Philippe Lahire, and Robert B. France. Slicing feature models. In *Proceedings of the 2011 26th IEEE/ACM International Conference on Automated Software Engineering*, pages 424–427. IEEE Computer Society, 2011.

[4] Mathieu Acher, Patrick Heymans, Philippe Collet, Clément Quinton, Philippe Lahire, and Philippe Merle. Feature Model Differences. In *Proceedings of the 24th International Conference on Advanced Information Systems Engineering*, CAiSE'12, pages 629–645, Berlin, Heidelberg, 2012. Springer-Verlag.

[5] Sven Apel, Florian Janda, Salvador Trujillo, and Christian Kästner. Model superimposition in software product lines. In *ICMT '09: Proceedings of the 2nd International Conference on Theory and Practice of Model Transformations*, pages 4–19, Berlin, Heidelberg, 2009. Springer-Verlag.

[6] Colin Atkinson, Joachim Bayer, and Dirk Muthig. Component-based product line development: The KobrA approach. In *Proceedings of the First Conference on Software Product Lines: Experience and Research Directions: Experience and Research*

Directions, pages 289–309, Norwell, MA, USA, 2000. Kluwer Academic Publishers.

[7] Colin Atkinson and Thomas Kühne. The role of metamodeling in MDA. In *Proc. UML 2002 Workshop on Software Model Engineering*, pages 67–70, 2002.

[8] Australian Institute of Quantity Surveyors. *Australian Standard Method of Measurement of Building Works*. Australian Institute of Quantity Surveyors, 5th edition, 1990.

[9] Don Batory, Jacob Neal Sarvela, and Axel Rauschmayer. Scaling step-wise refinement. *IEEE Transactions on Software Engineering*, 30(6):355–371, 2004.

[10] Jakob Beetz, Léon van Berlo, Ruben de Laat, and Pim van den Helm. BIMserver.org: An open source IFC model server. In *Proceedings of the CIP W78 Conference*, 2010.

[11] David Benavides, Sergio Segura, and Antonio Ruiz-Cortés. Automated analysis of feature models 20 years later: A literature review. *Information Systems*, 35:615–636, September 2010.

[12] A. Bertolino, A. Fantechi, S. Gnesi, G. Lami, and A. Maccari. Use Case Description of Requirements for Product Lines. In *International Workshop on Requirement Engineering for Product Line (REPL02)*, pages 12–18, September 2002.

[13] Jean Bézivin, Guillaume Hillairet, Frédéric Jouault, Ivan Kurtev, and William Piers. Bridging the MS/DSL tools and the Eclipse Modeling Framework. In *Proceedings of the International Workshop on Software Factories at OOPSLA*, volume 5, 2005.

[14] R. Binder. *Testing Object-Oriented Systems. Models, Patterns, and Tools*. Addison-Wesley, 1999.

[15] Barry Boehm. Software Risk Management. In C. Ghezzi and J. A. McDermid, editors, *Proceedings of 2nd European Software Engineering Conference (ESEC'89)*, pages 1 – 19, Coventry, UK, September 1989.

[16] Frederick P Brooks. *The Mythical Man-Month*, volume 1995. Addison-Wesley Reading, MA, 1975.

[17] Achim D. Brucker, Dan Chiorean, Tony Clark, Birgit Demuth, Martin Gogolla, Dimitri Plotnikov, Bernhard Rumpe, Edward D. Willink, and Burkhart Wolff. Report on the Aachen OCL Meeting. In *Proceedings of the MODELS 2013 OCL Workshop (OCL 2013)*, volume 1092 of *CEUR Workshop Proceedings*, pages 103–111, Miami, Florida, USA, 2013.

[18] buildingSMART. Industry Foundation Classes, Edition 3, Technical Corrigendum 1. http://www.buildingsmart.com, July 2007.

[19] Jordi Cabot and Martin Gogolla. Object Constraint Language (OCL): A definitive guide. In Marco Bernardo, Vittorio Cortellessa, and Alfonso Pierantonio, editors, *Formal Methods for Model-Driven Engineering*, volume 7320 of *Lecture Notes in Computer Science*, pages 58–90. Springer Berlin Heidelberg, 2012.

[20] Walter Cazzola, Jean-Marc Jézéquel, and Awais Rashid. Semantic join point models: Motivations, notions and requirements. In *SPLAT 2006 (Software Engineering Properties of Languages and Aspect Technologies)*, 2006.

[21] Franck Chauvel and Jean-Marc Jézéquel. Code generation from UML models with semantic variation points. In *Model Driven Engineering Languages and Systems, 8th International Conference, MODELS 2005, Montego Bay, Jamaica, October 2-7, 2005, Proceedings*, volume 3713 of *Lecture Notes in Computer Science*, pages 54–68. Springer, 2005.

[22] Franck Chauvel and Jean-Marc Jézéquel. Code generation from UML models with semantic variation points. In *Proceedings of MODELS/UML'2005*, Montego Bay, Jamaica, July 2005.

[23] M. Clauss. In *Workshop on Domain-Specific Visual Languages, OOPSLA 2001*, page 11.

[24] Curtis Clifton, Gary T Leavens, Craig Chambers, and Todd Millstein. Multijava: Modular open classes and symmetric multiple dispatch for java. *ACM Sigplan Notices*, 35(10):130–145, 2000.

[25] Alistair Cockburn. Structuring use cases with goals. *Journal of Object-Oriented Programming*, pages 35–40 and 56–62, Sept/Oct and Nov/Dec 1997.

[26] Steve Cook, Anneke Kleppe, Richard Mitchell, Bernhard Rumpe, Jos Warmer, and Alan Wills. The Amsterdam Manifesto on OCL. In *Object Modeling with the OCL*, volume 2263 of *Lecture Notes in Computer Science*, pages 115–149. Springer, 2002.

[27] Krzysztof Czarnecki and Ulrich W. Eisenecker. *Generative Programming: Methods, Tools, and Applications*. ACM Press/Addison-Wesley Publishing Co., New York, NY, USA, 2000.

[28] Paulo Anselmo da Mota Silveira Neto, Ivan do Carmo Machado, John D. McGregor, Eduardo Santana de Almeida, and Silvio Romero de Lemos Meira. A systematic mapping study of software product lines testing. *Information & Software Technology*, 53(5):407–423, 2011.

[29] Chris Daly. Emfatic language for EMF development. IBM alphaWorks, November 2004. http://www.alphaworks.ibm.com/tech/emfatic.

[30] Werner Damm and David Harel. LSCs: Breathing life into message sequence charts. *Formal Methods in System Design*, 19(1):45–80, 2001.

[31] Edsger W. Dijkstra. The Humble Programmer. *Commun. ACM*, 15(10):859 – 866, October 1972.

[32] Chuck Eastman, Charles M Eastman, Paul Teicholz, and Rafael Sacks. *BIM Handbook: A Guide to Building Information Modeling for Owners, Managers, Designers, Engineers and Contractors*. John Wiley & Sons, 2nd edition, 2011.

[33] Sven Efftinge and Markus Völter. oAW xText: A framework for textual DSLs. In *Workshop on Modeling Symposium at Eclipse Summit*, volume 32, page 118, 2006.

[34] Marina Egea and Vlad Rusu. Formal executable semantics for conformance in the mde framework. *Innovations in Systems and Software Engineering*, 6(1):73–81, 2010.

[35] Eva Van Emden and Leon Moonen. Java quality assurance by detecting code smells. In Arie van Deursen and Elizabeth Burd, editors, *9th Working Conference on Reverse Engineering (WCRE 2002), 28 October - 1 November 2002, Richmond, VA, USA*, page 97. IEEE Computer Society, 2002.

[36] Joshua M. Epstein. Why model? *Journal of Artificial Societies and Social Simulation*, 11(4):12, 2008.

[37] Sebastian Erdweg, Tijs van der Storm, Markus Völter, Meinte Boersma, Remi Bosman, William R. Cook, Albert Gerritsen, Angelo Hulshout, Steven Kelly, Alex Loh, Gabriël D. P. Konat, Pedro J. Molina, Martin Palatnik, Risto Pohjonen, Eugen Schindler, Klemens Schindler, Riccardo Solmi, Vlad A. Vergu, Eelco Visser, Kevin van der Vlist, Guido Wachsmuth, and Jimi van der Woning. The State of the Art in Language Workbenches - Conclusions from the Language Workbench Challenge. In *6th International Conference Software Language Engineering (SLE)*, volume 8225 of *Lecture Notes in Computer Science*, pages 197–217. Springer, 2013.

[38] Ralph Johnson Erich Gamma, Richard Helm and John Vlissides. *Design Patterns: Elements of Reusable Object-Oriented Software*. Addison-Wesley Professional, 1994.

[39] Andy Evans, Robert B. France, Kevin Lano, and Bernhard Rumpe. Developing the UML as a formal modelling notation. *CoRR*, abs/1409.6928, 2014.

[40] J-M. Favre, D. Gasevic, R. Lämmel, and E. Pek. Empirical language analysis in software linguistics. In *Software Language Engineering*, volume 6563 of *Lecture Notes in Computer Science*, pages 316–326. Springer, 2011.

[41] Robert E Filman and Daniel P Friedman. Aspect-oriented programming is quantification and obliviousness. In *Proceedings of the Workshop on Advanced Separation of Concerns, in Conjunction with OOPSLA'00*, 2000.

[42] Franck Fleurey, Oystein Haugen, Birger Moller-Pedersen, Goran Olsen, Andreas Svendsen, and Zhang Xiaorui. A generic language and tool for variability modeling. Technical report, SINTEF, 2009.

[43] Apache Software Foundation. The FreeMarker template engine. http://freemarker.org/, 2015.

[44] Martin Fowler. *Refactoring: Improving the Design of Existing Code.* Addison-Wesley Professional, 1999.

[45] Robert France, Franck Fleurey, Raghu Reddy, Benoit Baudry, and Sudipto Ghosh. Providing Support for Model Composition in Metamodels. In *EDOC'07*, Annapolis, MD, United States, October 2007.

[46] Robert B. France and Bernhard Rumpe. Model-driven development of complex software: A research roadmap. In Lionel C. Briand and Alexander L. Wolf, editors, *International Conference on Software Engineering, ICSE 2007, Future of Software Engineering (FOSE 2007)*, pages 37–54. IEEE Computer Society, 2007.

[47] Martin Gardner. The game of life, parts I-III. *Wheels, life, and other mathematical amusements*, pages 20–22, 1983.

[48] Dragan Gašević, Nima Kaviani, and Marek Hatala. On metamodeling in megamodels. In Gregor Engels, Bill Opdyke, Douglas C. Schmidt, and Frank Weil, editors, *Model Driven Engineering Languages and Systems: 10th International Conference, MODELS 2007, Nashville, USA, September 30 - October 5, 2007*, pages 91–105, Berlin, Heidelberg, 2007. Springer Berlin Heidelberg.

[49] Hassan Gomaa. *Designing Software Product Lines with UML: From Use Cases to Pattern-Based Software Architectures.* Addison Wesley Longman Publishing Co., Inc., Redwood City, CA, USA, 2004.

[50] Hassan Gomaa and Michael Eonsuk Shin. Multiple-view modelling and meta-modelling of software product lines. *IET Software*, 2(2):94–122, 2008.

[51] Marie Gouyette, Olivier Barais, Jérôme Le Noir, Cédric Brun, Marcos Almeida Da Silva, Xavier Blanc, Daniel Exertier, and Jean-Marc Jézéquel. Movida studio: A modeling environment to create viewpoints and manage variability in views. In Ileana Ober, editor, *IDM- 7éme journées sur l'Ingénierie Dirigée par les*

Modèles-2011, volume 1, pages 141–145, Lille, France, June 2011. Polytech, Université Lille 1, service reprographie de Polytech, Université Lille I.

[52] Timo Greifenberg, Katrin Hölldobler, Carsten Kolassa, Markus Look, Pedram Mir Seyed Nazari, Klaus Müller, Antonio Navarro Perez, Dimitri Plotnikov, Dirk Reiß, Alexander Roth, Bernhard Rumpe, Martin Schindler, and Andreas Wortmann. Integration of Handwritten and Generated Object-Oriented Code. In *Model-Driven Engineering and Software Development Conference (MODELSWARD'15)*, volume 580 of *CCIS*, pages 112–132. Springer, 2015.

[53] Hans Grönniger, Holger Krahn, Bernhard Rumpe, Martin Schindler, and Steven Völkel. MontiCore 1.0: Ein framework zur erstellung und verarbeitung domänenspezifischer sprachen. Technical Report Informatics-Report 2006-04, Software Systems Engineering Institute, Braunschweig University of Technology, 2006.

[54] Clément Guy, Benoit Combemale, Steven Derrien, and Jean-Marc Jézéquel. On model subtyping. In *Proceedings of the 8th European Conference on Modelling Foundations and Applications (ECMFA 2012)*, number 7349 in Lecture Notes in Computer Science, pages 400–415. Springer, 2012.

[55] Arne Haber, Katrin Hölldobler, Carsten Kolassa, Markus Look, Bernhard Rumpe, Klaus Müller, and Ina Schaefer. Engineering delta modeling languages. In Tomoji Kishi, Stan Jarzabek, and Stefania Gnesi, editors, *17th International Software Product Line Conference, SPLC 2013, Tokyo, Japan - August 26 - 30, 2013*, pages 22–31. ACM, 2013.

[56] Arne Haber, Thomas Kutz, Holger Rendel, Bernhard Rumpe, and Ina Schaefer. Towards a family-based analysis of applicability conditions in architectural delta models. In *Variability for You Proceedings of VARY International Workshop Affiliated with ACM/IEEE 14th International Conference on Model-Driven Engineering Languages and Systems (MODELS'11)*, volume TR-2011-144 of *IT University Technical Report Series*, pages 43–52, Wellington, New Zealand, October 2011. IT University of Copenhagen.

[57] Günter Halmans and Klaus Pohl. Communicating the variability of a software-product family to customers. *Software and System Modeling*, 2(1):15–36, 2003.

[58] D. Harel. Statecharts: A visual formalism for complex systems. *Sci. Comput. Programming*, 8:231–274, 1987.

[59] David Harel, Hagi Lachover, Amnon Naamad, Amir Pnueli, Michal Politi, Rivi Sherman, Aharon Shtull-Trauring, and Mark Trakhtenbrot. Statemate: A working environment for the development of complex reactive systems. *IEEE Transactions on Software Engineering*, 16(4):403–414, 1990.

[60] David Harel and Bernhard Rumpe. Meaningful Modeling: What's the Semantics of "Semantics"? *IEEE Computer*, 37(10):64–72, October 2004.

[61] Oystein Haugen, Birger Moller-Pedersen, Jon Oldevik, Goran K. Olsen, and Andreas Svendsen. Adding standardized variability to domain specific languages. *Software Product Line Conference, International*, pages 139–148, 2008.

[62] Florian Heidenreich, Jendrik Johannes, Sven Karol, Mirko Seifert, and Christian Wende. Derivation and refinement of textual syntax for models. In *Model Driven Architecture-Foundations and Applications*, pages 114–129. Springer, 2009.

[63] Mark Hills, Paul Klint, Tijs van der Storm, and Jurgen Vinju. *Objects, Models, Components, Patterns: 49th International Conference, TOOLS 2011, Zurich, Switzerland, June 28-30, 2011. Proceedings*, chapter A Case of Visitor versus Interpreter Pattern, pages 228–243. Springer Berlin Heidelberg, Berlin, Heidelberg, 2011.

[64] J. Hutchinson, J. Whittle, M. Rouncefield, and S. Kristoffersen. Empirical assessment of MDE in industry. In *Proceedings of the 33rd International Conference on Software Engineering*, ICSE '11, pages 471–480. ACM, 2011.

[65] Andrew Jackson, Olivier Barais, Jean-Marc Jézéquel, and Siobhán Clarke. Toward a generic and extensible merge operator. In *Models and Aspects Workshop, at ECOOP 2006*, Nantes, France, July 2006.

[66] Patrick Heymans Jean-Christophe Trigaux. Modelling variability requirements in software product lines: a comparative survey. Technical report, FUNDP Namur, 2003.

[67] Cédric Jeanneret, Martin Glinz, and Benoit Baudry. Estimating footprints of model operations. In *Proc. of ICSE'11*, 2011.

[68] Jean-Marc Jézéquel. Model driven design and aspect weaving. *Journal of Software and Systems Modeling (SoSyM)*, 7(2):209–218, May 2008.

[69] Jean-Marc Jézéquel, Benoit Combemale, Olivier Barais, Martin Monperrus, and François Fouquet. Mashup of metalanguages and its implementation in the Kermeta language workbench. *Software and Systems Modeling (SoSyM)*, 14(2):905–920, 2015.

[70] Jean-Marc Jézéquel, Noël Plouzeau, Torben Weis, and Kurt Geihs. From contracts to aspects in UML designs. In *Proc. of the Workshop on Aspect-Oriented Modeling with UML at AOSD'02*, RENNES, France, 2002.

[71] Ralph Johnson and Bobby Woolf. Type object. In Robert C. Martin, Dirk Riehle, and Frank Buschmann, editors, *Pattern Languages of Program Design 3*, pages 47–65. Addison-Wesley Longman Publishing Co., Inc., Boston, MA, USA, 1997.

[72] K. C. Kang, S. G. Cohen, J. A. Hess, W. E. Novak, and A. S. Peterson. Feature-oriented domain analysis (FODA) feasibility study. Technical report, Carnegie-Mellon University Software Engineering Institute, November 1990.

[73] Gregor Kiczales, John Lamping, Anurag Mendhekar, Chris Maeda, Cristina Lopes, Jean-Marc Loingtier, and John Irwin. Aspect-oriented programming. In *ECOOP'97 — Object-Oriented Programming: 11th European Conference Jyväskylä, Finland, June 9–13, 1997 Proceedings*, pages 220–242. Springer Berlin Heidelberg, 1997.

[74] Cornel Klein, Bernhard Rumpe, and Manfred Broy. A stream-based mathematical model for distributed information processing systems - SysLab system model. In *Workshop on Formal Methods for Open Object-Based Distributed Systems*, IFIP Advances in

Information and Communication Technology, pages 323–338. Chapman & Hall, 1996.

[75] Jacques Klein, Benoit Caillaud, and Loïc Hélouët. Merging scenarios. In *9th Int. Workshop on Formal Methods for Industrial Critical Systems (FMICS), ENTCS*, pages 209–226, 2004.

[76] Jacques Klein, Franck Fleurey, and Jean-Marc Jézéquel. Weaving multiple aspects in sequence diagrams. In *Transactions on Aspect-Oriented Software Development (TAOSD) III*, volume 4620 of *Lecture Notes in Computer Science*, pages 167–199. Springer, 2007.

[77] Jacques Klein and Jean-Marc Jézéquel. Problems of the semantic-based weaving of scenarios. In *Aspects and Software Product Lines: An Early Aspects Workshop at SPLC-Europe 05*, 2005.

[78] Jacques Klein, Jean-Marc Jézéquel, and Noël Plouzeau. Weaving behavioural models. In *First Workshop on Models and Aspects, Handling Crosscutting Concerns in MDSD at ECOOP 05*, 2005.

[79] A. Kleppe. *Software Language Engineering: Creating Domain-Specific Languages Using Metamodels*. Addison-Wesley Professional, 1 edition, 2008.

[80] Holger Krahn, Bernhard Rumpe, and Stefen Völkel. MontiCore: A Framework for Compositional Development of Domain Specific Languages. *International Journal on Software Tools for Technology Transfer (STTT)*, 12(5):353–372, September 2010.

[81] Ivan Kurtev, Jean Bézivin, and Mehmet Aksit. Technological Spaces: An initial appraisal. In *CoopIS, DOA'2002 Federated Conferences, Industrial Track*, Irvine, 2002.

[82] Philippe Lahire, Brice Morin, Gilles Vanwormhoudt, Alban Gaignard, Olivier Barais, and Jean-Marc Jézéquel. Introducing variability into aspect-oriented modeling approaches. In *Model Driven Engineering Languages and Systems, 10th International Conference, MODELS 2007, Nashville, USA, September 30 - October 5, 2007, Proceedings*, volume 4735 of *Lecture Notes in Computer Science*, pages 498–513. Springer, 2007.

[83] Philippe Lahire, Brice Morin, Gilles Vanwormhoudt, Alban Gaignard, Olivier Barais, and Jean-Marc Jézéquel. Introducing variability into Aspect-Oriented Modeling approaches. In *In Proceedings of ACM/IEEE 10th International Conference on Model Driven Engineering Languages and Systems (MODELS 07)*, Nashville, TN, USA, United States, 2007.

[84] Jaiprakash T. Lallchandani and R. Mall. A dynamic slicing technique for UML architectural models. *IEEE Transactions on Software Engineering*, 37(6):737–771, 2011.

[85] Leslie Lamport. *\LaTeX—A Document Preparation System—User's Guide and Reference Manual*. Addision-Wesley, Reading, 1985.

[86] Michael Lawley and Jim Steel. Practical declarative model transformation with Tefkat. In *Satellite Events at the MODELS 2005 Conference, MODELS 2005 International Workshops, Doctoral Symposium, Educators Symposium, Montego Bay, Jamaica, October 2-7, 2005, Revised Selected Papers*, volume 3844 of *Lecture Notes in Computer Science*, pages 139–150. Springer, 2005.

[87] Edward A. Lee. Cyber physical systems: Design challenges. In *11th IEEE International Symposium on Object Oriented Real-Time Distributed Computing (ISORC)*, pages 363–369, May 2008.

[88] Kenneth C Louden. *Compiler Construction: Principles and Practice*. Cengage Learning, 1997.

[89] Sean Luke, Claudio Cioffi-Revilla, Liviu Panait, Keith Sullivan, and Gabriel Balan. Mason: A multiagent simulation environment. *Simulation*, 81(7):517–527, 2005.

[90] Hidehiko Masuhara, Gregor Kiczales, and Christopher Dutchyn. A compilation and optimization model for aspect-oriented programs. In *Compiler Construction, 12th International Conference, CC 2003, Held as Part of the Joint European Conferences on Theory and Practice of Software, ETAPS 2003, Warsaw, Poland, April 7-11, 2003, Proceedings*, volume 2622 of *Lecture Notes in Computer Science*, pages 46–60. Springer, 2003.

[91] John D. McGregor. Building reusable testing assets for a software product line. In *Software Product Lines, 10th International Conference, SPLC 2006, Baltimore, Maryland, USA, August 21-24, 2006, Proceedings*, page 220. IEEE Computer Society, 2006.

[92] Bertrand Meyer. Applying design by contract. *Computer*, 25(10):40–51, Oct. 1992.

[93] Mira Mezini and Klaus Ostermann. Variability management with feature-oriented programming and aspects. *SIGSOFT Softw. Eng. Notes*, 29(6):127–136, 2004.

[94] MontiCore Website http://www.monticore.de.

[95] Brice Morin, Franck Fleurey, Nelly Bencomo, Jean-Marc Jézéquel, Arnor Solberg, Vegard Dehlen, and Gordon S. Blair. An aspect-oriented and model-driven approach for managing dynamic variability. In *Model Driven Engineering Languages and Systems, 11th International Conference, MODELS 2008, Toulouse, France, September 28 - October 3, 2008. Proceedings*, volume 5301 of *Lecture Notes in Computer Science*, pages 782–796. Springer, 2008.

[96] Brice Morin, Jacques Klein, Olivier Barais, and Jean-Marc Jézéquel. A generic weaver for supporting product lines. In *EA '08: Proceedings of the 13th International Workshop on Software Architectures and Mobility*, pages 11–18. ACM, 2008.

[97] Brice Morin, Gilles Perrouin, Philippe Lahire, Olivier Barais, Gilles Vanwormhoudt, and Jean-Marc Jézéquel. Weaving variability into domain metamodels. In *Model Driven Engineering Languages and Systems, 12th International Conference, MODELS 2009, Denver, CO, USA, October 4-9, 2009. Proceedings*, volume 5795 of *Lecture Notes in Computer Science*, pages 690–705. Springer, 2009.

[98] Pierre-Alain Muller, Franck Fleurey, Frédéric Fondement, Michel Hassenforder, Rémi Schneckenburger, Sébastien Gérard, and Jean-Marc Jézéquel. Model-driven analysis and synthesis of concrete syntax. In *Model Driven Engineering Languages and Systems*, pages 98–110. Springer, 2006.

[99] Pierre-Alain Muller, Franck Fleurey, and Jean-Marc Jézéquel. Weaving executability into object-oriented meta-languages. In *Model Driven Engineering Languages and Systems, 8th International Conference, MODELS 2005, Montego Bay, Jamaica, October 2-7, 2005, Proceedings*, volume 3713 of *Lecture Notes in Computer Science*, pages 264–278. Springer, 2005.

[100] Jonathan Musset, Étienne Juliot, Stéphane Lacrampe, William Piers, Cédric Brun, Laurent Goubet, Yvan Lussaud, and Freddy Allilaire. Acceleo user guide. http://acceleo.org/doc/obeo/en/acceleo-2.6-user-guide.pdf, 2006.

[101] Clémentine Nebut, Franck Fleurey, Yves Le Traon, and Jean-Marc Jézéquel. A requirement-based approach to test product families. In *Software Product-Family Engineering*, pages 198–210. Springer, 2003.

[102] Clémentine Nebut, Franck Fleurey, Yves Le Traon, and Jean-Marc Jézéquel. Automatic test generation: A use case driven approach. *IEEE Trans. Software Eng.*, 32(3):140–155, 2006.

[103] Clémentine Nebut, Yves Le Traon, and Jean-Marc Jézéquel. *System Testing of Product Families: from Requirements to Test Cases*, pages 447–478. Springer Verlag, 2006.

[104] Clémentine Nebut, Simon Pickin, Yves Le Traon, and Jean-Marc Jézéquel. Automated requirements-based generation of test cases for product families. In *18th IEEE International Conference on Automated Software Engineering (ASE 2003), 6-10 October 2003, Montreal, Canada*, pages 263–266. IEEE Computer Society, 2003.

[105] Changhai Nie and Hareton Leung. A survey of combinatorial testing. *ACM Computing Surveys (CSUR)*, 43(2):11, 2011.

[106] L.M. Northrop. A framework for software product line practice. In *Proceedings of the Workshop on Object-Oriented Technology*, pages 365–376. Springer-Verlag London, UK, 1999.

[107] Object Management Group. XML Metadata Interchange (XMI) Specification Version 2.5.1. OMG Document No. formal/2015-06-07, http://www.omg.org/spec/XMI/2.5.1/, June 2015.

[108] Object Management Group (OMG). MDA Guide Version 1.0. OMG Document no. omg/2003-05-01, http://www.omg.org/mda/, May 2003.

[109] Object Management Group (OMG). Human-Usable Textual Notation Specification Version 1.0. OMG Document No. formal/2004-08-01, http://www.omg.org/spec/HUTN/1.0/, August 2004.

[110] Object Management Group (OMG). MDA Guide Revision 2.0. OMG Document no. ormsc/2014-06-01, http://www.omg.org/mda/, June 2014.

[111] Object Management Group (OMG). Object Constraint Language (OCL) Specification Version 2.4. OMG Document No. formal/2014-02-03, http://www.omg.org/spec/OCL/2.4/, February 2014.

[112] Object Management Group (OMG). Meta Object Facility (MOF) Core Specification Version 2.5. OMG Document No. formal/2015-06-05, http://www.omg.org/spec/MOF/2.5/, June 2015.

[113] Object Management Group (OMG). Unified modeling language specifications (uml), version 2.5. OMG Document numbers formal/2015-03-01 http://www.omg.org/spec/UML/2.5/, Mars 2015.

[114] William F Opdyke. *Refactoring: A Program Restructuring Aid in Designing Object-Oriented Application Frameworks.* PhD thesis, University of Illinois at Urbana-Champaign, 1992.

[115] D. L. Parnas. On the criteria to be used in decomposing systems into modules. *Commun. ACM*, 15(12):1053–1058, 1972.

[116] D. L. Parnas. On the design and development of program families. *IEEE Transactions on Software Engineering*, 2(1):1–9, 1976.

[117] Terence Parr. *The Definitive ANTLR 4 Reference.* Pragmatic Bookshelf, 2nd edition, 2013.

[118] Gilles Perrouin, Jacques Klein, Nicolas Guelfi, and Jean-Marc Jézéquel. Reconciling automation and flexibility in product derivation. In *Software Product Lines, 12th International Conference, SPLC 2008, Limerick, Ireland, September 8-12, 2008, Proceedings*, pages 339–348. IEEE Computer Society, 2008.

[119] Simon Pickin, Claude Jard, Thierry Jéron, Jean-Marc Jézéquel, and Yves Le Traon. Test synthesis from UML models of distributed software. *IEEE Transactions on Software Engineering*, 33(4):252–268, April 2007.

[120] Klaus Pohl, Günter Böckle, and Frank van der Linden. *Software Product Line Engineering: Foundations, Principles, and Techniques*. Springer, 2005.

[121] K Popper. *The Logic of Scientific Discovery*. Routledge Classics. Taylor & Francis, 2002.

[122] Rodrigo Ramos, Olivier Barais, and Jean-Marc Jézéquel. Matching model-snippets. In *Model-Driven Engineering Languages and Systems, 10th International Conference, MODELS 2007, Nashville, USA, September 30 - October 5, 2007, Proceedings*, volume 4735 of *Lecture Notes in Computer Science*, pages 121–135. Springer, 2007.

[123] Awais Rashid, Ana Moreira, and João Araújo. Modularisation and composition of aspectual requirements. In *Proceedings of the 2nd International Conference on Aspect-Oriented Software Development, AOSD*, pages 11–20. ACM, 2003.

[124] Mark Richters and Martin Gogolla. OCL: syntax, semantics, and tools. In *Object Modeling with the OCL, The Rationale behind the Object Constraint Language*, volume 2263 of *Lecture Notes in Computer Science*, pages 42–68. Springer, 2002.

[125] Louis M. Rose, Dimitrios S. Kolovos, Nikolaos Drivalos, James R. Williams, Richard F. Paige, Fiona A. C. Polack, and Kiran Jude Fernandes. Concordance: A framework for managing model integrity. In Thomas Kühne, Bran Selic, Marie-Pierre Gervais, and François Terrier, editors, *Modelling Foundations and Applications, 6th European Conference, ECMFA 2010, Paris, France, June 15-18, 2010. Proceedings*, volume 6138 of *Lecture Notes in Computer Science*, pages 245–260. Springer, 2010.

[126] Louis M Rose, Richard F Paige, Dimitrios S Kolovos, and Fiona AC Polack. Constructing models with the human-usable textual notation. In *Model Driven Engineering Languages and Systems*, pages 249–263. Springer, 2008.

[127] Jeff Rothenberg, Lawrence E Widman, Kenneth A Loparo, and Norman R Nielsen. *The Nature of Modeling*, volume 3027. Rand, 1989.

[128] Bernhard Rumpe. A Note on Semantics (with an Emphasis on UML). In Haim Kilov and Bernhard Rumpe, editors, *Second ECOOP Workshop on Precise Behavioral Semantics*. Technische Universität München, TUM-I9813, 1998.

[129] Bernhard Rumpe. <<java>>ocl based on new presentation of the ocl-syntax. In *Object Modeling with the OCL*, volume 2263 of *Lecture Notes in Computer Science*, pages 189–212. Springer, 2002.

[130] Bernhard Rumpe. *Modelling with UML. Language, Concepts, Methods.* Springer International, 2016.

[131] Pierre-Yves Schobbens, Patrick Heymans, and Jean-Christophe Trigaux. Feature diagrams: A survey and a formal semantics. In *Requirements Engineering, 14th IEEE International Conference*, pages 139–148. IEEE, 2006.

[132] Bran Selic. UML 2 Specification Issue 6462. http://www.omg.org/issues/issue6462.txt, updates dating until 2008, 2013.

[133] Yannis Smaragdakis and Don S. Batory. Mixin layers: an object-oriented implementation technique for refinements and collaboration-based designs. *ACM Trans. Softw. Eng. Methodol.*, 11(2):215–255, 2002.

[134] Software Product Line Conference - Hall of Fame. http://splc.net/fame.html.

[135] Herbert Stachowiak. *Allgemeine Modelltheorie*. Springer-Verlag, Wien, New York, 1973.

[136] Jim Steel and Robin Drogemuller. Domain-specific model transformation in building quantity take-off. In *Model Driven Engineering Languages and Systems*, pages 198–212. Springer, 2011.

[137] Jim Steel, Robin Drogemuller, and Bianca Toth. Model interoperability in building information modelling. *Software and Systems Modeling (SoSyM)*, 11(1):99–109, 2012.

[138] Jim Steel, Keith Duddy, and Robin Drogemuller. A transformation workbench for building information models. In *Theory and Practice of Model Transformations*, pages 93–107. Springer, 2011.

[139] Jim Steel and Jean-Marc Jézéquel. On model typing. *Software and Systems Modeling (SoSyM)*, 6(4):401–413, 2007.

[140] Dave Steinberg, Frank Budinsky, Ed Merks, and Marcelo Paternostro. *EMF: Eclipse Modeling Framework*. Pearson Education, 2008.

[141] Frank van der Linden. Software product families in europe: The Esaps & Cafe projects. *IEEE Software*, 19:41–49, 2002.

[142] Markus Völter and Iris Groher. Product line implementation using aspect-oriented and model-driven software development. In *Software Product Lines, 11th International Conference, SPLC 2007, Kyoto, Japan, September 10-14, 2007, Proceedings*, pages 233–242. IEEE Computer Society, 2007.

[143] Thomas von der Maßen and Horst Lichter. Requiline: A requirements engineering tool for software product lines. In Frank van der Linden, editor, *Software Product-Family Engineering, 5th International Workshop, PFE 2003, Siena, Italy, November 4-6, 2003, Revised Papers*, volume 3014 of *Lecture Notes in Computer Science*, pages 168–180. Springer, 2003.

[144] M. P Ward. Language-oriented programming. *Software-Concepts and Tools*, 15(4):147–161, 1994.

[145] Mark Weiser. Program slicing. In Seymour Jeffrey and Leon G. Stucki, editors, *Proceedings of the 5th International Conference on Software Engineering, San Diego, California, USA, March 9-12, 1981.*, pages 439–449. IEEE Computer Society, 1981.

[146] David M. Weiss and Chi Tau Robert Lai. *Software Product-line Engineering: A Family-Based Software Development Process.* Addison-Wesley Longman, Boston, 1999.

[147] Jon Whittle, John Hutchinson, and Mark Rouncefield. The state of practice in model-driven engineering. *IEEE Software,* 31(3):79–85, 2014.

[148] Tewfik Ziadi, Loïc Hélouët, and Jean-Marc Jézéquel. Towards a UML profile for software product lines. In *Software Product-Family Engineering, 5th International Workshop, PFE 2003, Siena, Italy, November 4-6, 2003, Revised Papers*, volume 3014 of *Lecture Notes in Computer Science*, pages 129–139. Springer, 2003.

[149] Tewfik Ziadi, Loïc Hélouët, and Jean-Marc Jézéquel. Revisiting statechart synthesis with an algebraic approach. In *26th International Conference on Software Engineering (ICSE 2004), 23-28 May 2004, Edinburgh, United Kingdom*, pages 242–251. IEEE Computer Society, 2004.

[150] Tewfik Ziadi and Jean-Marc Jézéquel. Software product line engineering with the UML: deriving products. In *Software Product Lines - Research Issues in Engineering and Management*, pages 557–588. Springer, 2006.

[151] Tewfik Ziadi and Jean-Marc Jézéquel. Software product line engineering with the UML: deriving products. In *Software Product Lines*, pages 557–588. Springer, 2006.

Index